Gentle Medicine for Balance in Body and Peace of Mind

The Elements of Care® Program

Martha M. Libster PhD, APRN

Content Copyright© 2020 Golden Apple Publications

Cover Copyright© 2020 Golden Apple Publications

All rights reserved. No part of this publication may be reproduced, translated, stored in a retrieval system, or transmitted in any form or by any means, electronic, mechanical, photocopy, recording, Web distribution, information storage and retrieval systems or otherwise, without the prior written consent of the Publisher, except by a reviewer who may quote brief passages in a review.

Cover/Book Design and Artwork: Mark Gelotte www.markgelotte.com

Copy Edit: Julie Smith Taylor

Printed in the United States

Library of Congress Control Number: 2020939768
Includes bibliographical references and Index ISBN 978-09755018-9-4
Libster, Martha Mathews 1960-

1. Self - Help - Personal Growth, 2. Health & Fitness-Herbal Medications, 3. Gardening-Herbs, 4. Nature-Plants, 5. Body Mind & Spirit Hermeticism.

I. Libster, Martha Mathews author

Golden Apple Healing Arts dba Golden Apple Publications does not warrant or guarantee any of the products, recipes, or remedies described or discussed on its website, or in a seminar, webinar, or publication; nor has it performed any independent analysis in connection with any of the information shared in good faith with attendees, readers, and guests. Golden Apple Healing Arts does not assume, and expressly disclaims, any obligation to obtain and include information other than that which it deems important. The attendee, reader, or guest is expressly warned to consider and adopt all safety precautions that might be indicated by the activities described herein and to avoid all potential hazards. By following any educational instructions contained herein, the attendee, reader, or guest willingly assumes all benefits and risks in connection with such education.

Golden Apple Healing Arts makes no representations or warranties of any kind, including but not limited to, the warranties of fitness for particular purpose or merchantability, nor are any such representations implied with respect to the material set forth herein, and Golden Apple Healing Arts takes no responsibility with respect to such material. Golden Apple Healing Arts and its subsidiaries shall not be liable for any special, consequential, or exemplary damages resulting, in whole or part, from the attendee, reader, or guest's use of, or reliance upon, this educational material.

Information presented by Golden Apple Healing Arts and Golden Apple Publications is not intended to be a substitute for the services of a health care professional nor is it meant to authorize or endorse the use of herbs or other therapeutic modalities by the professional reader in the care of patients. Neither Dr. Martha Libster nor Golden Apple Healing Arts are responsible for any consequences incurred by those employing remedies. Botanical and other therapeutic knowledge is constantly changing. Different opinions by experts, continued research and clinical results, individual circumstances, and possible error in preparing educational content requires the attendee, reader, and guest to use their own judgment and other information when making decisions based on the material contained in or derived from Golden Apple Healing Arts resources and publications. Although Dr. Martha, contributor(s), and Golden Apple Healing Arts have, as is humanly possible, taken care to ensure that the information is accurate and up to date at the time of inclusion on this web site and in events and services, people are strongly advised to confirm that the information meets their unique needs and health patterns and complies with the latest legislation and health care standards where they reside in the world. Dr. Martha Libster and Golden Apple Healing Arts cannot accept any legal responsibility or liability for an attendee's, reader's, or guest's use of botanicals or any other therapeutic modality discussed during an educational service or event in the care of themselves or others.

Om wagi shori mum!

This mantra is homage to Manjushri, a Master of Speech in Buddhist tradition, who is the patron of writers in the arts and sciences.

Manjushri means "Gentle Glory."

May each word and the essence of the message written herein be infused with the gentle presence of Manjushri's discriminating wisdom and may each reader access the power, wisdom, and love of their own heart that enables them to choose their medicines wisely no matter how gentle that medicine may seem to be.

Table of Contents

Foreword by Catherine Dees
Preface by Martha Mathews LIbster
Chapter 1 Welcome Back to the Plant World 1
   Memories and Plant Partnership 3
      Gentle Medicine Self-Study #1 Plant Memories 3
   Plant Teachers 5
      Gentle Medicine Self-Study #2 When does food become medicine? 6
   Self-care in a Tiered Healthcare System 9
      Gentle Medicine Self-Study #3 Self-care Survey Question 11

Chapter 2 The Elements of Care® Program: A Guide for Self-Care 13
   Tea Tasting 14
      Gentle Medicine Self-Study #4 Managing Expectations with Mindful Tea Tasting .. 16
   Sentience and Common Sense 17
      Lesson from St. John's Wort 21
   Self-care with a Capital S 24
   Season for Climate Change 26
      Gentle Medicine Self-Study #5 Comfort Level with Change 27
      Gentle Medicine Self-Study #6 Change and Transition 28
      Gentle Medicine Self-Study #7 The Power of Perception 29
   Five Elements of Climate Creation 32

Chapter 3 The 5 P's of the Self-care Model 35
   The Self-care Model for Primary Prevention 35
      The Solution is Simples 38
      Gentle Medicine Self-Study #8 A Simple Lemon Compress for Fever Reduction 38
   Plants 40
      Plant Designs and Growth Patterns 40
         Plant Parts 41
      Plant Constituents 45
         Common Constituents of Plants 46
   Peace and Plant-like Gentleness 49
      Peaceful Safe Place 53
      Gentle Medicine Self-Study #9 Designing a Peaceful Safe Place 55
   Patterns in Health, Physics, and Paradigms 56
      Putting Energetic Patterns First 57
      Eight Principle Patterns 60
      Paradigms About Plant Partnership 64
         Biomedical Paradigm 65
         Traditional Paradigm 73
         Self-care Paradigm 78

Chapter 4 Start Your 5 Elements of Care® Self-care Plan 81
    Starting a Self-care Plan 82

Chapter 5 Entering the Earth Element 84
    Know Your Self – Anatomy, Physiology, and Pattern Science 84
    The Chlorophyll Connection 86
        Gentle Medicine Self-study #10 Entering the Green World 88
    Gentle Medicine Begins at Home 91
        Community Ethics and Cannabis, Tobacco, and American Ginseng 93
    Becoming Ecocentric and Green 96
        Protecting Your Self-care Green Pharmacy 98

Chapter 6 Awakening the Air Element 102
    Mindful Decision-Making and Problem-Solving 103
        Gentle Medicine Self-study #11 Breath and Body Scan 103
            Self-care Process for Problem Solving in Self-care 106
            Observations 107
            Pattern Recognition 109
            Planning 109
            Reframing Self-care Interventions 110
            Evaluation 111
    How to Decode Herbal Scientific Data 111
        Resposible Reporting and Writing 112
    Referral Beyond Self-care 116

Chapter 7 Welcoming the Water Element 118
    Recipes for Making Herbal Simples 119
        Healing Foods and Oral Remedies 120
            Teas – Infusions and Decoctions 122
            Soups 124
            Pills and Capsules 125
            Syrups 127
            Tinctures and Liquid Extracts 127
            A Note About Homeopathy 130
        Topical Applications 131
            Compresses 132
        Gentle Medicine Self-study #12 Comforting Ginger Compress 133
            Poultices and Plasters 135
            Infused Oils, Liniments, Salves, and Ointments 136
    Simples for Creating A Healing Environment 139
        Aromatherapy, Inhalations, and Steams 140
        Herbal Baths 141
        Five Element Foot Bath 142
        Healing Gardens 144

Chapter 8 Fanning the Fire Element **146**
    Evaluating Best Self-care Practice 148
    Guideline for Best Self-care Plans 152
    Five Rights of Precision Plant Partnership Self-care 153
        Right Plant 155
            Weighing Benefits and Risks 155
        Right Application 160
            Gentle Medicine Self-Study #13 Home Garden Medicine 162
            Common Sense and Complexity 162
        Right Time 163
            Interactions and Reactions 164
        Right Dose 167
        Right Person 170
    Putting Fear into the Flame 171

Chapter 9 Effecting the Ether Element **174**
    Alchemy and the Secret Essence of Lemon Bread 176
    Plant Alchemy 179
        Formulation 181
    Adaptogen Action and Thinking Plants 184
    Bach Flower Remedies 186
    Remember the Harmony of the Golden Ratio 188

Conclusion: The Way of the Thornless Rose **190**
    Self-talk 191
        Gentle Medicine Self-Study #14 Self-talk 191
    Wisdom of Elders 192
        Gentle Medicine Self-Study #15 Power Object 193
    Learning from the Lemon Balm Lawn 195
    Simples for Turning the Dial 196

Next Steps **198**
Endnotes **199**
References **205**
Index **211**

Experiential Guide **221**

Foreword by Catherine Dees

The plant kingdom was the original medicine cabinet, Nature's pharmacy, given to us by God or the gods. The world's sacred traditions speak of the blessings that plants are endowed with, as nourishment and medicine for the body, mind, and spirit. From deep antiquity – and still known to indigenous peoples – there has been a hallowed compact between humans and the plant kingdom. If we have distanced ourselves from that understanding, that sublime partnership, it's not the fault of the plants; they are here for us, as they have always been. It is up to us now to learn from them, engage all our senses, let them know we see and love and respect them. When we touch a plant, let it be with acknowledgment and gentleness and receptiveness – and a sincere desire to hear what it has to tell us. What we have to learn will be beyond price.

Martha Libster's Elements of Care® program, which is the focus of this extraordinary book, can be a life-changing experience. Be ready to encounter a deeper awareness of the body you inhabit and its profound energetic resonance in partnership with plants. Be ready for a shift in perceptions as you enter the beautiful world of "gentle medicine."

The healing effect of a conscious partnership with plants operates on levels far beyond what we think of as the physical; it extends to the emotional and spiritual. It is a pathway to "balance in body and peace of mind," as the book's title tells us. It is difficult to adequately describe the scope of this self-care program, except to say that a person who engages with it may never look at a plant or one's worldview, quite the same way.

Dr. Martha is a Clinical Nurse Specialist, a Nurse-Herbalist, and an Herbal Diplomat®. She is also a scholar of the long history of the healing arts and its practitioners. The Elements of Care® program represents thirty years of her integrative insights. Her life's work is the healing of the Self, in all its magnificent, majestic wholeness.

Throughout her book we find Gentle Medicine Self-Study lessons to guide us into an intimate conversation with the plants around us...to learn how to enter the Green World and become apprentices in a process of lifelong learning. And what a master class this is! Can food be medicine? Of course it can. Can what we call a weed be medicine? Of course it can. "...[E]very substance (including plants) has the potential to be medicine," Dr. Martha writes. The modern medical paradigm has moved away from these primary, traditional avenues of self-care and self-healing, in its embrace of the dominant biomedical way of healthcare. Should it be a choice between one or the other? Not at all, she tells us. She is here to teach a new healing paradigm of inclusion, "a balance of biomedical, traditional, and personal plant partnership experience."

So, how does this training work? It has to do with such concepts as mindfulness, sentience, common sense, intuition, insight. It's about going into yourself and knowing that "partnering with plants requires full communion as an open two-way channel" – a tuning of the self "deliberately, consciously, and enthusiastically to plants." We don't "use" plants in this self-care paradigm, she says, we "apply" them.

And we keep the two-way channel open. "In essence, what and how we observe something, and what we think when we observe it, changes 'it.'" If that sounds like Quantum Theory, it is, but it is also what is understood in indigenous cultures around the world. Your touch, your thought, your intention, affects your relationship with a plant. You could call that scientific, or spiritual, or simply mysterious. But Dr. Martha witnesses it every day of her life.

Self-care, as she sees it, is primary prevention. Her program of plant partnerships is "a foundation for a healthcare reform movement that seeks … to ensure a more sustainable healthcare system for the future."

Gentle Medicine for Balance In Body and Peace of Mind is an important – I would say essential – book for these times. It is entirely possible that you will come away armed with new skills, new awareness of the plant consciousnesses all around you – and of the subtle vibrational ocean we and our plant partners swim in. Together.

This is a book of wisdom and peace – a glorious how-to on so many levels. It is as calming, hopeful, informative, surprising, enlightening, life-affirming and joyful as anything I have ever read. It brings forth the ancient truth of what "healing" is and should be, but often is not.

If you want to wrap your arms around a brilliant, beautifully written, "old-new" way to be fully alive to Nature's healing ways – and expand yourself from the inside out – start here. And be sure to read about Dr. Martha's multi-generational secret recipe for lemon bread, a creation that apparently lives in its own wondrous, alchemical reality.

Peace,

Catherine Dees
Co-Producer - Continuum: The Immortality Principle
Senior Editor - St. Lynn's Press
Author - Omm Sety's Egypt

Preface

Historically, many people's cultural values include the freedom to explore all health options and to discover what "works."[1] Self-care, the first tier in all healthcare systems is a healing tradition in America and around the world. This book is about precision self-care with plant medicine for common health concerns, life transitions, and excessive stress. In the Elements of Care® gentle medicine program detailed throughout this book, you will follow the roots of ancient wisdom and healing traditions. You will learn a new language that can change your life with recipes and remedies for Self-care practices leading to greater energy as balance in body and peace of mind. Your laboratory for personal growth resides in your own kitchen and garden!

This book seeks to add a new dimension to your current knowledge of health, healing, and Self-care. *Gentle Medicine for Balance in Body and Peace of Mind* takes an energetics-first approach to understanding health patterns that form the foundation for partnering with plants in the creation of a precision Self-care plan. You will master the use of the five familiar Elements of Care® – ether, fire, air, water, and earth– while selecting and creating simple herbal remedies.

Drinking a cup of cool water or sipping a cup of tea, tasting a favorite childhood food, and singing a memorable song are just a few of the thousands of examples of simple remedies, acts of kindness, one can give to oneself in times of stress, sadness, confusion, pain, and thirst. Kindness is the remedy of remedies. Nurses have known this to be true for over 300 years.[2] Picking the precise remedy for use at the right time and place can be a catalyst for healing. A healing process always involves change. Plant medicines are gentle but powerful catalysts for change and therefore healing. Herbalism as partnership with plants in human healing has stood the test of time. Gentle medicines with plants as partners are often familiar and accessible too. Simple, familiar, and accessible gentle medicines are the formula for successful Self-care. Therefore, the Elements of Care® program for balance in body and peace of mind begins with re-entering the world of plants.

Martha Mathews Libster, PhD, MSN, APRN-PMHCNS, APHN-BC, FAAN
Wauwatosa, Wisconsin

CHAPTER 1

Welcome Back to the Plant World

How beautiful everything is! Gardens, forests, mountains, deserts, and even the oceans and rivers are alive with the plant life that grows in, on, and around them. As you think about plants in Nature, try to recall any fragrances, colors, shapes, tastes, or textures associated with your experiences. The teachings in many cultures' healing traditions on the partnership between humans and plants suggest that it is this sensory experience that is key to understanding a plant's medicine. Some scientists suggest that the memories humans have from engaging with plants over millennia for the purpose of care and cure have become encoded impressions on human DNA. This might explain why plant medicines are so familiar and therefore perceived as safe. Plants, although quite powerful in their action, have earned the reputation throughout history as "gentle" medicine. Many, if not most plants, mainly when applied in the whole form following tradition, do, have extensive safety records. Regardless of the history, genetic memory, and an appearance of plant-like gentleness, safety with plants requires first-hand knowledge. A proper introduction is essential!

Establishing a relationship and being introduced to the personality of any healing plant is a foundation for safe and effective plant partnership. Getting to know the personality of a plant is similar to getting to know your physician or nurse. The more a health practitioner knows about you, the better they are at providing care that addresses your unique needs. Healthcare systems stress the importance of relationship-centered care because it is well documented that addressing individual patient needs increases the potential for safer and more effective care that does not over- or under-estimate any health benefits or risks of care. A more intimate understanding of a plant leads to a more informed, knowledgeable, and judicious partnership in care and comfort.

As communities become more industrialized, moving away from farming and their daily connection with the land as their source of food and medicine, people become less likely to remember their families' plant medicine traditions. Children are taught to buy a product at a store and may not know what is in that remedy or how it was made. They will not have had the experience of getting to know plants through gardening, tea tastings, plant walks in the forest, or preparing foods and simple medicines from what they find in Nature or cultivate in their gardens. Reading about a plant or its medicinal constituents does not prepare one to choose from hundreds of plants on the planet as does direct interaction with Nature, be that in a garden, the woods, or growing a plant in a pot on a patio.

The best gentle plant medicines are those we know from experience. Those experiences are remembered and conveyed as stories of how the plant heals us. An understanding of plant medicine develops through learning growth patterns as well as observing through the senses, human physical and energetic responses when in the presence of any given plant. Is the medicine of a plant only within the plant? Those whose emphasis is on industry and patent medicine would say that the medicine of the plant lies only in its biochemical constituents. History and tradition say otherwise. The "medicine" of a plant lives in the stories shared of the enduring relationships between people and plants. There are many stories.

As you read this, do you remember any of your own stories of some plants that you have come to know? Each memory of plant medicine resides in the story as shared with others for whom we care. Safety, benefits, and risks are recorded in that story that can have more meaning in a moment of need than what is read in a book or online about another's experience at a distance.

Many sources of information help us learn about the gentle medicine of plants and are referenced throughout this book. Still, ancient wisdom suggests that at the beginning, the safest and most beneficial route is plant introduction through personal sensory experience. This book provides you that opportunity for personal self-study of your relationship with the plant world, to begin to make your own medicine, and create stories of healing. Everyone's stories of the plant world are welcome.

Interacting with healing plants is a highly sensory experience that has been known throughout history to inspire healing as balance in body and peace of mind. How are the plants able to inspire? By and through a relationship with plants, you will learn just how. Just as each person has a different personality, so too does each species of plant have different qualities which they demonstrate in the way they affect humans, such as how they smell, look, taste, and feel. If you do not remember having had an experience of plant partnership that inspires, this book, *Gentle Medicine for Balance in Body and Peace of Mind*, offers you an opportunity of a lifetime! It guides you through the Elements of Care® (EOC) gentle medicine program to cultivate your connection with medicinal plants and design your Self-care plan. Start with one plant as your focus for a relationship, perhaps one for which you have a memory from childhood. Try Gentle Medicine Self-study #1. For those who *do* have memories of plant partnerships, this guide is an invitation and orientation to become certified in the EOC gentle medicine Self-care program with plants as partners.

—*Memories and Plant Partnership*—

Gentle Medicine Self-study #1: Plant Memories

What are your earliest memories of plants? How old were you?
What happened with the plant(s)?
What did you learn about the plant?
Use a journal to record your memories and reflections.

Relationships with plants often leave lasting impressions, mainly when they feed and heal us. Human experience with plants is stored away on DNA while imprinting a memory of the environment that is familiar and, therefore, safe. Safe memories of plants are communicated over generations through stories about beliefs, knowledge, and practices that hold meaning for peoples of every culture. Plant-people partnerships are universal. While the histories are vastly different from culture to culture, within the essence of those stories is the comfort that familiarity with plants as foods and medicines offers.

Have you ever thought about how plants affect your life? This program is a guide for deep reflection on your life experience of healing plants, flowers, and trees and for creating your unique Self-care plan. It is a guide for those who want to "stop and smell the roses" and mindfully enter the plant world in a new way. Many have forgotten their plant partnerships with flowers, trees, and plants. It is time to restore the knowledge of healing traditions with plants. We need it. Our children need it.

For the past two centuries, people in industrialized nations have moved away from their direct connections with plants. This disconnection from plants is now having an impact on children. There are children in America who live in rural areas where agriculture is a way of life, who do not know that broccoli is a vegetable and who cannot say from where the tomatoes on their pizzas come. I have taught them in my classes and had the awesome opportunity to introduce them to the plants that give them foods and medicines. Some children I have met are afraid to play outdoors in Nature and instead spend hours on their computers and cell phones so that they will not, as they have been told, develop allergies or illnesses due to environmental exposures. How has it happened that children are afraid of being in Nature and are subsequently losing direct connection with the plant world?[3]

My earliest memory of a plant partnership is of myself eating little clovers with tiny yellow flowers on the side of the road in front of our house in Massachusetts. I am not sure how I knew to eat them at age four, but they were delicately sour and satisfied my love of sour foods that I had as a child. I also loved to eat dill pickles and then drink the pickle juice in an aperitif glass! I have other early memories of plants. My mother taught me about collecting the sap running from maple trees and how to find and eat checkerberries in the mountains, but we are not sure how I knew about clovers and dill. Some children are born with a gift of math, music, or sports. Mine was the plants. My grandmother told me stories of her memories of my relationships with plants even before age four. She told me that I was in a restaurant for my third birthday, where I was asked by the server what I wanted for my birthday dinner. She told me that I put my little nose up in the air and said with a smile, "artichokes!" I remember my mother teaching me when and how to cook and eat an artichoke. She also taught me to drink milk after eating an artichoke because it makes the milk taste sweet. She said that was due to the iron in the artichoke.

I still eat artichokes, especially in the spring. The artichoke is the flower bud of *Cynara cardunculus*, a thistle plant cultivated as a food. I love the *process* of eating the green bud as much as the artichoke itself. I do not grow them, but I enjoy choosing them at the market. I pick the ones with the widest stems, which I have found often signifies a larger heart, the core of the artichoke. I also find peace in holding the artichoke in my hands, the process that happens when I connect the plant with the memory of my grandmother and mother's teachings. The taste, smell, and texture trigger positive memories and health as balance in my body.

Partnership with plants in Self-care and comfort of others is my life work. It is my calling to help those who desire a relationship with plants so that they, too, can learn the best ways to partner with healing plants in the care of self and humanity. If plants are your personal or professional interest, an idea of fun, or even a passion, then you have found the right book!

This book will guide you, step-by-step and element-by-element, to re-enter the world of medicinal plants in a way that you cannot get from surfing the internet. This is a whole program in one place. It also is the result of more than thirty years of experience in my work as a nurse.

My research on nurses' and the public's knowledge of healing plants demonstrates that plant partnership in Self-care is an enduring healing tradition. According to the last World Health Organization (WHO) study in the 1980s on the subject of traditional healing, 80 percent of the world's population still used their traditional methods of healing, including medicinal plants.[4] Yet, that knowledge has become all but lost in more industrialized societies. The disconnect from the plant world, with their own medicine stories, has caused many to suffer, though they may not realize that to be one cause. Reconnection with the gentle medicine of the plant world requires no previous experience. This book, *Gentle Medicine for Balance in Body and Peace of Mind*, is designed to serve as a guide on your journey - a reintroduction to Self-care with healing plants as partners. Welcome back to the plant world!

—*Plant Teachers*—

Plants provide a vessel for carrying out our hearts' intentions for healing, energy, and comfort in the care of Self and others. Plants are partners in this work and, therefore, also are "teachers" in this program. In the EOC program detailed in this book, you will learn what plants have taught me as a person and a nurse. I am their student, called time and again, to enter their green and flowery world. You, too, can engage plants to be your teachers! It is possible to have a personal relationship with a plant, even a single plant, that will bring you so much understanding of the beauty of the Creator and the creation— human, animal, and plant—that healing can occur at all levels of your being. People can heal spiritually, mentally, emotionally, and physically from experiences with a single plant. I have witnessed these many times. Some of those stories are included here. I hope that they make you smile.

I also hope that they help you to remember your connection with plants and how you think about and relate to them. How have you learned to care for yourself and others over the years? What do you believe and think about healing plants? Do you talk about plants when someone asks you how you take care of yourself? You can now! To get started, think about your knowledge of plant foods. Take oranges, for example. Do you drink orange juice for cold or flu symptoms because you think that it is a "good source of vitamin C"? What beliefs or knowledge do you have about orange juice, whole oranges, or growing orange trees? Do you have other health beliefs about how to take care of yourself when you have a common cold or the flu? Do any of those beliefs include plants either as foods or medicine?

Gentle Medicine Self-study #2: When Does Food Become Medicine?

Pick or purchase a fresh orange (Citrus sinensis). Wash it thoroughly. Cut the orange into quarters. Set a timer for 5 minutes. Quiet yourself in a comfortable chair. Use all of your senses to focus mindfully on the orange. Smell, feel, look at, listen to, and taste the outer peel, the inner peel, and the fruit.

- What are the qualities of the orange?
- Is it "medicine"?
- When is a plant food and when is it medicine?
- Who decides? How is this decided?

Record your reflection.

By definition, a medicine is "a substance or preparation used in treating disease; something that affects well-being."[5] Therefore by definition, just about any substance on the planet could be a medicine if it is used to treat disease or it affects someone's well-being in some way. Water, for example, is a substance for treating illness. Water is used to prepare medicines and wash the bodies of the sick. Drinking water also affects the well-being of a person. Without water, people cannot survive. Does this mean that water is medicine? It can indeed be used medicinally in the care and treatment of the ill. And some who have sampled the special mineral waters found in the western United States, for example, or at Lourdes in France, says that water itself can indeed be medicine. When does water become medicine and not just a fluid, we need to drink every day to survive?

A substance becomes a medicine when people decide to call it "medicine." What is medicine varies from culture to culture. Water becomes medicine at Lourdes in France because many people have witnessed that water heal the lame and the dying. This is an example of how an everyday substance can become medicine. As a healing substance, water becomes medicine because people assign healing properties to it. People believe the substance to be healing. Thus, every substance (including plants) has the potential to be medicine.

The age-old definition of a weed is "a plant for which no use has been discovered yet." Because humans often do not value a plant until it has meaning for them, there are many plants deemed weeds! For example, St. John's Wort (*Hypericum perforatum*), one of the most healing plants I know and one for which I have many fond memories, is deemed a "noxious weed" in numerous countries because it can be invasive. Invasive plant species are deemed as such because they are said to be a threat to the natural resources in an ecosystem or the human use of those resources. If the healing benefits of St. John's Wort were well known and weighed against the risks, the plant might be exonerated.

There are five types of plant- human partnerships:

1. Weeds—no partnership
2. Ornaments—aesthetic partnership
3. Foods—nourishing partnership
4. Medicine—care and cure partnership
5. Recreational and Abused substance—can lead to excessive partnership

St. John's Wort

Assigning the title of "medicine" to a plant may be one of the highest human honors bestowed on a plant. When a plant becomes "medicine," it then becomes an object of power. Plants that can heal are valued in societies because they have the potential to heal and extend life. The plant is no longer an ornament, a pretty object growing outside the backdoor. It is no longer a food used to nourish the body alone; it can be a commodity and a resource that cures and heals. The plant becomes a source of revenue because of its healing properties. Countries that value plants as medicine have regulatory bodies whose job it is to determine safety standards for those plant medicines. Determining standards includes being able to decide on the nature of plant partnership.

Plants deemed a weed are either ignored or destroyed. Plant partners for recreation and excessive use, such as opium poppy (*Papaver somniferum*) and marijuana (*Cannabis sativa*), are often easily identified in society. They get a lot of attention through the media. The plants of these partnerships can be highly valued (and expensive) for their ability to create a particular effect on the body and mind, such as euphoria. Still, they can be plants of potential abuse when they are associated with addictive behavior or excessive recreational use. Plants used as ornaments and foods are identifiable as well. Ivy (*Hedera sp. L.*), for example, is a common ornamental house plant. It is not eaten as are raspberries (*Rubus idaeus L.*).

The ability to discern when a specific plant moves from a food to a medicine partnership is often more challenging, especially for the governmental regulatory bodies charged with protecting the public from harm due to plants. In reality, people frequently partner with many plants as both food and medicine, mainly when the term "medicine" implies more than substances that are ingested. Medicines are also applied topically and environmentally, meaning through the other senses of sight and smell. Examples of topical applications of plant medicines are salves and poultices. Environmental applications are baths and steams. Plant medicine applications will be discussed later on in greater detail.

A plant's application does not determine its categorization as a food or medicine because plant medicines can be eaten or drunk just as plants are for food. How a plant looks or how much it costs cannot help determine whether it is a medicine or food either. The difference between a plant as food and plant as medicine lies in the *intent* of the person who is partnering with the plant. When a plant becomes a medicine, valued for its ability to heal, there is intention for care and cure.

Grape (*Vitis vinifera*) is one of many examples of a plant that is represented in all five areas of partnership. Grapes are just a weed to those who have the vines growing in their yard but cannot identify the plant as grape. Red, purple, and green grapes are eaten as fruit. The leaves also are included in Greek and Middle Eastern cuisines. Grapes also are medicine. They have anti-inflammatory and pain-relieving properties ascribed to constituents such as ferulic acid, salicylic acid, ascorbic acid, and quercetin. Traditionally grapes, fresh or dried (raisins), are known to relieve discomfort related to arthritis and migraine. Wine is also produced from grapes, which has a number of medicinal benefits. Wine was historically prescribed and administered by nurses[6] as a remedy often referred to as *Spiritus fermentae*. Grapes, as wine, also can be drunk excessively. Wine is another example of a plant partnership in which the intention is food and medicine as it can be drunk as medicine in the same way it is drunk as part of a meal. The difference is in the person's purpose or intent.

—Self-care in a Tiered Healthcare System—

The human intent to heal with plants has been traced back to the earliest days of our species' evolution. The remains of medicinal plants, the pollen grains of eight plants including *Ephedra sp.* are said to have been discovered in the burial site of a Neanderthal man. Before the creation of antibiotics and other pharmaceuticals, plant medicines were what nurses, physicians, and other healers all used in healing practice. Plant partnership is not new to the world of science and technology. It is not a passing fad within the domain of alternative or complementary medicine.

History clearly shows the influence plants have had in the development of healing practices of the public and professional health care providers, drug development, and sustainability of health care systems of nations over the centuries. People partner with plants in Self-care and comfort of others because the plants are accessible, inexpensive, empowering, and effective remedies. People make their own whole-plant remedies, such as juices, extracts, compresses, poultices, teas, syrups, soups, plasters, steams, and baths. Plants not only play an important role in healing. They provide us with food, spiritual inspiration, and oxygen and therefore are intrinsic to life itself. They are a source of energy for a life that cannot and will not become burned out. Plants are essential partners in the design of a Self-care practice that supports and nurtures an energized, vibrant life.

A four-step tiered system[7] of healthcare exists within communities that starts with Self-care as the first tier. When changes occur in health, prompting a person to seek greater balance in body and peace of mind, their first step is searching their memory for how to deal with the change. If the change and the remedy to support balance are familiar, (i.e. they are present in one's memory), then there can be peace of mind in the knowledge that they can take care of themselves. A person practicing Self-care can restore or promote their own health by making lifestyle and dietary changes and by making Self-care simple medicines from the elements found in Nature in the form of fire or warmth, water, and plants. Terms often used to refer to this first step are "conservative care" or "watchful waiting."[8] Another term, "self-limited disease"[9] has been used since the 19th century by nurses and physicians who suggested that to avoid over-treatment, it was often preferable to first observe and support patients as they practice their own Self-care and let "Nature" run its course rather than suggest immediate biomedical intervention. Florence Nightingale wrote in her advice book *Notes on Nursing* in 1859 that: "Nature alone cures... and what nursing has to do in either case, is to put the patient in the best condition for Nature to act upon him."[10] She echoed popular sentiment among community caregivers and the public alike at a time in which people recognized the value of watchful waiting in the case of self-limited diseases as a judicious response to moderating perceptions of over-treatment by physicians using "heroic therapies," such as bloodletting and elemental mercury called "calomel."[11] However, self-limited disease and watchful waiting do not suggest that people should be doing nothing. The first tier is a vital time for Self-care, managing one's environment within and without. This tier is the focus of this EOC program.

It is also essential to understand the position of the other three tiers involved in health decision making. When a person or their family's resources, Self-care with lifestyle, food, and home medicines do not meet their health needs for care and cure, they begin the search for assistance outside of the home. The second tier is seeking the advice of family, friends, along with books and websites. The web has become an excellent rapid source of health information that is not without its risks. The third tier is seeking help from knowledgeable caregivers in the community, such as a nurse for their support, experience, and knowledge. The purpose of engaging the community caregiver in the third tier is to help navigate health choices, weigh the benefits and risks of those choices, implement and evaluate the effectiveness of chosen remedies, and then create and manage decision points for knowing when and if ever to move to the fourth tier. The fourth tier is biomedical care, that includes pharmaceutical drugs, surgery, radiation, and other diagnostics and treatments that require specialized knowledge.

Gentle medicine with conservative, watchful, and active Self-care is a foundational part of any healthcare system that promotes people's faith in their ability to take care of themselves and their families. Some do not know the history of medicine and the value and purpose of Self-care as the first tier. Some have entirely abandoned the possibility of a tiered health system and, with it all responsibility for their health. They may rely solely on fourth-tier biomedical care in all situations at all times. Relying exclusively on biomedical care is not judicious, nor is it feasible or sustainable for any community or nation.

Nurses witness the satisfaction of people, young and old, who have set an intention to learn how to care for themselves whenever possible. When I ask people if they would prefer to be *asked* what they would like to do about their health or *told* what to do about their health, most people want to be asked rather than told. People know that they are responsible for their health – body, mind, emotion, and spirit. Each person is responsible for the health choices that they make. Yet, there are times when people do want and need someone to tell them what to do. Typically, this is when they are in the most urgent or emergent of situations when they need compassion and access to a more considerable body of knowledge of healthcare.

Gentle Medicine Self-study #3: Self-care Survey Question

Would you rather be asked what you would like to do about your health or told what to do about your health? Ask this question of yourself or a friend or family member you are helping. The answer serves as an indicator for the tier of care that may be required.

Note to Reader: Please consult a reputable resource for triaging the advisability of engaging in Self-care. The Elements of Care® Self-care program is a resource for best designs in Self-care when the first tier of care is warranted. Recommended resources for triage: Fries, J. & Vickery, D. Take care of yourself and Fries, J. & Vickery, D. Take care of your child.

Memories of gentle medicine plant partnerships endure. While peoples' intent to heal with plants may not have changed over time, how people partner with medicinal plants in Self-care has undergone many changes. Technology has had a significant impact on development of herbal supplements and pharmaceuticals. As you proceed through the EOC program and do the Self Studies in the chapters that follow, you will learn some critical strategies for making informed choices about gentle medicines, most specifically about a partnership with plants in precision Self-care. These strategies draw from many sources from the biomedical to the traditional worldviews or paradigms. You will also learn the health beliefs, culture, and language associated with these paradigms so that you, too, can teach others about plant partnerships in precision Self-care from a highly informed perspective that includes a balance of biomedical, traditional, and personal plant partnership experience. The beliefs, perceptions, and practices associated with plant partnerships exhibited by the three distinct plant perspectives will be discussed in more detail as you read on.

The significant social changes of the 1800s in the United States when being self-reliant and "being one's own doctor" as the first step in health care was a deeply held spiritual value and publicly pronounced ethic[12] has been replaced by technology including pharmaceutical drugs. That climate is changing. The invention of the electric light, modern plumbing, and water filtration plants have altered the course of human history and improved public health in so many ways. Unfortunately, people are realizing once again that rapid industrialization and the overall shift away from connections with Earth, plants, and seasonal growth cycles has taken its toll. The current biomedical healthcare culture that equates a preeminent healthcare system with primary care (1:1 provider treatment), technological innovations including pharmaceuticals, and hospital treatment has led to the creation of the most expensive system of medicine. While the biomedical culture and system often dominate public conversation, Self-care culture is still prevalent in society. It has been called the *hidden healthcare system*.[13] In the EOC program, I suggest that you consider all paradigms.

Re-entering the plant world and beginning to think in terms of the first tier of Self-care, does not oppose the biomedical. It does help to put the biomedical in perspective, however. The knowledge, ability, and freedom to take care of Self in body, mind, emotion, and spirit is one of the greatest gifts we have and can offer to our children. Self-care is a gift that "keeps on giving." The EOC program outlined in the next chapters demonstrates the essential role plant partnerships have in precision Self-care that would promote greater balance in body and peace of mind.

CHAPTER 2

The Elements of Care® Program: A Guide for Self-Care

The Elements of Care® (EOC) program is for anyone from young children to families, health professionals, and scientists, to teachers and public servants. The Self-care discussed in the EOC is not the information that fills the internet, which only provides resources and information. *Self-care is a science* with a strong research base, primarily in nursing and sociology.[14] The EOC program incorporates scientific understanding, from bench to bedside. It will help you apply information and resources in the design of your precision Self-care plan that reflects your unique health patterns and, therefore, is profoundly meaningful. The EOC, based in centuries of nursing history of expertise in the art and science of Self-care,[15] also represents my thirty years of *integrative insights* as a Clinical Nurse Specialist, Nurse-Herbalist, and Herbal Diplomat®. I hope that you will find the references to my experiences working with people and their nurses around the world who partner with plants for Self-care and in the care and comfort of others helpful.

The plant world is so very full of beauty, color, fragrance, and extraordinary design. Entering the healing world of plants can inspire integration and insight. Integration is the ability to *embody* or make something a genuine part of our whole being. Being embodied is easy when we interact with a world that is beautiful and fragrant, and no danger would cause us to raise our defense mechanisms. Integration is also a quality of heart that supports the desire to broaden one›s consciousness to move mindfully beyond preconceived ideas, feelings, and experiences. Insight is the understanding, sensitivity, heightened awareness, and humanity that become possible as a result of this broadened state of consciousness.

Learning how a particular plant heals, *integrative insight* suggests that many ways of knowing be employed. Knowledge of plant medicine comes from growing them and harvesting them in their natural surroundings, making different remedies from their seeds, fruits, leaves and roots, and experiencing them with human senses in the care of self and family. Reading botanical research on the constituent parts of plants as well as clinical trial research done with the whole plant or its constituents is yet another way of knowing. Staying mindfully receptive to learning and actively inviting knowledge of a plant›s medicine through experiences in body, mind, emotion, and spirit will challenge any preconceived human expectations of the natural world. The mindfulness practice of managing expectations is a strong basis for integrative insight. One way to cultivate the ability to manage expectations about plants is to do a blind tea tasting in which a person does not know what tea they are tasting.

To do the mindful tea tasting managing expectations Self-study, you will need to make two teas [See Gentle Medicine Self-study #4]. It is best to use cinnamon (*Cinnamomum verum*) and peppermint (*Mentha piperita*) because they are food grade as well as medicinal plants and are quite differently energetically, as will be explained. No one is ever required to participate in a Gentle Medicine Self-study. If you or a person you are doing this Self-study with smell something about the tea that causes concern, then you can decide to opt out.

A small amount of each tea is poured into separate cups without any indication of what the tea is, except that the teas are made from plants that could be found in a kitchen. Instruction for part one of the Self-study:

- Please suspend your effort to name the teas / the plants.
- Do not try to search your memory to name the plant.
- If you recognize the plants, do not state aloud what they are.
- Instead, focus on your senses.

Part two of this mindfulness Self-study is the tea tasting and recording your experiences.

—*Tea Tasting*—

While taking tea is a global culinary tradition, "tea tasting" for medicinal purposes is the scientific process used for centuries to determine the energetic medicinal qualities of plants. For example, I learned tea tasting when I studied Traditional Chinese Herbal Medicine (TCM). Over about fourteen months, I tasted about 240 herbs. Tasting is an integral part of plant partnership education. The term *tasting* is something of a misnomer as all of one's senses are engaged in the process of experiencing the plant in addition to the sense of taste. A tasting traditionally begins with meditation and ends with reflection. The meditation period is a time of preparing the body to act as a barometer for the action of a plant in the body. Before meditation, the herb is cooked, extracted (decocted or infused) in water. The cooking and preparation of the tea for tasting is also a meditation. Plants are handled with awareness and gratitude. Consider the growth of the plant and the effort and energy it took, human and plant, for the petals, twigs, roots, seeds, or leaves of any given plant to available for tea. Gratitude and appreciation open the heart and all of the channels in the body. It is in this open state that a tea is tasted. Tasting can be simple. There are two primary questions to ask when tasting herb tea:

1. Where do I/you feel the effects of this plant in my/your body?
2. What is the thermal nature of this plant?

Question 1, in the TCM tradition, is answered in terms of the three "burners": upper, middle, and lower. The upper burner is the head and upper chest area, the middle burner is the abdomen and chest area, and the lower burner is the lower abdomen. While the focus is on the torso and head areas, you can also report any sensations in your limbs. Peppermint, for example, is typically felt in the upper burner, but many also feel the effect of peppermint in the middle burner. Take a moment to remember tasting the first (peppermint) tea. It often helps to close your eyes to block some of the visual stimuli from the environment. What do you remember about the tea entering your body? Did it open your sinus and head channels? Second - What is its thermal nature?

The energetic scale for this Self-study is a hot to cold scale: Hot......Warm....Neutral....Cool.....Cold. Whether peppermint tea is served as a (temperature) hot or cold beverage, peppermint is considered *energetically cold*. By comparison, spearmint *(Mentha spicata)*, a plant in the same genus as peppermint for example, is not as cold. It is energetically cooling. Then taste the second tea – the cinnamon *(Cinnamomum verum)*. In which burner(s) do you feel it? What is its thermal nature? Some herbs may be felt in more than one burner. Cinnamon is warming and enters the middle burner and all channels. That's one reason why cinnamon is so popular on holidays during winter months!

Monks who conducted the tea tastings reached consensus long ago about the energetic classification of herbs, such as peppermint and cinnamon. There are hundreds of herbs that are classified similarly and are recorded in the TCM *Materia Medica* (book of herbal remedies). Over time, people have reconfirmed the value of the experiential process of tea tasting. Tea tasting and energetic classification of herbs ultimately result in a more precise choice of herbs in Self-care. The energetics of an herb is part of its profile or personality that is important to understand when attempting to establish plant partnerships.

Gentle Medicine Self-study #4: Managing Expectations with Mindful Tea Tasting

Cinnamon Decoction
Purchase 5 small or 2 large cinnamon sticks (the bark of *Cinnamomum spp.*) Wash them thoroughly and place in small pot. Cover with spring or distilled water. Raise water to the boil and take off stove. Cover with lid and allow to sit for at least 4 hours as the herb expands. After expansion period, check water level and add enough water so that the level is about 2 cm above the herbs. Decoct (gentle boil) the herb for 45 minutes at a temperature where the steam just rises from the water – not a rolling boil. The water level should be about ½ of the original level after the cooking. Strain the decoction and discard or compost the herb. Sip the tea at room temperature. Cinnamon is classified as opening and warming the energy channels in the body. Record your reflection of cinnamon decoction – body, mind, emotion, spirit.

Mint Infusion
Harvest or purchase fresh or dried mint leaf (*Mentha piperita*). Chop the fresh leaf or gently crush the dried leaf prior to infusing in boiled water. Put 1-2 teaspoons of fresh or 1 teaspoon of dried herb in a tea pot or tea ball. Pour one cup of boiled water over the herb. (Put the herb in the cup first and splash with the water rather than put the water in the cup first and try to submerge the leaf.) Strain and sip. Peppermint is energetically cold and opens and cools the channels of the head (upper burner). Record your reflection of the mint infusion.

Since childhood, people are taught to use their minds to name things in their environment: dog, cat, momma, chair, etc. Knowledge of the environment is demonstrated in what and how much we know to name over time. Past experiences of the environment also can set up preconceived expectations of what happens next in our interchange with our environment. When re-entering the world of medicinal plants, many people have numerous expectations that sometimes are negative about the plants that may not originate from their personal experience. Their expectations may be projections or thoughtforms originating from the experience and memories of others. This tea tasting Self-study is one example of a way to give potential plant partners a fair chance to show us what they are and what they offer us. We have the opportunity to clear the memory of past projections so that we can more mindfully engage with a plant in the present moment. Clearing our memory can be the beginning of the partnership.

This book is neither encyclopedic nor exhaustive in terms of how many plants I know. Rather, it is pointed to what plants I know are best from my clinical work and research in partnership. More specifically, I have included those plants that have a very real affinity for applications in Self-care and comfort. These include oral applications, such as herbal teas, soups, alcohol extracts, syrups, and floral waters; topical applications, such as compresses, poultices, distillates, infused oils, ointments, and salves; and environmental applications, such as footbaths, full baths, healing gardens, steams, and aromatic inhalations.

Precision Self-care with plants in the EOC program starts with learning the energetics or physics of plants rather than the biochemistry of their constituents that can be known through personal Self-study, such as a tea tasting that uses the body as a barometer. This is a safe, efficient, and practical approach. Knowledge of the energetics of plants as foundation for choices in plant partnership can be discerned through patterns: symptom–sign–symbol patterns in persons and the energetic patterns of the plants as well. Traditionally, the medicine of a plant is described energetically by the story of its patterns. History is a record of patterns over time. The histories of plant medicines demonstrate that the unique energetics of each plant can be discerned. Plants are energy fields and sentient lifeforms.

—Sentience and Common Sense—

When people consider plant partnership, it is often because of a perceived need for the benefits of the plant. Knowledge of the general benefits of a plant must be balanced with caution and common sense. Common sense is a critical component of one's ability to be cautious. Wise and safe partnership with plants often depends upon common sense. Common sense is defined as "sound and prudent but often unsophisticated judgment."[16]

People do not have to have extensive formal herbal education to be able to reason about how they might partner with a plant. They can access their common sense. Common sense, if it is not repressed, can help determine the appropriateness of an herb. Common sense is demonstrated as an intuition or insight related to a particular experience. For example, if someone decided to eat cayenne pepper *(Capsicum frutescens)* to improve circulation, but they took it in capsule form, they could block one way that commonly measures dose—taste. Taste and other sensory experiences can activate one's common sense. If a person eats whole cayenne peppers and experiences the hot spicy taste of the herb, they would, at some point, say, "I think I've had enough." Common sense works best when the plant is experienced fully by the senses. Common sense can be our own personal, natural regulatory agency!

Nurses can use all five senses to learn about healing plants. Taste the plant as long as it is not poisonous. Look closely at the pattern of growth and smell the fragrance it may emit. Touch the plant's leaves and feel its edges and boundaries, how it is defined in space. Interact with the energy field of the plant, although you may not be aware of it. Human beings and the environment are energy fields that are in constant relationship with one another. Plants as part of the environment are also energy fields. The energy field of a plant can be sensed by our own bodies in much the same way we feel the presence or energy field of another human being. The energy field or life force of a plant can even be measured. The book, *The Secret Life of Plants*,[17] outlines numerous studies of plants utilizing scientific instruments such as those that measure electrical voltage, demonstrating that plants exhibit a life force or energy field. Studies also demonstrate that plants specifically relate to their environment in ways such as adapting to human wishes, responding to music, and communicating with humans. They move very slowly, so they must be observed very closely in addition to being measured by instruments.

Scientists have found that many plants have special abilities. For example, Tompkins & Bird found that "Plants are even sentient to orientation and to the future...a sunflower plant's, *(Silphium laciniatum)*, leaves accurately indicate the points of a compass. Botanists at London's Kew Garden found that Indian licorice, *(Arbrus precatorius)*, can predict cyclones, hurricanes, tornadoes, earthquakes, and volcanic eruptions."[18] Indigenous healers often teach that with plants, just as with humans, the *whole* is greater than the sum of the parts. Just as people are not only identified by their livers or some other organ or cell, and people with cancer have a greater identity and personality that is well beyond that of their cancer cells and disease, whole plants found in their natural state are more than their plant constituents or their taste or their leaf patterns.

It is possible to connect with plants. Many cultures who hold plant life sacred, suggest that we are able as humans to connect with the spirit of a plant as well as its material substance. It is often the body of the plant, which is most often thought of as the medicine when in actuality, it is the spirit or essence of the plant as well as the constituents of its body that heal. It is our breath, movements, and spirit that activates and inspires any medicinal action of a plant. With respect and consideration, we enter the quiet sentient lives of plants to form a partnership. They are receptive and responsive. Scientists to shamans have concluded from their knowledge of plants that plants are also intelligent and feeling. This sentient plant world is a ready source of inspiration and natural instruments for creating Self-care.

The beauty of plants can raise us up when human suffering stifles the senses. Exploring their world with all of the senses, engaging with them, and partnering with them, can provide some wonderful scientific experiences and existential moments. Commune and communicate directly with plants and give an equal platform to the "voice" of plants. Then focus on protecting your plant populations just as you learn the safest ways to partner with plants.

Plants require our protection because they are vulnerable. As they are non-verbal, we protect them by attuning to them and by learning their growth patterns and personalities [See Chapter 3]. Plant attunement, as well as knowledge, is a foundation for integrative insight. In return for attuning to plants, they provide us with insight into the opportunities they provide for balance in body and peace of mind. Plant remedies affect the body, mind, emotion, and spirit. This is why plant partnership is the focus of the EOC Self-care program that offers direct access to *holistic common-sense* Self-care with plants as teachers as well as partners.

Although plants do not use a voice, they often teach with clear instructions to those who are willing and able to tune in to their patterns of non-verbal communication. Plants communicate through behavior and our ability to perceive and interpret that behavior is what determines whether we learn from them or not. We recognize their "instructions" through different ways of knowing, such as insight. Psychological science informs us that this way of knowing and communicating that occurs in the non-verbal world, does so at the level of the subconscious and unconscious mind with all of its sensory experience, symbolism, and patterns.

We use our senses to interpret non-verbal behaviors that manifest as patterns of movement, sound, and energy. If you are having trouble imagining plant communication, consider human babies. Babies do not use formal language, yet parents interpret their behavioral cues and vocalizations so that they can communicate with and learn from their infant. As time passes since the day of birth, parents begin to recognize a pattern in their baby's cries, movements, and energy levels. For instance, a mother might realize that her infant is starting to get sleepy because the baby begins to yawn, rub its eyes, and make short puffing sounds.

The major difference between plant and infant communication is that plants do not vocalize. Therefore, one must become quite adept at observing plants' behavior patterns over time. As we work with plant patterns, we begin to understand the plant's presence and their abilities to help us in healing. The first step in mastering plant communication is to engage all of one's senses and use them to recognize and affirm the presence of plants. Plants are everywhere! They are in the houses we live in, the foods that we eat, and the medicines we apply. They are part of our celebrations and rituals: holly at Christmas, horseradish at Passover, bay leaf in victory, and rose petals at baptisms. These examples represent the human perspective. However, partnering with plants in healing requires full communication as an open two-way channel.

Think about the presence of plants from their perspective that is without a connection to human events of any kind. Become aware of the presence of plants by becoming an active participant in their world. Use your senses to validate the patterns of their existence. This is a highly subtle process because this work is done in the non-verbal world, the realm of the subconscious and unconscious mind. The process involves attuning one's self deliberately, consciously, and enthusiastically to plants.

Start with observation and simple acknowledgment of the plants in your environment, and then as you grow in your plant communication connections, you will understand more about this subtle world of plants and their power to heal. You will come to experience first-hand that the healing power of plants is much greater than merely providing substance for human remedies. They are sentient life with a story to tell. That story is as healing, in my experience, as their chemical constituents. They can heal in a way that is unique. One way to understand their healing ways is to be with the plants and to listen to the stories of people who have insights into their world.

But experiencing plant patterns in the subtle world is a skill that has to do with the ability to enter the plant world where the vibration of existence is very different from that of humans. That vibration is gentle, quiet, and delicate in comparison with the human world. This description holds even when referring to the presence of gnarly vines or trees with the toughest of barks. One must change vibration to enter the world of plants. Vibration change and communication occur as a result of change in consciousness. This skill is not unknown to people. The ability to change vibration is observed in adult to infant communication. The human relationship with plants is most often unconscious, if not nonexistent. Openness to integrative insight and a commitment to mindful reflection is an invitation for a synergistic understanding of the plant world, an engaging human-plant relationship, and a rich learning experience of the healing potential that can result from engagement with the plant kingdom.

Understanding and communicating with plants and sharing their stories are a lost part of the science and art of plant partnership in precision Self-care. It is in the story, the history, that we can learn the healing power and energetic properties of plants very quickly. We employ the knowledge of plant partnerships that has been cultivated, treasured, and preserved in recipe books, domestic guides, and sick room management books. The plant kingdom is a vibrant, colorful, aromatic, and quiet world of sentient life that has provided some of the simplest and yet powerful remedies, which people have used in Self-care and comfort practices throughout the centuries. Welcome to the vibrant world of the seeds and sound, fruits and fragrance, leaves and colors, flowers and flavor, roots, and textures that will amaze you. Connect through your senses to them, and the plants will lead you where you need to go and to what you need to learn. Enter the garden, meadow, forest, desert, ocean, or river, and you will find them—the plants—awaiting connection and quietly and eagerly ready to show you what they are.

LESSON FROM ST. JOHN'S WORT

Any expectations I still had about plants changed in 1997 when I had a transformative experience with plants that changed my worldview about the life force and sentience of plants forever. At the center of this lesson from the plant world was St. John's Wort *(Hypericum perforatum)*.

Many years ago, a friend and teacher of mine taught me what the scientist Paracelsus and other renowned teachers of plant medicine, including 20th century American herbalist John Christopher, maintained: that "the plant medicines we need grow outside our backdoor." The theory seemed reasonably abstract to me when I first heard it, and I simply tucked it away in my mind thinking that someday, somehow, I might be shown evidence of the truth of the statement. Many theories, such as this, are taught today as a routine part of herbalist education.

The backdoor theory was proved for me in a vivid experience when I was working as a nurse on a postpartum labor and delivery unit in a suburb of Denver, Colorado. For several weeks, physicians had delivered several babies on the unit by performing a fourth-degree episiotomy on the mothers. The number of episiotomies concerned everyone because it was not typical to do so many fourth degrees, and the women who had to undergo the procedure were so uncomfortable after delivery. I was also concerned because I knew that fourth degrees were often avoidable.

You see, over the years, I observed the results of deliveries performed by a British-educated nurse-midwife who massaged the perineum of her laboring mothers with St. John's Wort oil (infused oil) to help relax the cervix. My observation was that the oil prevented the need for an episiotomy, let alone an extensive one. I also had prepared and included the oil in my nursing practice for many years in the healing of wounds and injuries to the nervous system and in trigger point therapy for clients with fibromyalgia. I knew the healing properties of the plant and thought that it would help the women in Denver. As they came into my care at the hospital, I could not help but wish that I knew how to convince our labor and delivery team to consider another approach, such as that used by the midwife with whom I had worked. At that time, I was knowledgeable about nurse-herbalism but knew nothing about creating hospital systems policy changes. Even though I cared so much about the women, I found myself very intimidated to speak up about my years of knowledge in the prevention of episiotomy.

One morning, there was construction at the hospital. I was told that I had to park *behind* the hospital (we parked near a field), and I looked up in the hazy sunlight to see an entire field of small, yellow flowers. Every year, I had wildcrafted St. John's Wort flowers to make oil and tinctures for my clients, family, and friends. But that year, there had been no flowers. My herbal colleagues and I could find no plants in the mountains at all. It had been a very peculiar year in that regard. As you might imagine, when I went to investigate the flowers in the field, I found that the yellow flowers were indeed St. John's Wort. There was a huge field of the flowers growing literally outside the back door of the hospital, just as the herbal teachers had said the herbs that we need do. Never before had I seen such a massive demonstration of a theoretical proving. The medicines we need really do grow outside our back door. I have seen it many times since then.

What was particularly interesting about this situation with St. John's Wort was that I had tried to find the flowers in the mountains as I had done in years past. There did not seem to be any flowers for harvest on the feast of St. John, June 24th, as there should have been. By July, when I discovered the field of plants outside the hospital in that suburb of Denver, it appeared as if all of the plants had magically come down from higher elevations to grow right outside that hospital unit where I had prayed for assistance from that very flower. It was such a powerful spiritual experience in understanding the consciousness and sentience of healing plants, as well as my connection to the plant world. I remember speaking to the nurse manager about the appearance of the St. John's Wort. But even with her support, we could not figure out a way at that time to create the change that we knew could help the doctors and nurses as well as the women facing episiotomy. I vowed to dedicate my life to figuring out a way to create that very system change and to tell this story— St. John's Wort's story—wherever and whenever I could.

While elated with the affirmation of this plant connection, I was quite distraught at the outcome in the hospital. Unfortunately, the labor and delivery staff never did take advantage of the healing power of the St. John's Wort. My husband, friend, and I harvested what we needed for our remedies and left the rest. When I went back the next year to the field behind the hospital, not a single St. John's Wort plant could be found. Although they had appeared at the hospital's back door wanting to help us, the door was not yet open to them. Since that time, I have worked to open those doors for plant partnerships. This experience and many others like it are the reason I use the term "plant partnership." My experiences have shown me that plants are sentient or aware lifeforms and their healing effects are expressed *in relationship* with people—a dimension of healing yet to be fully explored by the sciences. Because plants are sentient, I try to be conscious of the language I use when referring to them. For example, I often say that people "apply" plants in self-care and comfort rather than saying that we "use" plants.

This book, *Gentle Medicine for Balance in Body and Peace of Mind*, seeks to dispel any lingering myths and misconceptions, ambiguity, and intimidation associated with a partnership with plants that would impede experiencing the joy and healing that is available to those who would enter the natural beauty of the plant world through the EOC program. The EOC program advocates *plant partnership* in precision Self-care to address common health concerns experienced in everyday life. The EOC approach is rooted in common sense, botanical knowledge, and healing traditions, as demonstrated for generations in the science and art of Self-care with a capital "S."

—Self-care with a Capital S—

Although Self-care is powerful, the substances and applications required to create even the smallest shift in health in body, mind, emotion, or spirit are minimal and can be quite gentle in nature; hence the reference to those medicines that come from Nature, such as water and plants, as gentle medicine. Nature cure has been the tried-and-true respected focus of Self-care and the creation of healing environments for centuries.[19]

Self-care is a healing tradition, as well as a science. Throughout history, people have engaged natural elements in the care and comfort of themselves, their families, and communities before seeking advice from others. The word "care" comes from the Old English word *Carian*, which means "to feel concern."[20]

Care is communicated through actions. How people *demonstrate* care for themselves and others is one way that they manifest their personality and the essence of their being.[21] Self-care is a spiritual path, the essence or purpose of which is a greater understanding of Self, *with a capital "S."*

The Self with a capital "S" refers to that which ancient philosophers referred to as the essential self. The essential and enduring Self is in all, is interdependent, inseparable, and part of a cosmic whole and therefore represents a spiritual individuality in unity with the Creator. The self with a lower case "s" is the perishable self that is the personality and the ego, that which is individuated from the whole. Fritjof Capra describes the self as an "abstraction devised by our discriminating and categorizing intellect."[22] It is the essential and enduring Self within that reincarnates in a series of perishable selves. To understand how Self-care, as attention to the essential and enduring Self, actually leads to balance in body and peace of mind, we need only look to the many ancient wisdom traditions, such as in religion and healing. We also look to the findings of those in the scientific field of physics, such as J.S. Bell, Henry Stapp, and Alain Aspect.

Physics is the domain of science that studies the energy-matter universe (the environment) within and without. Physics is the study of relationships on an atomic level that has led to the revelation of the basic oneness of the universe.[23] The worldview of modern physics explores the same elements at the heart and center of all spiritual and religious study east and west, namely a consciousness recognizing the unity and interrelatedness of all phenomena that is all things and events in the world as a cosmic whole. Quantum physics has added new dimensions to our understanding of thoughts or consciousness and the impact that consciousness has in and on the environment and others within that environment. In essence, what and how we observe something and what we think when we observe it changes "it."

Capra shows in his work of relating east and west, spiritual/religious tradition and science that the mystical – scientific path that leads to an *experience* of the oneness of all things is that which brings one balance in body and peace of mind. This path of seeking to "bring together" or "samadhi," as it is called in the yogic tradition, is a central notion in meditation practice in which one experiences the unity or non-duality of the Divine. This experience of union is taught in religious and mystical tradition to be a gift or *grace* from God, the Creator. It is also taught that the *effort* that persons make in seeking union, yoga, balance, and peace of mind prepares one to receive the gift as the reconciliation or union of opposites, "as above - so below." The path of Self-care is one of spirit (grace) and practice (effort); it is spiritual *and* practical. Peoples' choices of Self-care have demonstrated this integration of the spiritual and the practical.

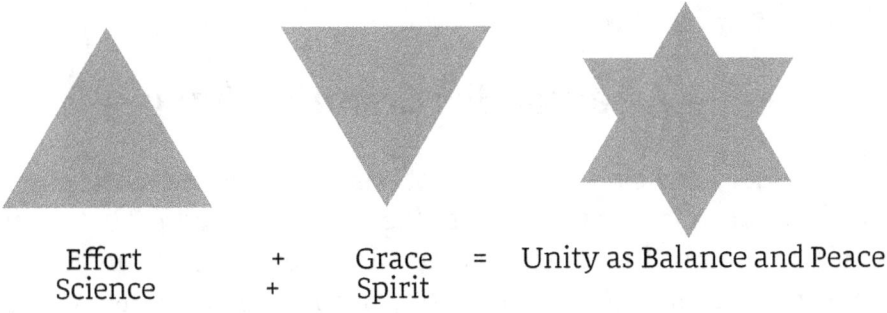

Effort   +   Grace = Unity as Balance and Peace
Science +   Spirit

It is quite common for people to incorporate healing knowledge from tradition and emergent science in Self-care as an integrative process. The insight gained from such reconciliation of seeming opposites, science and tradition, produces a greater understanding of the unified whole, that results in integrative insight.

Partnership with healing plants provides easy entrée into the process of the integration of science and tradition. The result of the interplay of experience between reading about and tasting plant constituents on one hand and experiencing their healing stories and the beauty of their presence in Nature on the other, informs the overall understanding and integrative insight of their medicine that is potent and yet gentle at the same time—the union of opposites. The essence or outcome of this integrative Self-care process is greater unity or a sense of belonging and the peace that can come from the experience of the union of opposites or unity. The pursuit of Self-care as a balance in body and peace of mind also supports a nurse's effort to serve humanity. This effort is the spiritual thread of the work of Self-care with a capital S. Self-care embraces the creative process of metamorphosis exemplified in plant growth, that of contraction (pushing upward through the soil toward the sun) and expansion (blossoming outward). Goethe wrote about the benefit of observing these alternating polarities of energy in the plant world. He wrote, "through an intuitive perception of eternally creative nature we may become worthy of participating spiritually in its creative processes" and that perceiving the essence of metamorphosis will "likely involve a beneficial metamorphosis in the essence of the perceiver."[24] This study and celebration of this essential connection between people and plants and the spiritual, as well as physical benefits, is at the heart of an enduring historical partnership in evolution as the reconciliation and unity of opposites. This is how plants have endured as foundational to Self-care and why they are the focus of the EOC precision Self-care program.

—*A Season for Climate Change*—

Consider your own memories of past experiences with Self-care. You may have been trying to prevent illness or generally feel better in health. Similarly, your self-care efforts may have been to maintain your strength while moving through or recuperating from an illness or injury. All pursuits in health and healing, from prevention to recuperation, require some form of change. Self-care requires a certain level of comfort with independent decision making, self-determination, and the will to create change.

The word "change" often provokes anxiety simply because of its connotations. People frequently associate change with some type of adverse or uncomfortable event in which something is given up, such as a personal habit, object, practice, belief, thought, or action. The change also may be perceived as that which happens in life that is against one's own will or desire. However, people serve as agents of change in their own lives by the decisions that they make in the first place. Personal choices lead to change.

Change does not necessarily require that a person give up something. It can also be about adding something to one's life or a simple shift or movement from one point to another. Consider, for example, a watercolor painting of a landscape set in an oak frame. If you were asked to "change the painting," you might not even consider painting over it or throwing the painting away, although that would fulfill the requirement for "changing" the painting. You might readily consider other possibilities for creating change, such as changing the frame to a walnut frame or decorating the frame in some way that is complementary to the painting that would improve the painting. Most changes in health begin with re-framing. There are at least three approaches to re-framing: "adding to," "giving up," or "moving things around."

Gentle Medicine Self-study #5: Comfort Level with Change

Try this change Self-study with some friends and family. First have each person select a partner to work with. Have each one face their partner and study the appearance of the partner for 30 seconds. Then have the partners turn back to back and give them the following simple instruction: "Change Your Appearance in 3 Ways." After one minute, have the pairs turn around to face each other and give them a few minutes to discover what changes were made. After everyone finishes the Self-study, have them sit down and record on a board the number of changes in which the person either added to, gave up, or moved around something in their appearance.

Having done this Self-study with groups on numerous occasions, I have found that most people have a habit of interpreting "change" to mean that they must give something up. People give up or remove their glasses rather than move their glasses to their pocket. They remove an earring rather than move the earring to their buttonhole. Even more rarely do people pick up an object in the environment around them and add it to their appearance as a form of change. Change, whether taking away from, adding to, or shifting something in the "picture," is the beginning of the process of transition, the process during which we adapt to the change. There are three stages in the process of transition:[25]

1. <u>Letting Go</u> of old ways and identities or breaking old habits.
2. <u>Neutral Zone</u> – After letting go of old habits but before the re-patterning has taken hold.
3. <u>Renewal</u> – Coming out of the transition with new energy, new identity, renewed sense of purpose.

Gentle Medicine Self-study #6: Change and Transition

Reflect on your Self-care practices as they are today. What would you change—that is add, give up, or move around? Write down your vision for change.

1. Change – Relinquish:

2. Change – Add:

3. Change – Move around

Where are you in the process of transition?

4. Letting Go:

5. Neutral Zone:

6. Renewal:

As you participate in these Self-studies, you are reflecting upon the change and transition process that is part of your everyday life. Change is so common that we often forget that it is our response to change and our ability to transition in a way that maintains harmony and peace that often defines us as individuals, communities, and nations.

Plants are catalysts for change in body, mind, emotion, and spirit. The plants in our houses and gardens serve as reminders to us that everything in life changes over time and that there are seasons and cycles in life. Plants evolve from seeds to shoots and leaves, and then to brilliantly colored flowers, plants, or trees. Plant evolution includes the process of plant death when they transform into a new layer of topsoil with the help of insects and microbes.

Herbal remedies can create powerful changes in behavior, energy flow, circulation, digestion, respiration, thought process, emotional and spiritual awareness. These changes are often subtle, occurring gently over time, and are often best understood through observation of health patterns. Herbs catalyze changes defined in herbalism as adaptogen[26], stimulant, cathartic, carminative, sedative, tonic[27], diuretic, demulcent[28], hallucinogen, alterative[29], aphrodisiac, counterirritant, vermifuge[30], febrifuge, emmenagogue, emetic, and vulnerary[31], actions to name just a few.

Reflection and re-framing in Self-care can catalyze an ability to perceive the positive experiences that the change and transition process brings. Perception is influenced powerfully by consciousness, habit, and momentum. This next Gentle Medicine Self-study demonstrates the power of perception.

Gentle Medicine Self-study # 7: The Power of Perception

FINISHED FILES ARE THE RESULT OF YEARS OF SCIENTIFIC STUDY COMBINED WITH THE EXPERIENCE OF MANY YEARS.

How many F's do you see? I have shown this Self-study as a slide at conferences and asked people to count the F's that they see. On the count of three, I ask them to call out the number of F's that they see. People call out numbers from two to six. They then look around wondering how people in the room can see different numbers of F's on the same slide!

There are, in fact, six F's in the sentence, and yet few people see the six Fs. Moving slowly from word to word, I point out the F's using a laser pointer. I also tell them that studies on perception suggest that on any given day, we may or may not see all six F's. However, once someone points out the Fs to us, our brains cannot "un-see" the actual number of F's.

This Self-study causes people to think about perception and mind. People realize that we may not always see what is right in front of us. The lesson of this Self-study can be applied to plant partnership and Self-care as well. How many plants are there in front of us that we step on, not even perceiving that we have just crushed some medicine beneath our feet until someone—a healer or teacher—points them out to us? Until we practice Self-care, do we have any idea about the power that resides within us to create change, healing, and peace right here and now? Consider what compels you to make changes in your life and health that you perceive as leading toward greater balance in body and peace of mind. What forces keep you from making those changes?

Figure 2-1 is a simple diagram of the forces of change identified by social scientist Kurt Lewin. Driving forces can be persons, ideas, attitudes, actions, incidents, customs, and interactions that incite a desire or will for change. Change is movement and driving forces that move us toward that change. Restraining forces represent persons, ideas, attitudes, actions, incidents, customs, and interactions that maintain a certain state or habit. The image of the forces of change shows balance or the status quo. The driving forces for change are equal to the restraining forces.

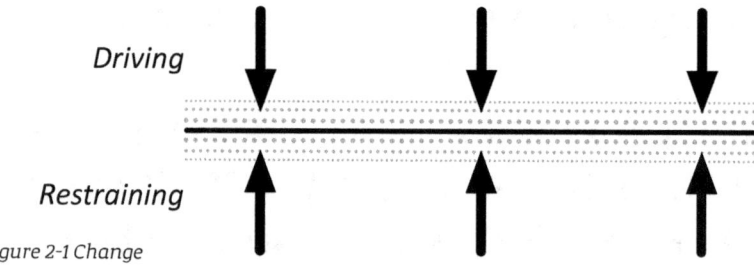

Figure 2-1 Change

For a change of any kind to occur, the forces must shift. Restraining forces must decrease or driving forces must increase. There must first be a desire or reason for the change.

The perception of illness and disease is often a powerful driving force for change as can a greater desire for well-being. Health as a process describes a continuum of constant change from wellness to illness. Gentle medicine with plants as catalysts supports the change and eases transitions in balance within the Self and in the environment in which the Self resides.

Environmental or climate change, with its cycles and seasons, is constant throughout life. Climate changes are potent actions that are experienced by individuals, families, communities, nations, and the planet as a whole. Climate change and change, in general, is often a challenge for people. The human brain, as part of a body coded for survival and adaptation to changes in the environment, interprets climate change as unfamiliar and therefore sets in motion responses, such as fear and anxiety. These "normal" emotional responses to change are perceived in the cells of our bodies, minds, and spirits as a call to action. This change response focuses on adaptation as its goal.

The process of adapting to changes in climate as the environment within and without is essentially the same whether the focus is personal human change, such as a shift in perception, or physical shifts in planetary patterns. Over time, people can learn to consciously engage in the highly creative process of adaptation to environmental climate changes both within and without. Mastery of fear and anxiety is achievable though not without challenge. The result can be a greater balance in body and peace of mind. The last chapters of this book focused on each of the five elements describe how the elements provide the framework for designing the specific changes that one wants to make in one's life defined here as precision Self-care with a capital S.

Unfortunately, today the phrase "climate change," rather than referring to the normal process of adaptation, transformation, and evolution as a change in patterns and relationships within Self and the environment, has been deemed "unprecedented" by a media suggesting that there is no historical record. The term can serve to encourage negative thoughtforms, projections, and predictions rather than normalize efforts to master climate changes within and without as fully precedented in human history.

History is filled with dire predictions of destruction during times of powerful planetary changes, be they humanly constructed world wars or natural "disasters." Amid all the scientific and religious discussion and debate, activism, legislation, and power struggle, there is a simple truth. Climate change is what life is about! Changing one's internal climate or environment is what children are doing when they go to school to further their education and eat the foods prepared for them.

There is a reciprocal relationship between the internal and external environments. The impact of interior changes cannot help but have an effect on the external environment. There is communication and exchange between the two. We are "Selves-in-relation" to the environment in which we live and act in the world. Therefore, becoming an agent of climate change through Self-care is just not a philosophical exercise. Climate change agency in Self-care is about engaging in a spiritual and practical path of life study of the environment within and without as engagement with the five elements of creation: fire, air, water, earth, and ether. Climate change is not only an event that happens outside of us. Climate change is happening within us; it is us. This is an ancient wisdom teaching of deep love and truth that evokes a greater responsibility and respect for life and a frame of reference for individual and collective purpose as human beings who share the same planetary space.

Shifts in consciousness do accompany significant climate change within and without. People do indeed adapt. All people hold the potential to use their physical strength, cognitive function, emotional courage, and spiritual insights to meet their unique responsibility for being and creating climate change. None are exempt from a relationship with the environment within (Self) and without. That relationship begins as we become aware of the warmth, smell, and sound of our mother's womb. Infants to elders learn to create relationships with Self, others, earth, and environment. Learning to change and how to adapt and to transition is a life-long pursuit that nurses witness in their patients as well as in themselves. The difference in adaptation responses typically relates to consciousness, how one perceives the five elements of Self, and creating the environment within and without.

—*Five Elements of Climate Creation*—

Ancient wisdom traditions describing both material and spiritual existence have focused for millennia on the five elements of all creation as a model for defining, describing, and discussing life on planet Earth. The five elements are fire, air, water, earth, and ether. The foundations of science and medicine in many cultures are recorded in terms of understanding these five elements and the numerous relationship patterns between the elements as they are expressed in the creation of environments within and without.

Physical transformation corresponds to the earth element. Environment or climate change of the earth element is seen in physical and behavior change. Mental transformation, corresponding to the air element, includes shifts in thought patterns, knowledge development, social and cultural beliefs, and values. Emotional transformation, corresponding to the water element, can be observed as fluctuations in emotional engagement in relationship to self and with others. Spiritual transformation, corresponding to the fire element, is observed as a change in consciousness, perceptions, and relationship to the Creator and creation—all that is material and spiritual.

Ether, the fifth element, is the essence of all four elements. Ancient Greeks describe it as "pneuma," which means "breath." It is perception, essence, and consciousness that enables us to derive meaning from climate changes experienced throughout life as the patterns expressed in the five elements of creation. Ether sustains consciousness as it resides in the body. The Upanishads, ancient sacred Hindu teachings, describe consciousness as the "expression of the soul, the light within the heart."[32] Changes in relation to the Creator, the soul, and the light within the heart, and the spiritual dimension of perception can be observed and measured in patterns connected with the expression of physical, mental, and emotional behaviors. How the physical, mental, and emotional changes are perceived is an expression of consciousness. Changes in perception often signal a spiritual shift in consciousness.

The five elements describe primary energetic health patterns in people as well as the remedies or therapies that are given, and the environments for healing that are created and maintained. For example, the main energetic pattern of a person with a fever or the herbal remedy cayenne pepper is "hot." Balance of the elements as they manifest in a person is created by harmonizing their internal and external environments. Thus, if they were fevering or hot, they might seek to cool themselves with hydrotherapeutic applications, such as a cold compress or cooling peppermint tea to drink. The healing environment includes the quality of temperature (fire), air, fluid (water), and substance (earth) both within and around a person. Lifestyle patterns, such as activity, sleep and rest, and diet, are known to have a direct effect on the balance of the internal environment of the person with the external environment. The EOC program supports the path to becoming more conscious and aware of the ways that you, as a human being, your family, or your community, can affect climate change, the environment within and without. The EOC program is a framework for engaging in gentle medicine precision Self-care for climate change, a movement toward harmony in personal and planetary health patterns that can be expressed as greater balance in body and peace of mind. From this EOC Program, you will be able to:

- Communicate knowledge of the Elements of Care® program for precision Self-care
- Utilize the five elements structure in health promotion and precision Self-care for common health concerns
- Develop a personal gentle medicine chest or apothecary filled with your favorite plant-partner Self-care recipes and remedies
- Demonstrate how to apply the EOC program in pursuit of greater balance in body and peace of mind utilizing a precision Self-care plan that you have designed

The EOC precision Self-care program consists of two parts. The first part, chapters 1 - 3, provides the background information you will need about the 5 P's used in the EOC program: Primary Prevention, Plants, Patterns, and Peace. The second part, Chapters 4 – 9 and the Conclusion, guides you in designing your five elements Self-care plan.

CHAPTER 3

The 5 P's of the Self-care Model

Discussions about healthcare, and related topics about the economy, politics, and social change, typically focus on disease and death prevention and navigating tier four interventions. The EOC program with plants as partners is a foundation for a healthcare reform movement that seeks to change that focus to include tier one, to ensure a more sustainable healthcare system for the future. The focus for creating change with the EOC program is the 5 P's of the precision Self-care Model: primary prevention, plants, peace, and patterns.

—The Self-care Model for Primary Prevention—

The EOC precision Self-care model utilizes education, resources, and information to support everyday health decisions. A goal of plant partnership in precision Self-care is to make the most informed decisions about choosing the best herbs and applications. "Herbs" is a broad term most often used to refer to both culinary and medicinal plants. Herbs have traditionally applied to whole plants or whole plant materials, whereas "herbal products" is a term that refers to the result of the processing of the plant. There are differences in their applications, and therefore, it is crucial to identify which is being talked about, whole herbs or herbal products.

	Whole Herbs	**Herbal Products**
Source	Gardens, Herb Companies, Wild-crafting	Herb or Pharmaceutical Company
Production	Whole Fresh or Dried Plant Referred to as "Bulk" herbs.	Made of whole fresh or dried plants. Also made from plant constituents extracted from whole plants
Dosage	Follows traditional knowledge	May be based on clinical trials or national materia medica and pharmacy documents
History of Use	Long-term evidence to draw on. Tradition and Folklore recorded in herbals[33], recipe/receipt books, diaries, oral history	Short-term evidence. Because of production technology, herbs may be sold in new forms undocumented in history and folklore.

35

Some people only know of herbalism as represented by the herbal supplements sold in pharmacies and health food stores as capsules. They often relate herbalism only to the plants that are ingested and have no experience of applying herbs topically or taking them in the numerous forms that make up the body of herbal science and art of herbal medicine making. An herbal tea made from the flower of a plant, such as chamomile (*Matricaria chamomilla*), harvested from a garden would not be an herbal product or supplement. A chamomile ointment would be. Whole herb chamomile that the consumer can use in making an herbal compress or steam might be sold in a grocery store, but a chamomile compress cannot. An onion is an herb, as well as a vegetable. An onion poultice is referred to as an herbal application or remedy as opposed to an herbal product. Onions are products sold in the marketplace, but onion poultices are not. Neither onions nor onion poultices are referred to as herbal products. Informed consumers understand the nuances of terms by being informed about how plants are applied in Self-care.

There are thousands of plants on the planet. Everyone has plants unique to their sphere of influence. Plants also bring people together. We share plant medicine recipes and stories of healing as a way of getting to know each other. Essential to the precision Self-care model is an ability to discern the best herbal information and resources for supporting Self-care. Healthcare providers working in the biomedical system may have little to no direct knowledge or experience of a plant, herbal product, or an herbal application in question. People often have extensive cultural knowledge about plants that they or their family members have partnered with for generations. What they need is support in matching the best plant or plant formula with their own unique health patterns.

A common question people ask because they are more used to dealing with healthcare practitioners in the biomedical system who ask the same thing is, "what herb is good for this disease" (and they name the disease). This question is a sign that they should refer themselves to a health practitioner who may have some knowledge and experience with herbs. That practitioner should be someone who knows pathology or disease and can treat illness. The EOC program self-care model does not require one to know about biomedical diagnosis or disease. *Health patterns* are the domain of precision Self-care, and Self-care is "primary prevention." Informed decisions about primary prevention can shift to changing unhealthy behaviors to promote health rather than treat disease after it has already begun to take root. Secondary and tertiary prevention, as the treatment of disease, is practiced in the biomedical system. As the particular focus of biomedicine is disease diagnosis and management, many do not refer to that system as a "healthcare" system. A healthcare system must include health promotion and disease prevention.

One of the central beliefs of the biomedical culture is the value of clinical trial research. Nurses and other biomedical practitioners may state that they will not provide information to their patients about an herb until that herb has been researched through clinical trials for specific disease and "proven safe." This may be well-meaning in that nurses believe in research as the best source of information for a care design that they think better ensures public safety. Some engage in Self-care with the same belief; however, let's look more closely at this belief and what it means. There are many scientific, ethical, and professional reasons why research may be an inappropriate goal for Self-care with plant partnerships for disease prevention and health promotion.

In general, clinical research does not and cannot fully "prove" safety for the person as the Food and Drug Administration (FDA), and any researcher can attest. Alternative language to the word "prove" is used when referring to the scientific process. A study might "suggest" or "indicate a possible relationship." Quality science always acknowledges the limitations of the research. There are many. Research is a tool of the scientist. It is one way of knowing about the object of discovery, which in this case, is an herb or herbal product. Waiting for proof through research before engaging in giving and receiving information and resources about healing herbs could mean that one would *never* accept any herbal information and resources. Herbal medicine is not the only healing art for which there may be no clinical trial research. There are many remedies and interventions used commonly in the health sciences that have not been "proved" by formal clinical trials research. Even using prescription-only drugs, "off label" (that is experimental and without research) is a well-known occurrence in healthcare. A study done in the 1990s by the United States Office of Technology Assessment found that only 20 percent of *common* medical interventions at that time had been shown effective through research.[34]

What about other forms of evidence that might increase knowledge and thereby lower risk? Many of the herbs that are commonly applied in Self-care have centuries of traditional evidence for support. Some countries ask about the necessity of conducting clinical research on those herbs at all when there is already a centuries-old body of evidence of safe human use. Besides, it is not feasible to study all of the herbs in everyday practice. A trial of any single herb applied in Self-care is, as a trial of any pharmaceutical drug, time-consuming and expensive. There are alternatives. This chapter discusses the complementary alternatives to focusing on clinical trial research as the only way of knowing about the safety and efficacy of herbs. The EOC program will guide you in starting to develop multiple methods for gathering evidence and information from several sources to be used in health decision-making. In herbal medicine, the first solution is simples.

THE SOLUTION IS SIMPLES

The most common herbal remedy in Self-care plant partnership is the single herb remedy, known as a "simple." Examples are raspberry leaf tea for toning the uterus during the third trimester of pregnancy, elderberry syrup for alleviating early symptoms of influenza, and calendula salve for diaper rash. Lemon compress for fever is another very common whole herb simple that has been demonstrated effective through numerous clinical trials. [See Gentle Medicine Self-study #5] People are often quite comfortable working with simples, such as lemon compresses made from whole herbs, which they can learn and then apply in Self-care very easily.

Gentle Medicine Self-study # 8:
A Simple Lemon Compress for Fever Reduction

Try this Self-study in cooling the body. Lemon Compress is a topical application of an herbal infusion (water extraction) of lemon using a cotton, silk, or wool material. The temperature of the room should be regulated so that the person is not chilled by drafts or by the room temperature itself. The person is covered for warmth. A woolen cloth with safety pins attached is placed on the bed in preparation for being placed around the lower legs. Place another piece of soft material on top of the wool that will fit around the legs. Then the dipping cloth is prepared. A bandage-type material that will go around the lower legs is folded to fit the legs and then rolled on both sides up to the middle. Place the bandage on another cloth that can be used to wring out the bandage. This cloth should have both ends rolled, too. Place tepid water, temp 37.6 °C / 99°F, in a bowl and, using a fork to hold a lemon submerged in the water, use a paring knife to cut the lemon in half into a star shape. Use the base of a glass or small bowl to press the lemon halves. The lemon is cut under water so that the volatile oil does not escape. Then put the cloth with the bandage on it in the lemon water, holding onto the rolled ends so that they do not get wet. Wring out until cloth is not dripping. Use the cloth to sponge the person who is fevering. Begin sponging by wrapping the ankles in the cloth. Flip the compress as soon as the cloth draws heat from the body. The compresses are wrapped around the lower leg from the top of the metatarsals to below the kneecap and left in place for 60 – 120 minutes while the person is reclining. Monitor temperature, blood pressure, and perspiration to be sure that the person's temperature is lowered gently.

Another common question people have is about how and when to choose herbal products that contain multiple ingredients. These formulations may rely upon traditional recipes used in many people over time, or they may be the result of the ingenuity of an herbalist, Phyto-pharmacy scientist, or research and development team. In the Self-care model, formulations represent more significant challenges than do simples. In a formulation, the energetics of each herb is taken into account. A formulation, for example, could be a concoction of herbs known to support a specific system such as the cardiovascular system. Many herbs fall into this category in Western herbalism. But an herbalist has other criteria than this system's approach that they use when formulating for a client. The best precision Self-care approach is to treat each herb in the formula as a simple and focus on the energetic appropriateness of each one of the herbs in the formulation. Additional guidelines for herbal decision making are provided in Chapter 6 *Awakening the Air Element*. In addition to tea tastings, we can get to know the energetics of a plant's personality by learning basic botany.

Plants

When human beings decide to partner with someone, they get to know the other person first. One way to get to know plants as partners in precision Self-care is to learn botany. Botany, or "the properties and life phenomena exhibited by a plant,"[35] is an entire field of study devoted to understanding plants. Plants, like humans, have their own "personalities." A brief overview of botanical science and plant personalities are explained here highlighting the following areas: (1) plant designs and growth patterns, and (2) plant constituents.

PLANT DESIGNS AND GROWTH PATTERNS

Using Latin names in botanical science serves many purposes. First, botanical names often describe some aspect of the growth pattern of the plant. For example, the Latin name for red clover, *Trifolium pratense*, describes the plant as having *tri-*, or three, *folium-*, or leaves, three leaves. Second, Latin names provide a clarifying, common language for identification of plants and sharing that information from person to person. Both purposes lead to the overall goal of being able to accurately identify a plant as useful for human consumption either as food or medicine. A plant has only one Latin name, but it may have numerous common names that vary from culture to culture. The Latin name allows one to communicate about medicinal plants internationally because the plant name is standardized all around the world.

The Latin binomial nomenclature for plants is credited as the work of Carl Linnaeus, a Swedish botanist (1701–1778) who wanted to create a universal way of communicating about plants. In learning to recognize and identify plants, it is best first to practice identifying plants and their growth patterns by family, then genus, and then species. One example of a plant family is the *Rosaceae* or rose family. Apples, raspberries, and roses belong to this family. The family name is always capitalized. The genus is the first name of the plant and is always capitalized. The second name assigned a plant is the species, and it is written in lower case unless the second name is the name of a person, then it may be capitalized as well. Both genus and species names are italicized.

After genus and species, the variety of the plant may be listed. For example, one species of the common herb, thyme, has the Latin name *Thymus serpyllum*, and the white flower variety is called *Thymus serpyllum var. albus* (white). When referring to a group of plants with the same genus name, the genus name can be abbreviated to the first letter, followed by a period after spelling out the genus name the first time. For example, *Thymus serpyllum* would appear as *T. serpyllum*. If a particular document discusses a group of plants with the same genus and different species, then the name will appear as the genus followed by the abbreviation "*spp.*," which means species plural. "*Spp.*" also can be used when writing that many plants within a specific genus are applicable.

PLANT PARTS

Seeds

Plants can be identified in various stages of development, although some are easier to identify at times than others. Plants can be identified by their seed. For example, compare an apple seed and a dill seed that you might have in your kitchen. Notice the differences in color, size, outer coating, and markings. Seeds are dormant and capable of germination. Seeds can survive environmental conditions that their parent plants could not. They are tiny packages of tremendous potential. When a seed germinates and begins the growth process, cotyledons, or seed leaves, are formed. The seeds of flowering plants contain either one or two cotyledons, identifying it as a dicot (two cotyledons) or a monocot (one cotyledon). Angiosperms, or flowering plants, that make up the largest group in the plant kingdom called a "division," are either monocots or dicots. The word "angiosperm" is from the Greek "angeion" (vessel) and "sperma" (seed), indicating that these plants have seeds that are formed inside vessels, or as we call them, fruits. Angiosperm are sophisticated life forms that supply most of the vegetables in the human diet and our supply of hardwood. Monocots include grasses, cereal grains, sugar cane, lilies, aloe, iris, and orchids. Dicots, the larger of the two groups, include roses, other flowering plants, and trees of all sorts. The other major division of plants known as "Gymnosperms" (or naked seed division) produces seeds in cones, such as a pinecone. *Thuja occidentalis* and *Ginkgo biloba* are members of the Gymnosperm division.

The seed feeds itself by absorbing water, doubling in size, and breaking down starches, proteins, and fats present in the cotyledons and endosperm, a food storage structure of the seed, which it then sends to the embryo where new structures of a seedling can be formed. The seed sends out roots as it uses oxygen in the soil for the germination process. As the small leaves burst through the soil and are exposed to light, germination ends. The seedling is capable of photosynthesis and therefore is capable of feeding and sustaining itself, a process known as "autotrophic nutrition." Humans are heterotrophic organisms; that is, we rely on foods formed from other sources.

Roots

Gardeners often ignore the root systems of ornamental plants for the appeal of the plant's colorful blossoms and intricate leaves. But in herbal medicine, the roots of plants are essential medicine. Roots serve three purposes for the survival of the plant.

1. Roots keep the plant anchored to the soil.
2. Roots store excess food for the potential future needs of the plant.
3. Roots enable the plant to absorb water and minerals from the soil
4. environment.

Some roots are edible, such as the root of *Angelica sinensis*, but many roots are not traditionally eaten whole or in a powder form in a capsule. They usually are decocted, extracted with water, and heat, either because it is safer than eating the root or because the healing constituents are more available through decoction. A plant usually has either a fibrous root or a tap root system. Some plants have both. The fibrous system, such as is found in grasses, is composed of numerous thin-branched roots. A taproot has one or two longer, sparsely branched roots that go deeper into the soil. Carrots (*Daucus carota*) and horseradish root (*Armoracia rusticana*) are examples of taproots. These types of root systems can be vast. At the other extreme, cacti have very shallow fibrous root systems so that they can catch every drop of moisture possible that passes through their hard desert soil.

Roots are considered strong medicine in some cultures. We witness their strength not only in their potent medicinal actions but also in the way they grow, often pushing their way through concrete sidewalks and buildings. Each branch of root is an exact replica of the root that created it. The constituents of the food found in the roots of plants are discussed further in the section about plant constituents. Roots of medicinal plants are often harvested in the autumn when the energy and nutrients of the plant have returned fully to the root rather than being in the stems, leaves, and flowers. Some plants' roots are harvested in the spring. The roots of biennials, plants that grow leaves during the first years and then flower and bear fruit and die during the second year, are harvested in the autumn of the first year or spring of the second year. Allowing the plant to stay in the ground over the winter helps turn the starches in the root to sugars, making the harvest in the spring more flavorful.

During the second year, after the plant has achieved the full maturity of a summer season, the medicinal principles of the plant travel to the aerial or above-ground parts, leaving the root hollow and of little if any medicinal value. The roots of perennials, plants that come back year after year, enduring the seasons, can be collected in the autumn after the aerial parts of the plant have died back, demonstrating that the energy of the plant has gone back into the root. Burdock (*Arctium lappa*) is an example of a perennial in which the root is collected and dried the first year in the fall. Some herbalists prefer to collect the roots of individual plants the following spring after the herb has had a full winter of garnering its strength in the root. Many perennial plants are best harvested for medicine after at least two years of growth. Tubers and rhizomes, which are underground stems, are sometimes collected in or just after the flowering season of the plant or in the fall after the aerial parts have died back.

Shoot System

The shoot system of a plant includes the stem, branches, and leaves. To ensure that each leaf receives necessary sunlight and air circulation, the plant stem sections called "internodes" stretch and spread the buds and subsequent leaves apart. Three basic leaf patterns or arrangements on the stem occur with plant growth—alternate, whorled and opposite.

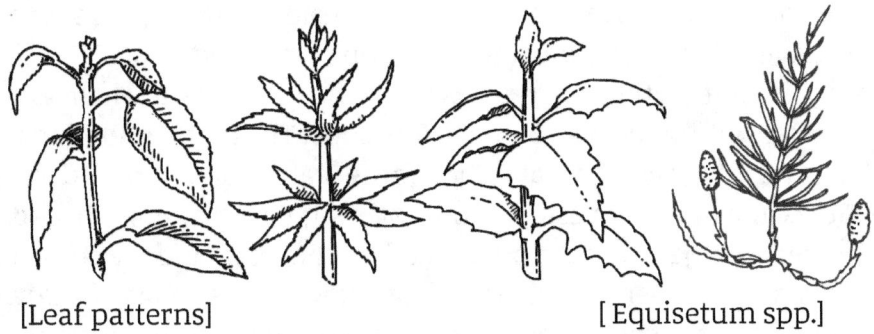

[Leaf patterns]   [Equisetum spp.]

The stem functions as a support for the leaves so that they get adequate light for photosynthesis, except for horsetail (*Equisetum spp.*), in which the stem is photosynthetic. In general, the difference between a tree and a shrub is that the tree has one main trunk to support its leaves, and shrubs are smaller with many woody stems. The bark of a tree or shrub is the place on the stem where it thickens and turns brown and rough.

The leaves of plants are truly miraculous. They are designed to capture light to be used in photosynthesis. The three parts of the leaf are the (1) leaflets; (2) the petiole, or small stem that attaches the leaflet to the branch; and (3) the stipule, the anchor for the petiole on the branch. Not all plants have stipules. The leaflets also have identifying patterns. Some leaflets are simple, and some are compound. They are pinnately compound where the leaves are organized alongside a central axis, such as the plants in the pea family (*Fabaceae*). They can be palmately compound where the multiple leaflets extend out from one central point like the fingers on the palm of a hand such as maple (*Aceraceae*). It is unknown how a plant design, including the leaf pattern, is created.

Flowers

Echinacea spp.

The intricacies of Nature shine in the design of the flowers plants produce. Flower structures are created at the tip of the flower stalk or pedicel. The stem tip, known as the "receptacle," bears the flower parts. Flowers arrange themselves within the bud in rings or whorls. The outer whorl is called the "calyx" and has several sepals. The words "calyx" and "sepal" derive from the Greek meaning "covering." This covering sheds or curls backward as the flower emerges from the bud. Together, the calyx and the corolla, layers of petals, are considered the perianth of a flower. The petals of a flower can be many different colors and can add to the data used to identify a plant. The flower color and shape often relate to the type of insect or animal with which the flower has a symbiotic relationship. Pollination among many plants occurs as a result of an insect recognizing a plant by its color, leaf or petal pattern or markings, and scent.

The male reproductive structures called "stamens" that emerge from the center of the petals are composed of long thin stalks called "filaments" and little terminal bulbs called "anthers." Pollen, which contains the sperm cells, develops in the anther. The female part of the plant is called the "pistil." At the tip of the pistil is a sticky surface called a "stigma" where the pollen attaches. The style is the long, stem like attachment to the stigma, and it secures the pistil at the base known as the "ovary." The pollen germinates and enters the style and then the ovary. The ovary is the part of the flower, which has the potential to turn into fruit. Not every plant contains all reproductive parts.

The plant can use the scent of the flower to attract insects or animals that assist in pollination or to deter predators. Those animals and insects that are welcomed by a plant are rewarded with food (nectar), setting up an essential symbiotic relationship. Plant growth patterns are often a result of some protective process between the plant and animals or the environment from which they both benefit. For example, cacti have spines to keep away predators and to act as condensers for any moisture that might be present in the atmosphere. Their color camouflages very few plants, but many emit noxious odors or other chemical defenses that act against predators. These substances are known as "secondary products" or "metabolites" produced by the plant.

PLANT CONSTITUENTS

In addition to the plant's metabolic work to extract energy from its food by the process of photosynthesis, it also makes starch, fats, cellulose, and proteins. Among the proteins the plant produces are enzymes that catalyze chemical activities that enable healthy cellular function within the plant. Various biochemical processes lead to the synthesis of several secondary plant metabolites that function as chemical defenses in the plant. These secondary plant metabolites are often the biochemical indicators used to distinguish one species or family of a plant from another.

Understanding a plant's constituents also helps us understand its potential medicinal personalities or qualities. However, dissecting plants into their numerous components does not necessarily lead to a better understanding of a particular plant's healing action in a specific person. Every healing plant has multiple plant constituents. Understanding plant constituents may guide Self-care decisions to some degree. However, whether or not a particular herb is appropriate for a specific health pattern at a specific time is ultimately determined by many factors related to the total personality of the herb and an individual's needs, not just the individual plant constituents.

COMMON CONSTITUENTS OF PLANTS

Acids

One of the most common plant acids is called *tannic acid* or "tannins." Tannins bind with proteins causing water to leave the cell and constriction of tissues creating an "astringent" effect. It is not surprising that plants with tannins often have a recognizable puckering and drying effect on the tissues. Some examples of tannin-rich plants are tea (*Camellia sinensis*) and raspberry leaf (*Rubus idaeus*). Tannins are generally antiseptic, antioxidant, antiviral, coagulant, and anti-inflammatory. The tightening of tissues is a tonifying effect. *Oxalic acid* is also astringent and is sour tasting and found in rhubarb (*Rheum rhaponticum*), for example. *Oxalic acid* can be very irritating to the digestive tract. It can combine with calcium in the bloodstream, forming insoluble calcium oxalate, which can deplete the body's calcium levels and also can lodge in the kidneys. Citrus and other fruits contain citric acid. *Formic acid* is the acid that enables stinging nettle (*Urtica doica*) to sting upon contact with a passerby. This acid loses its bite when the plant containing it is cooked.

Alkaloids

Alkaloids contain nitrogen and are bitter tasting, water-soluble, and usually basic (pH) in nature. The majority of plant alkaloids are known to have a narcotic, analgesic, or sedative effect on the central nervous system and have played an essential role in the development of human medicine. Valerian (*Valeriana officinalis*), an herbal sedative, contains *terpenoid alkaloids*. Some alkaloids, like caffeine, are stimulants and can be addicting. One alkaloid often mentioned in the scientific and medical literature is the *pyrrolizidine alkaloid*. This alkaloid, found in plants like comfrey (*Symphytum officinale*), is toxic to humans and may cause liver damage. Other common alkaloids are quinolines as are found in quinine and the *isoquinolines* from opium poppy (*Papaver somniferum*) that are found in morphine and codeine. Some of the most common alkaloids, *methylxanthines*, are caffeine, theophylline, and theobromine. The names of alkaloids can be recognized by their ending "-ine."

Carbohydrates

Carbohydrates are aldehyde or ketone alcohols containing hydrogen, carbon, and oxygen in which the oxygen and hydrogen are usually in the same ratio as water. Carbohydrates are classified into two groups: sugars and polysaccharides. Sugars, such as fructose, are identified by their sweet taste. Plant polysaccharides include mucilage, the slimy moist substance found in plants such as aloe and psyllium (*Plantago spp.*); *inulin*, often found in the root of plants such as dandelion (*Taraxacum officinale*); *pectin*, a complex polysaccharide found in plants such as apples and citrus fruits; gum, thicker and stickier than mucilage and found in Agar for example; and *cellulose*, the polysaccharide from which wood is made.

Glycosides

Glycosides are involved in the regulatory, protective, and sanitary functions of the plant. Glycosides are made up of a sugar and an aglycone molecule. Most glycosides, except saponins, are inactive unless separated from the sugar. Mustard and other plants are known for their skin-irritating property on humans are examples of *sulfur glycosides*. Peach and apricot pits contain *cyanhydric glycosides*, which occur widely in Nature and contain nitrogen, hydrogen, and carbon. They react with cytochrome oxidase, an enzyme that links oxygen to individual cells and causes the cells to asphyxiate. Although the body has a way of dealing with minimal amounts of cyanide by adding a sulfur molecule, excessive amounts of this glycoside are poisonous to the human body. Carbon-based *phenol glycosides*, the last group of glycosides, include *flavonoids*, the plant constituents found in many fruits and vegetables, well known for their antiviral, anti-inflammatory, and antioxidant qualities; *saponins*, recognizable by their ability to form foam in water, are found in plants such as potatoes (*Solanum tuberosum*) and tomatoes (*Lycopersicon esculentum*). Although they can destroy the cell membrane of erythrocytes, they are poorly absorbed by the human digestive system, so they usually pass through the body. They also can be easily broken down when cooked. *Saponins* often have anti-inflammatory or immunostimulant effects.

The *anthraquinone glycosides* found in plants such as Senna, aloe, and rhubarb are digested by bile, absorbed by the small intestine, and excreted through the colon, thereby having a laxative effect; however, some plants, such as St. John's Wort, that contain this glycoside are not laxatives because they are not fat soluble. *Cardiac glycosides*, as found in plants such as *Dig-*

italis, stimulate the contractions of the heart muscle. All of these are considered dangerous and not to be used by the uneducated. *Coumarins* are phenol glycosides that are sweet-smelling, like freshly cut hay, and may be found in plants in the parsley (Apiaceae) family. There are numerous types of coumarins in the plant world that fall under the general classifications of coumarins: hydroxycoumarins, methoxycoumarins, furanocoumarins, pyranocoumarins, and dicoumarols. Coumarin does not have the same action as an anticoagulant drug. Because dicoumarols destroy vitamin K, they are the type of coumarins that act as anticoagulants. Coumarin-type anticoagulant drugs were created based on a model of the coumarin that was found in fungal contamination of sweet clover.

Essential or Volatile Oils

Volatile oils also referred to as essential oils, are unstable and separate easily from the plant and evaporate into the air. They are the cause of the fragrance associated with the plant. Volatile oils are combinations of aromatic molecules of which there are thousands in existence in the plant world. For example, eucalyptol is an *oxide* found in the Eucalyptus tree. Oxides are a chemical classification within the larger group of plant constituents known as "essential oils." Other types of volatile oils include, but are not limited to, alcohols, aldehydes, esters, ethers, ketones, phenols, and terpenes.

Resins

Resins, like pine pitch and myrrh, are formed from oxidized volatile oils. They are sticky, not soluble in water, and are secreted from the plant when it is injured. Resins are often used medicinally as astringents and antiseptics.

Latex

Latex is the milk like or yellowish sap that oozes from plants such as dandelion stem and leaf. Latex is acrid and sometimes bitter as well. Latex, from the Latin word for "fluid," contains small particles of rubber and historically has been the source of natural rubber. The presence of latex in a plant often is a signal that the plant is medicinal. The presence of latex also can mean that the plant can be very irritating to the skin.

Acrid Substances

Plants with acrid substances include horseradish (*Amoracia rusticana*) and mustard (*Brassica spp.*). Acrid substances in these and other plants are related to the glycosides and taste hot or pungent.

The wisdom that emanates from the natural world is felt, tasted, seen, heard, touched, and smelt as one enters a partnership with a plant. As you enter the world of plants, remember to use all of your senses as you get to know the herbal remedies that come from these exquisite life forms called "plants," each with their own personality. To understand something of the personality of any plant, we learn the growth pattern of the plant and about the plant's inner workings or constituents. We also need to understand the plant's preferences that are demonstrated non-verbally in the way it grows and interacts with its environment, including humans. Although plants can convey powerful medicine and messages as did the St. John's Wort behind the Denver hospital, they are, as a whole, recognized for the gentle peaceful, presence that they convey to humans from the natural world.

—*Peace and Plant-Like Gentleness*—

The mid-1800s in the United States was the last significant populist period in history when major social changes occurred. People had endured war and pandemics and were seeking a more peaceful existence. Women's literature of the period, in particular, often referred to the pursuit of "plant-like gentleness," a harmonic, reign of peace, and an end to violence in all areas of life, including medical practice.[36] Today, many seek balance in body and peace of mind as major planetary and personal changes continue to challenge us to keep our peace with ourselves and each other.

The pursuit of peace as recorded in religious and ancient wisdom traditions of east and west begins and ends with an understanding of Self. Intuition and insight allow for a deep connection between the realm of spirit and the Creator and the individual Self as embodied in the realm of matter. Enduring wisdom traditions suggest the possibility of the unity of opposites, such as the unity of spirit and matter, as the foundation for peace. The possibility of unity is rooted in the transformation of gnosis and mystical experience as in the experience of the union of opposites, the foundation of Hermeticism.

The word hermeticism comes from the name Hermes Trismegistus, a philosopher whom the Greeks considered to be a messenger of the Gods. Hermeticism is not religious doctrine; it is a living tradition that serves as a stimulant in the spiritual life of humanity and a guardian of the life and soul of religion, art, and science. Hermeticism is a philosophy of the five elements of all creation that suits every creed, philosophy, and health belief and clashes with none. The ancient Greeks believed a healthy person to be one who experienced the proper balance of the four elements with the activity of pneuma, the fifth element. These five elements appear in the ancient philosophy, *The Emerald Tablet*.[37] Hermes Trismegistus translated the text of the Tablet. According to legend, there have been three incarnations of Hermes. The third Hermes (Trismegistus) was Balinas, who may have authored the earliest translation of *The Emerald Tablet*. These Hermetic texts have been read by scientists, philosophers, and healers from Socrates to Paracelsus to Nightingale.[38]

Hermetic texts, documenting the oldest living tradition in the West, have inspired Judaism, Christianity, Islam, Paganism, and Gnosticism. In Celtic tradition for example, the five elements of Self are described as "doorways into an infinite universe."[39] Eastern religions and philosophies such as Buddhism, Taoism, and Hinduism also share similar concepts and terminology. Hindu scripture, written between the 4th and 8th century BCE speaks of the elements this way:

> All things find their final peace in their inmost Self, the Spirit: earth, water, fire, air, space and their invisible elements; sight, hearing, smell, taste, touch, and their various fields of sense; voice, hands, and al lpowers of action; mind, reason, the sense of 'I', thought, inner light, and their objects; and even life and all that life sustains…He who knows, O my beloved, that Eternal Spirit wherein consciousness and the senses, the powers of life and the elements find final peace, knows the All and has gone into the All.[40]

These teachings form the foundation for the traditional medicine of India called Ayurveda, the "science of life," as recorded in the *Caraka Samhita*.[41] The balance or harmony among the five natural elements influencing health and peace is also foundational to the practice of TCM, Japanese Kampo medicine, Persian Unani medicine, and the medicine wheel of First Nation peoples of the Americas.

Foundational to Hermeticism is the emphasis on Self-knowledge and the understanding of Self, and all matter, as a manifestation of the elements of creation, fire, air, water, and earth. Ancient Greek philosophers, such as

Aristotle, described these four elements or four fundamental "archetypes" of "first matter" as that which originated from the "One Thing." Ether, as the essential element found in other traditions, is comparable to the Greeks' notion of the "One Thing." Their unique qualities described the four archetypal elements. Fire is hot and dry and in isolation is naturally active, violent, destructive and combustive. Water is cold and moist and in isolation is naturally passive, receptive, and unstable. Earth is cold and dry and in isolation is naturally neutral, inert, and absorptive. Air is moist and hot and in isolation is naturally harmonic, generative, temperate, and maturing.[42] By altering any of these qualities, one would effect change in the elements. For example, one could turn water into steam by applying heat. This underlying philosophy was applied to the healing arts. Early Greek medical theory, known as "humoral" theory, the foundation of modern Western medicine and early professional nursing, associated health with balance in the four humors. The four humors: choler, sanguis, phlegm, and melancholer, corresponded with each of the four elements fire, air, water, and earth respectively.

Hermeticism has, like many philosophical paths and religious traditions, had its history of perversions through individuals who would seek the ecstasy of mystical experience without understanding the Self or the Creator and without using those experiences to bring healing and peace in service to humanity. Some seek only to learn the elements of Self to aggrandize the self (little s) of the ego. Rather than to bring unity and peace, that ego expression has designs to separate itself in the world. And while the ego may be relevant on the physical level as to incarnate fully, the peace we seek is, according to ancient wisdom, found in our union and unity of opposites.

"You have the power within you to heal your Self!" Those were the words spoken to me in a dream nearly thirty years ago when I was seeking peace as I had been struggling for some time with problems in my own body, mind, and spirit for which biomedical physicians had no cure. Those dedicated to the healing arts know that there are many disorders and diseases for which there is no cure. By "cure," I mean eradication and removal of uncomfortable symptoms. People endure all sorts of maladies ranging from everyday aches and pains to toxicity and disease. It is in the perseverant search for balance in body and peace of mind that people come to the healing arts.

At the heart of healing arts, is the understanding of suffering as a part of life. Suffering can be a very personal and lonely experience. Sometimes there is a cure, an opportunity for the removal of the suffering. Still, often, there is not, especially when one considers all of the common illnesses and injuries people endure throughout life. What sometimes adds to human suffering is the belief that people should be able to identify one cause for any form of suffering, from cancer to depression to freckles, and that there should also be one cure for that one cause of disease.

One-cause, one-cure is a philosophy promoted by medical men of the 18th and 19th centuries, such as Benjamin Rush. While their intentions to find the one cause and one cure may have been honorable and compassionate, the record of results is incomplete at best. There is no one-cause, one-cure for the common cold yet. Nor is there a cause and cure for cancer, dementia, or anxiety. Humanity is in the process of exploring causes and cures. The demand for a cure continues to be heavily embedded in society that, more recently, has turned to technology for the answer, including pharmaceutical drugs.

Those who suffer when there is no known cause or cure often suffer in silence at the margins of health care systems dedicated to the pursuit of a one-cause, one-cure. While humanity waits for science to find the cure, people can find relief from suffering in the science, art, and spiritual path of Self-care. The nursing profession exemplifies the benefits of support for the Self-care path. It has centuries of expertise in persevering with people by providing education in Self-care when there has been no hint of cure.[43]

The world is full of instruments that support the practice of Self-care that are fashioned from the five elements: fire, air, water, earth, and ether. These gentle medicines of comfort and care are highly accessible in times of suffering for they are within us and all around us. These five elements are a platform for healing the Self with a capital "S." The pursuit of knowledge of the healing power within the Self, with a capital S, is a solution to suffering, as was suggested in my dream.

The impression that was left by that inspirational dream was one of hope. The pursuit of hope is so compelling that I have spent my life in study of that healing "power" within all of us which I have found tied to the five elements of care. The remedies made from those five elements with their unique energies promote the expression of that power within that will address suffering at all stages of life. The result of this understanding as the EOC program is exemplified in this book with the simple purpose for restoring hope in the path of Self-care with plants as partners. I invite you to begin this program where I was taught to begin. Seek the peaceful, safe place in the garden of your own heart.

PEACEFUL SAFE PLACE

Seeking Self-care for balance in body and peace of mind is a spiritual path associated with shifts in consciousness, so simple and common that they can be easily overlooked as insignificant. The experiences and results of the path of Self-care can also be extraordinary and ecstatic. Healing environments are those safe places nurses can create to support Self-care practice and the associated shifts in consciousness that accompany the pursuit of balance in body and peace of mind.

Knowing the right plant or plants to engage and how to apply them at the precise time in the most precise healing way in care and comfort is the focus of this Self-care program. Partnering with plants in healing, comfort, and care takes time. Although they are of the same elements as human beings, plants are distinct. They also differ from one another just as people differ from one another. Each person-plant partnership for healing is distinct. Understanding the five elements provides foundational understanding for making informed choices about Self-care with plants as partners to create greater balance in body and peace of mind for yourself and your family.

Plant partnerships informed by knowledge, experiences, and beliefs about healing plants as well as by the insight that comes from our relationships with plants. Step by step, element by element, this book guides you in the creation of your precision self-care plans rooted in knowledge, experiences, and insights gleaned as you enter the plant world with curiosity, compassion, caution, and common sense.

The five elements are your guides. Use the elements chapters to design your precision Self-care plan. There are more Gentle Medicine Self Studies and reflections that complement the content you read. The Gentle Medicine Self-studies deepen your understanding of your plant partnerships. Our creative responsibility in Self-care is not to design a new "medicine" or therapeutic practice. Be at peace! There is a wise teaching that, "There is no new thing under the sun" (Ecclesiastes 1:9). Self-care and the five elements are not new at all. What makes Self-care so appealing and why it and the hermetic tradition of the five elements have endured throughout history is how each person expresses or demonstrates the union and unity of the five elements in precision Self-care. The unique mindful way in which you design your

Self-care plan with plants as partners using the five elements and the EOC program as a guide is what will make that Self-care more meaningful and memorable for you. The next step is to design a peaceful, safe place for your Self-study and partnership with plants.

GENTLE MEDICINE SELF-STUDY # 9: DESIGNING A PEACEFUL SAFE PLACE

Design a peaceful "safe place" for doing the next phase of your Self-care Self-study work – within and without. Find a physical space in your home or elsewhere where you can close your eyes and know that you will be completely safe and not be interrupted or disturbed. Take a comfortable position and close your eyes. Place your fingers on your radial pulse and notice the rhythm and rate of your pulse. Then move your awareness to the center of your chest and your heart – the heart that beats as pulse. Using your memory and imagination, find or create a place in your mind in which you are completely safe ... and by yourself. Carefully note all sounds, shapes, colors, smells, sensations, and tastes associated with your safe place. Take your time. Notice any plants in your safe place. As with the tea tasting Self-study, do not attempt to name the plants. Remember their color, shapes, smells, taste, and sensations that you experience with them in your safe place. After your creative reflection, try to synthesize this reflection of creating a safe place into one word that represents the essence of the safe place. Breathe in and out and move your awareness back to your radial pulse. Notice the rhythm and rate of your pulse now. Note the name of your safe place in a journal dedicated to your plant experiences and Self Studies. Be sure to research any plants that you found in your safe place. What is its botanical name and personality? Where does it grow? Does the plant or any of the botanical patterns have meaning for you? Record what you learn about the plant in your journal. You can re-create this safe place at any time of the day and anywhere you go. Lock it in to your memory now for future reflection.

As technology-based practice has grown, as manifested primarily in the reliance on pharmaceutical drugs, plant partnership has waned and, in some industrialized countries, fallen out of use altogether. A premise of this book is that humans rely on plants for their existence, and therefore partnership with plants is essential to Self-care. Re-establishment of partnership with plants is possible. The scope of the precision Self-care plan, however, varies from person to person according to their health patterns and the environmental patterns in which they live.

—*Patterns in Health, Physics, and Paradigms*—

Pattern is a regular formation. In the natural world, patterns are perceived and remembered through a combination of sensory experiences of images, sounds, tastes, smells, and kinesthetic sensations. Some patterns repeat, but not all. For example, those who have experienced snow, know what the general pattern of the snowflake is and can recognize it as "snow." But each snowflake is different in its crystalline pattern. Recognition of patterns is fundamental to an understanding of health and the ability to engage in precision Self-care.

Physicists study many kinds of material and energetic patterns. The word physics, derived from the Greek word "physis," means to perceive the nature of all things. Physics is the branch of science seeking to understand perception and how the constituents of the universe (all Nature) interact. Quantum physics is concerned not only with discerning patterns within the observed but also within the observer.[44] The ability to perceive patterns comes from within the observer.

Biologist Dr. Rupert Sheldrake proposes that Nature is mostly habitual in that all natural systems or "morphic units" from plants and crystals to human societies inherit a collective memory that influences their patterns in form and behavior. Morphic resonance, with its repeating patterns in personal and race memory, may account for how Self-care with plant remedies works and how they have endured so many generations as a healing tradition.

Resonance is rhythmic vibration in response to an environmental stimulus. Morphic resonance is the influence of previous activity on a subsequent similar event organized by morphic fields. Sheldrake defines morphic fields as "fields of information."[45] They exert a "region of physical influence" in which matter and energy are "interconnected"; "matter is energy bound within fields."[46] Morphic resonance occurs between rhythmic structures of activity based on similarity. The influence of morphic resonance accumulates over time. Memory, conscious or unconscious, is due to morphic resonance. As memory is experienced by one person or many in society as a collective experience known as history, it takes shape or form. It carries with it the power to affect human experiences, such as belief, action, and feelings. What this means is that recognizing patterns becomes easier over time. That is excellent news for those who strive to make memories of safe and effective partnerships with plants.

People's memories of Self-care partnerships with plants can be pleasant, fuzzy, fragrant, tasty, stimulating, and even ecstatic. They also can be unpleasant, thorny, stinging, and bitter. People's experiences of the same plant can also be very different at any given time. I learned this plant lesson at an early age! My sister and I were on Mount Washington in New Hampshire, with our mom searching for checkerberries (*Gaultheria procumbens* – another common name is wintergreen). Mom pulled out her penknife to cut the one tiny red checkerberry that we had found into four pieces for us, our brother, and her. I loved the flavor, but my sister spit it out. She has never liked the smell, let alone the taste of wintergreen, aka checkerberry. Over-the-counter digestive aides that flavored with wintergreen have the opposite effect for her because she finds that plant's smell pattern unpleasant. My perception is that wintergreen is wonderful! My favorite ice cream is checkerberry chip, and I am still teaching about the analgesic qualities of the salicylates in the *Gaultheria* leaf and the elegant taste of the berry today. "One man's meat is another's poison." Pattern recognition—health, plant, and energetic patterns—is so vital to Self-care safety and efficacy, especially with plants.

PUTTING ENERGETIC PATTERNS FIRST

Think about your Self-study with the orange. That was a Self-study in pattern recognition. Some might be able to recognize and name the orange with their eyes closed relying only on their sense of smell to discern the orange pattern. Patterns are observable characteristics and discernable interrelationships that represent the energetics of persons and plants. Consider the orange Self-study and recall again if you can identify the experience of the "vitamin C" in the plant. There is vitamin C in the plant, but the way one knows this is not through the senses or experience of energetic patterns. We learn about vitamin C and its role in health promotion. Using the senses is a scientific way of knowing the energetics of the plants that are closer to the field of physics than it is to biochemistry. So much of the focus on plant medicine in highly technological nations is on the biochemical constituents of plants. Energetic understanding through the senses is highly accessible. It has a high degree of accuracy, whereas to be exact that one is getting enough vitamin C, for example, one would need a blood test. High degrees of certainty are why traditional systems of Self-care focus on energetic patterns first in decision making rather than relying on theoretical knowledge of biochemistry, which one cannot experience in one's body as well as the sensory experience of energetics.

Health is described in terms of patterns. According to the humoral theory of Greek physicians, such as Hippocrates and Galen, health was defined as the balance of four patterns known as 'humors': blood, bile, phlegm, and choler. Avicenna (980–1037) and Culpeper (1616–1654) were considered experts in the science of astrology, planetary patterns, to determine which plant was applied for the care of a particular patient.[47] The study of the science of astrology is not only to match the plant pattern with the person's pattern but also to understand order in Nature. It is a sense of order that often influences peace of mind, as we can observe in young children. Plants and stars are both believed to be linked to the natural order of the universe. Biodynamic gardening incorporates the knowledge of astrological patterns when growing and harvesting herbs for medicine making.[48]

Another historical theory applied in discerning the best plant partnership is the Doctrine of Signatures associated with the work of Paracelsus, a Swiss-German physician (1493–1541). The Doctrine of Signatures states that each plant has a pattern that he called a "signature," which he defined as something in the way the plant looks or how it grows, that lets the person know the healing purpose of the plant. For example, potatoes have "eyes" and are, therefore, could be considered for use in the healing of the eyes. The shape of the *Panax ginseng* root looks like the shape of the human body. This signature of the whole body suggests that ginseng's healing properties support the entire body. And indeed, ginseng is traditionally used to promote energy or "qi" in the whole body. The signature of violets is that they hide from the sun and love the shade; therefore, they are of benefit to the migraine sufferer whose individual signature pattern is a sensitivity to light and seeking the solace of a darkened room.

In the Doctrine of Signatures, there is a matching of signatures in the plant with the symptom-sign patterns observable in a person. One of the plant remedies that demonstrates the Doctrine of Signatures is grape *(Vitis vinifera)*. The signature of the grape is associated with the lungs: the large stem representing the main stem bronchus and the grapes the alveoli. Green grapes are cooling to the lungs, and red or purple grapes warm the lungs. Green grapes cool the lungs when a person's sputum is yellow or green, which are symptoms of heat, and red or purple grapes for a "cold" cough when the sputum is white.

Observing and interpreting symptom-sign health patterns adds dimension to the level of science exemplified in the humours, astrological, and Doctrine of Signatures approaches. Symptom-sign health patterns organize perceptions and observations of behaviors as well as changes in those behaviors over time. Naming one's symptom-sign health pattern is simply a summary description of observed behaviors as opposed to a medical diagnosis, which is a judgment of those same behaviors as "healthy" (good) or "disease" (bad).

Medical diagnoses, by definition, describe patterns of pathology in cells, tissues, organs, mind, or emotion. The one cause -one cure health belief, now fundamental to biomedical healthcare systems today, suggests that there is in illness one pattern, and in the cure, there is one pattern. Nature suggests otherwise most especially in Self-care, where disease is not the focus.

Changes in body, mind, emotion, and spiritual behaviors do not necessarily have to suggest disease. Those who seek health promotion, wellbeing, and wellness can focus instead on a symptom-sign health pattern summary that describes evolutionary movements toward a self-styled goal that holds meaning for balance in body and peace of mind for the person. The Elements of Care® program focuses on the recognition of symptom-sign health patterns in Self-care rather than medical diagnoses as more supportive of and specific to achieving personal goals. The EOC program assists you in transitioning from a disease focus in your life and nursing practice to a symptom-sign health patterns approach.

While there is nothing inherently wrong with biomedical belief and the associated healthcare practices and disease focus, a commonly held belief in the health sciences and healing traditions is that solutions need to be able to address the complexity of health patterns of energy flow that human beings express within themselves and in relation to their environments. Energy flow in human beings and throughout the matter universe manifests as the five patterns known as elements: Fire, Air, Water, Earth, and Ether. Applying inductive thinking to identify health patterns using the five elements is a starting point for teaching and learning how to be a Self-care change agent when addressing common health patterns, such as sleep and rest, mobility, pain, energy, emotions, and thought, hormone balance, and nutrition. Applying the five elements as a framework for pattern recognition is the focus of many culture's traditional knowledge used in the healing of self and others. An easy-to-learn healing tradition that supports the application of symptom-sign health patterns in Self-care is the ancient system called *8 Principle Patterns in Traditional Chinese Medicine "TCM."* This is used in teaching and learning health pattern recognition in the EOC precision Self-care program.

EIGHT PRINCIPLE PATTERNS

The TCM system is based on the principle of balance, a major concept in Taoist philosophy, and on the recognition of patterns of symptoms and signs unique to a given person. It is a philosophy of care that can be applied by the public in Self-care with plants as partners as food or medicine. TCM has its language-related to symptom-sign patterns and classification of foods and herbs. Westerners can quickly learn the language and underlying philosophy of the system to be able to apply the principles and methods of the system effectively. First, is the study of TCM energetics of foods. I recommend the book, *The Tao of Healthy Eating* on TCM diet therapy[49] as people can readily recognize the energetic pattern of common food, such as a chili pepper, (the energetics of which are hot and spicy), that they have eaten many times. Also, lifestyle and dietary changes are always recommended first in the classical TCM tradition. If the imbalance is not affected by those changes, then herbs and other modalities are introduced. I have practiced TCM nurse-herbalism for over 25 years and found that adherence to this basic system is highly effective in Self-care and in nursing practice, specifically when doing an assessment. The publication on the *Tao of Integrative Nursing Assessment*[50] provides more details about the application of TCM philosophy in the care of patients.

One of the earliest organizing structures for TCM is known as the 8 Principle Patterns. There are four groups of two patterns, each that comprise the 8 Principle Patterns. They are heat/cold, excess/deficiency, interior/exterior, and yin/yang. The four groups describe general energetic qualities; however, no one group is sufficient to provide a holistic representation or diagnosis of a person's pattern. In TCM, the energetic qualities are grouped, such as in the diagnosis of "Interior Heat Deficiency" (Called Yin Deficiency). The purpose is to utilize interventions, such as a simple herbal application of the herb that will move the pattern toward greater *balance*. For example, if someone has heat in the head, one might consider balancing the heat in the head with a cooling herb that traditionally affects the head area. One example is peppermint (*Mentha piperita*) tea, an herb, as discussed previously, that is energetically cold and known to affect the head area.

The terms heat and cold do not refer to actual body temperature. They represent the opposite ends of a thermal energetic continuum—perceptions of heat and cold—with neutral (neither hot nor cold) in the center. Everyone experiences symptoms of heat and cold and points in between during the day. It is when a quality, particularly an extreme quality such as heat or cold, is consistently present that an imbalance exists, and the quality is inferred. One of the best indicators of heat/cold pattern is the tongue. A normal tongue, such as that of a healthy school-age child, is typically pink with a white coating. That coating is neither too thick nor too thin or spotty.

Cold pattern includes:
1. The person feels cold or dislikes cold.
2. The person prefers to drink warm or hot drinks.
3. Urine is light in color, and stools are loose.
4. The application of heat relieves discomfort.
5. Movements and speech are often slow.
6. The person acts withdrawn.
7. Pulse is slow.
8. Tongue tissue is pale and the coating white.

A healthy tongue coating is white. Therefore, that symptom alone is not sufficient for inferring cold. Several symptoms must be present for deciding that the pattern is "cold," but not all on the list must be present. It is also possible for a person to have symptoms of both heat and cold at the same time. For example, a person may feel hot in the head and cold in their feet. They may walk slowly but talk fast—a symptom of heat.

Heat pattern includes:
1. The person feels hot and dislikes heat.
2. The person is thirsty and prefers cold drinks.
3. Urine is dark in color, and they may be constipated.
4. Cold applications reduce pain.
5. Movement and speech are rapid.
6. The person is outgoing.
7. Pulse is rapid.
8. Tongue tissue is red and the coating yellow.

Excess and deficiency, like heat and cold, are points on a continuum and can exist simultaneously in one person. The thickness of the tongue coating is one of the most critical symptoms differentiating excess and deficiency.

Excess pattern includes:
1. Uses energy forcefully.
2. A person's breathing is heavy.
3. Pressure and touch aggravate pain.
4. Movements are forceful and speech is loud.
5. A person is outgoing and sometimes aggressive.
6. Pulse is strong.
7. The tongue coating is thick.

Deficiency pattern includes:
1. The person is fatigued and perspires easily.
2. A person's breathing is shallow, and they may be short of breath.
3. Pressure and touch help relieve pain.
4. The person's movement is weak, and speech is quiet.
5. The person is often passive.
6. Pulse is weak.
7. The tongue coating is very thin.

The terms "exterior" and "interior" refer to the relative depth or superficiality of illness in relation to the entirety of the symptom-sign pattern rather than to the physical expression in the body. Interior, for example, is not a literal term referring to the center of the anatomy, and exterior does not correctly refer to the skin.

Exterior pattern includes:
1. Sudden onset of acute illness; chills and a low fever.
2. Sinus congestion and discharge.
3. Dull pain in the head and muscles.
4. Pulse is floating (a specific profile in which the pulse is felt more strongly at the surface of the skin and diminishes with increasing pressure).
5. The tongue typically has a normal tongue coating and tissue.

Interior pattern includes:
1. Chronic illness; acute illness that has become more severe.
2. Sensations of excessive cold or heat; high fever.

3. Abnormal changes in breathing not related to exercise.
4. Abnormal urination and bowel symptoms.
5. Pain in the trunk of the body.
6. Changes in speech and behavior.
7. Abnormal pulse.
8. Any abnormality in tongue tissue or coating.

Yin and yang are central concepts to the Taoist philosophy of harmony and balance. They are relative concepts that are explained by their relationship rather than by absolutes. In terms of physical health, yin is the ability of the body to calm and cool itself, and yang is the ability of the body to heat and energize itself.

The 8 Principle Patterns organize observations, identifying, and naming/communicating health patterns perceived as both health and illness behaviors. Clear energetic pattern recognition leads to best choices in precision Self-care, such as the best choice of an herb. Here is an example of Self-care coaching that I provided to someone who had a medical diagnosis of uterine fibroids and persistent pelvic pain that was worse when she touched her abdomen (excess-interior). Her tongue coating was thick in the back of the tongue, suggesting excess, specifically "dampness," in her lower abdomen or "burner" as it is called in TCM as discussed previously. The purple hue of her tongue tissue and menstrual history suggested "blood stagnation" also in the lower burner, which would result in accumulated dampness.

When I asked her about her lifestyle and diet patterns, she mentioned that she ate a sweet potato every day. The young woman was healthy, very active, and very health conscious. Sweet potatoes would not seem to many in the biomedical field to be a risky food. But from a symptom-sign pattern perspective, the food was a concern for this woman. Think about sweet potatoes for a moment. The ones that the woman was eating were orange (warm color as opposed to blue or green), sweet, and a bit gooey (damp). They may not be as damp as a block of cheese or a scoop of ice cream (colder), but they are damp all the same. Self-care pattern diagnosis was "Blood and dampness stagnation" in the "lower burner" potentially aggravated by the daily ingestion of sweet potato. The potato had not "caused" the dampness, but it was a part of her everyday lifestyle that was building and aggravating rather than moving and draining the dampness. She did a Self-study and abstained from eating sweet potatoes for one week while monitoring her pain level.

Her pain diminished exponentially within a few days. In this case, simple abstention from a food rather than herbs or over-the-counter pain medications was all that was necessary for creating greater balance in the body. She also had peace of mind knowing that her Self-care choice to change one plant food in her diet was effective. Symptom-sign pattern recognition and the 8 Principle Patterns will be referenced again in subsequent chapters.

PARADIGMS ABOUT PLANT PARTNERSHIP

Effective change and positive experiences reinforce people's belief in the choices that they make in health care. Over time, patterns of thinking take hold in cultures and reinforce a worldview or paradigm. Science and healing are part of the culture. The word culture comes from the Latin *cultus* meaning "care" and the French *colere* meaning "cultivate."[51] Cultivation is a term commonly used in the plant world when referring to the nurturance of plant growth. *Ur* in Hebrew means "light." A synthesis of the roots of the word suggests that culture is of significant concern in the healing arts because it is, in essence, "the practice of the cultivation of light" in Self-care and healthcare. Culture, as defined in the dictionary, is "the integrated pattern of human knowledge, belief, and behavior that depends upon man's capacity for learning and transmitting knowledge."[52] Health cultural diplomacy is the active expression of the internalized qualities of awareness of one's culture as the practice of cultivating light in the care of Self and others.

Health culture diplomacy suggests acknowledgment of the diversity of health beliefs and practices as represented in the belief patterns and paradigms discussed here and the need to build bridges between diverse groups through education and diplomatic example. The goal of health culture diplomacy is to build long-term relationships that can lead to an increasingly peaceful global community. The purpose of health culture diplomacy is improving communication and understanding between those acting according to biomedical, traditional, and Self-care cultures. Because people of all paradigms relate to plants, plants have the potential of bringing people of different health cultures, beliefs, and practices together! The EOC program recognizes the importance of knowing the three paradigms that impact Self-care with plants as partners: Biomedical, Traditional, and personal Self-care.

BIOMEDICAL PARADIGM

Some of the strengths of the biomedical paradigm include valuing cure, a persistent attempt to find the cause (diagnosis) of the disease in need of curing, and the innovative use of technology to make discoveries on the cellular level. A cure is highly valued because it is equated with life and health. Research, as discussed previously, is one means of determining the efficacy of the cure. The biomedical paradigm includes a conviction regarding the benefits of proper research in supporting the clinical provision of safer and more effective health care. The gold standard of research is believed in the west to be the randomized, double-blind, placebo-controlled trial because it is a form of inquiry that focuses on a particular variable and seeks to isolate that variable so that its unique qualities can be recognized. Research questions are often answered through the evaluation of quantifiable data. These common questions demonstrate the biomedical paradigm:

- Are there any clinical trials on the use of this herbal *drug*?
- How safe is this herbal drug for human consumption?
- How efficacious is this herbal drug in curing specific disease?
- What is the dose of the herb used?
- What are the active ingredients/constituents in the crude herb-drug, and can they be synthesized?
- What are the risks of harmful interactions between herbs and other therapies prescribed, such as drug and diet therapies?

You might be thinking, "these are the questions that anyone considering plant medicines *should* be asking." These are the critical questions asked by nurses, physicians, and pharmacists. These questions stem from the underlying values of the biomedical paradigm. The problem is that if answers don't come from these questions, the herb seems suspect, even useless. In industrialized societies, this biomedical dominance can lead to the closing of the heart and mind to curiosity about plant partnerships rather then add to the knowledge of the plant under consideration in Self-care. Those who would integrate the biomedical paradigm can practice re-framing the biomedical questions.

In general, the biomedical view is that each plant is a potential drug. Historically, the plant's constituents have been more highly valued than the plant as a whole. The overarching question of the biomedical paradigm about herbal remedies can be summarized as "What makes this healing plant work?" The following sections discuss four views of the workings of healing plants from the perspective of the biomedical paradigm.

Plants as Potential Drugs

Plants are viewed as potential drugs. Most pharmaceutical drugs are derived from plants and their constituents. Only a small number of the more than 250,000 species of flowering plants on the planet have been studied and registered as drugs with some type of experimental confirmation of their biological activities.[53] Some of the prescription and over-the-counter drugs for which plants or their derivatives are used include caffeine, opium, tincture of benzoin, oatmeal, chlorophyll, reserpine, scopolamine, vincristine, morphine, ipecac, psyllium, digoxin, ephedrine, and theophylline. These and many more drugs have brought relief to people over the years, and they are the result of the hard work and vision of those with a biomedical worldview. In the United States, there is still some effort placed on plant-based drug development. Still, other governments in countries such as South Africa actively support and fund the development of traditional herbal medicines.

The cost of a new prescription drug going through the research and development phases and the formal approval process set forth by the Food and Drug Administration in the United States is estimated to be between hundreds of thousands to millions of dollars. The total cost depends on the number of phases of clinical trials to be undertaken and the drug test. The FDA is one of the most expensive drug approval systems in the world today. If drug companies were to put this kind of money into the development of plant drugs, they could only recoup their costs if they held exclusive rights or a patent on the herbal medicine to sell it. However, plants are not patentable because they are familiar, are used by many, and often grow outside our back doors. Drug companies can patent extraction techniques, or they can modify some natural compounds to make a semi-synthetic from a natural starting material. Although people may prefer a natural drug, drug companies prefer a synthetic that they can legally protect. Although some pharmaceutical companies have begun to take a second look at plant medicines, there are still some huge issues with the approach of searching for the active compounds.

Medicinal plants have very complex chemical structures. Identifying one unique active constituent that can create a specific health-giving action in the human body is not easy. Herbs deliver a smorgasbord of biochemical constituents to the body, and biomedical technology may not be able to identify how they work in multiple pathways at one time. The researcher may pay top money for the research and development of an herb or herbal formula only to end up with more questions about a particular plant's biologic and medicinal activity.

The consumer saves money with herbal remedies, however. One paper on the costs of herbal medicines to health care organizations reported that if St. John's Wort were given to depressed patients instead of Prozac and were effective only in 25 percent of cases, the cost savings estimated to the third-party payers would be $250,000.[54] The paradox is that although the research and approval of a pharmaceutical drug made from a plant may be valued and desired, the reality is that it is often economically impractical for drug companies to promote the very products those in the biomedical world may want.

Researching Safety and Toxicity

The other view of the biomedical paradigm is that plant medicines be submitted to the same rigorous testing and research controls used for drugs. It is often implied that the potential for harm to a patient taking plant medicines is just as great as if they were using a pharmaceutical drug. Therefore, toxicity, dosing, and standardization should be established for all herbal medicines. Some warn that herbs should not be used until such data are thoroughly collected and evaluated. Historical data demonstrate the opposite. Although there are herbal remedies that can cause harm if used improperly, such as applying a mustard plaster too long on the skin, community and health care records show that herbs have been considered gentler than pharmaceuticals that are often made of specific chemical compounds. Part of the reason for the safety record of plants as gentle medicine is due to their complexity discussed in Chapter 8.

So often biomedical practitioners suggest that herbs be recommended only if they can be proven safe and efficacious by randomized clinical trials (RCTs), the gold standard of biomedical science designed for use in the testing of pharmaceutical drugs that are single constituent products. The cost to support clinical research on every herb is positively prohibitive. There are some pros and cons to holding herbs to the same standards as pharmaceutical drugs. First of all, herbs do not have the same history as pharmaceutical drugs. Plant therapies often have been applied extensively in one culture or another, sometimes for hundreds of years by humans, whereas new drugs have not been used at all. Denying the use of drugs that have not been thoroughly studied is reasonable when they have never been used in humans. But is it reasonable to suggest that herbs that have been safely applied by humans for hundreds of years should now be allowed only based on whether or not studies have shown that they are helpful and not just executing a placebo effect?

Secondly, the concept of the standard RCT is not acceptable to all cultures. For example, scientists in some countries do not agree philosophically with the concept of using a placebo. Is it reasonable to believe that all cultures will honor and value the RCT as the gold standard for good science or good herbal practice? It may seem culturally biased to some that the RCT is the only truly acceptable measure of safety and efficacy of an herb.

Questions have been raised within the biomedical community about the feasibility and the effect of holding the RCT as the gold standard for health science in the first place. RCTs are very expensive and logistically challenging. The concept of the standard RCT is not acceptable to all cultures. In fact, RCTs have not been carried out for many of the medical treatments in existence. And even when RCTs are available, it is difficult to extrapolate the findings to the individual patient because the entry criteria into the RCTs are usually very stringent and the clinician may never find an RCT that matches the patient seeking treatment. Some have suggested that single patient trials (SPTs), or "N-of-1" studies, may be more feasible and more helpful in directing patient care. The SPT provides evidence to support the care of the *individual* patient.

Outcomes measurement, evidence-based practice, and research in general are an ongoing concern for biomedicine. Although clinical trials have been done with herbal medicines, there are questions as to whether or not these studies actually promote understanding of the herbal *therapy*. Many studies that help in identifying plant constituents that are possibly responsible for the action of a medicinal plant are done as *in vitro* studies in a laboratory. Can understanding the mechanism of action of a plant or its constituents give a clinician a reasonably good understanding of the safety and efficacy of the plant as a remedy or healing modality? Studies that lead to a greater understanding of the relationship of the plant in the healing rituals of an individual may be just as insightful as the studies that lead to greater understanding of the inner workings of the plant itself. Integration of understanding gained from biomedical and traditional research may be the most reasonable approach to informing precision Self-care.

Sharing the Evidence

The public, although interested in scientific research, is often uninformed regarding the variety of methodologies used to study herbs. It is the ethical responsibility of health practitioners and researchers to report findings clearly and includes any limitations of the study to the consumer. Meaning that if a large clinical trial on an herb shows favorable, generalizable responses, the public must understand that they are not assured benefit. Likewise, lack of identifiable benefit based on an RCT does not negate that traditional herbalists or a community have used for hundreds of years, then there is no health benefit. RCTs are very specific, and the results must report the study's inclusion criteria, the herb(s) included in the study, and how they were applied. For example, if the RCT involved the use of a standardized extract of a particular constituent from an herb such as alliin from garlic (*Allium sativum*), it should not be reported in a way that would leave the public with the impression that whole garlic or other garlic products would have the same results.

One example of ethically flawed reporting occurred with the release of results of an *in vitro* study of four herbs' effect on the penetration of *hamster* oocytes (eggs) and the integrity of donor (presumably human) sperm deoxyribonucleic acid.[55] The results of the *in vitro* study were that flooding the oocytes with a "concentrated herbal solution" of each of the four herbs resulted in reduced or zero penetration of oocytes. Exposure of sperm cells to some of the herbs resulted in the denaturation of DNA. One well-known American physician appeared on a major national news program and reported to the public that anyone trying to conceive should not take any of the herbs evaluated in the study. He mentioned that many herbs are not "studied" and therefore are potentially unsafe. No one reported that the research was on hamster instead of human cells. The physician did mention in passing that the study was an *in vitro* study, but he did not clarify that this meant only an experiment in a dish in a lab. The essence of the report was that the four herbs had not been studied; they are unsafe and pose a danger to those trying to conceive. The report was made without consideration of the need for a clear, unbiased representation of research findings.

Reports about research findings or evidence related to herbal remedies

should include the following plant science perspective when being shared orally or in written form:
1. A Plant Perspective
    a. Botanical names should include scientific name if known.
    b. Format for botanical name: Common name (*Scientific name*)
    c. Include relevant information on the historical and traditional applications of the plant or plants discussed.
    d. Be sure to distinguish whole plant from plant constituents and their applications when discussing botanical therapies.
2. Control Bias –Health sciences literature in which plants are discussed should follow guidelines for professional scientific reporting and writing.
    a. Discuss the data and avoid gross generalizations from unsupported data, which imply or state a risk from using botanical therapies
    b. Call for further research as is customary in scientific writing rather than debunk a plant, its use in health care or herbalism in general.
    c. Be fair to plants and cultural traditions and rituals that include them. Just as scientific writing calls for sensitivity to marginalized humans, respect should be shown to plants that are important to cultural traditions. Slurring of any plant, botanical therapy or cultural tradition is not appropriate.

Standardization

Another value of the biomedical paradigm is that of controlling the quality and quantity of plant constituents using a standardization process (such as European phyto-pharmaceuticals). Standardization is thought to provide for safer and more effective herbal remedies. A standardized extract is a plant preparation in which an active constituent, if identified, has been standardized or made uniform from individual product to individual product. Standardization is seen as beneficial by those thinking from a biomedical view in which the belief is that the active constituents in a plant are identified, extracted, purified, and standardized. This process is thought to make the remedy more like a pharmaceutical drug than any other plant preparation and better able to control quality and dose of medical constituents. Having the plant remedy standardized means that the practitioner can prescribe a specific dose of a "known" active constituent with the benefit of the constituent being in a "natural" form, as compared to synthetic drugs.

Many practitioners and people prefer drugs that are from a natural source. However, the ability to produce a standardized herbal medicine rests upon the ability of researchers to identify the active constituent of a plant. In some plants such as Senna *(Cassia senna L.)*, a plant that has been traditionally used for constipation, an "active constituent" has been identified. In Senna, the active constituent that seems to have a bowel irritant or stimulant effect is identified as "sennosides." Standardization of sennosides means for the consumer that taking a certain amount of herbal product should have a laxative effect. Because the sennosides are identifiable, the sennoside constituents are studied in much the same way a pharmaceutical drug would be.

The controversy is that sennosides are not the whole plant. The history of relatively safe use of Senna has to do with the traditional use of the whole leaf not sennosides. It is also argued that in many plants, a goal of identifying a single constituent is not possible and that the standardization of plant medicine to a single constituent is, therefore, misleading regarding efficacy and safety. It is well known in plant science that there are "normally more than one (or one type of) active component in a natural product" and that "standardization based on one particular type of chemical component is not representative of the total activity of the product. Consequently, these arbitrarily selected components can only be useful as a 'marker' of product quality. And these 'markers' are only valid for extracts that are total extractions of the herbs concerned."[56] Standardization does consistently assist in identifying the quality of a particular herb.

Plants grown even in the same field can vary in the potency of certain active constituents. Quality markers can help growers identify potential potency of the whole medicinal plant. Whole plants are, in general, less potent than an individual plant constituent. For comparison, take the apple. Most people who have eaten an apple remember the strong outer skin and the crunching sound when biting into the fruit for the first time. There is a lot of pectin and fiber in the apple skin. Now recall eating the fleshy part of the apple. Although some apples are tarter than others, they are a sweet fruit. The sugars in fruits are known as fructose. When extracted from the fruit and processed, fructose looks much the same as the white crystallized cane sugar you might eat. Think about what it might be like to eat a spoonful of fructose sugar. How might your body respond? Sugars are known to give the body an energy boost. Does your body get the identical energy boost from an apple as it does from a spoonful of fructose? Common sense tells us that extracted (standardized) fructose is not the same as an apple and it does not have the same total effect on the body either.

An example of when standardization may be helpful is in liver damage due to toxic substance exposure from acetaminophen, environmental pollutants, or mushroom poisoning, for example. Milk thistle seed *(Silybum marianum)* has been selected traditionally for more than 2000 years for illness related to the liver. Milk thistle products are standardized to silymarin, a hepatoprotective and antioxidant constituent. According to research, a therapeutic level of silymarin cannot be achieved by taking teas or simple alcohol extracts of the milk thistle seed because silymarin cannot survive the breakdown by digestive juices and enter the bloodstream via the intestinal wall.[57] Because silymarin is not very soluble in water and is poorly absorbed from the gastrointestinal tract, a concentrated, standardized extract or injectable form of the plant is used to provide the desired effects. Despite this biomedical evidence, herbalists and traditional healers may disagree that standardization is necessary for a person to receive a health benefit from milk thistle. Some herbalists are concerned about the risks related to standardization. Some people with chemical sensitivities have reported negative responses to standardized products because of the chemical residue in the product from the standardization process. More research is needed to fully determine the benefits and risks of using standardized herbal products.

Standardized herbs when sold in capsule or tablet form, are similar to pharmaceuticals. The consumer is not required to handle whole herb products or know how to prepare them for their healing applications. Some people may believe that taking a pill is more comfortable and enjoyable (i.e., no odd taste). Even though biomedical practitioners may think they are providing a service to these patients, some questions about the risks involved do still exist.

While clinical science in botanical medicine began in the 19th century in America and England, standardization is still relatively new. Doctors and nurses knew how to choose plant medicines for people and knew their standard dosages, which were individualized. The use of standardized plant extracts, and the movement away from the traditional paradigm with its ways of knowing about plant safety, efficacy, and dosing, is now being promoted by some as the professionalization of botanical medicine. Yet, those who adhere to a biomedical paradigm must, according to the values and standards of that paradigm, also question any unstudied biomedical beliefs that a standardized herbal preparation is somehow inherently better or safer than a remedy that is not standardized.

TRADITIONAL PARADIGM

History demonstrates some of the vast differences between traditional healers' and biomedical views of healing, health care, and medicinal use of plants. Biomedicine has striven to separate itself as *the* science[58] within the broader culture of the healing arts. Biomedical science often distances itself from the people and their traditions in an attempt to increase objectivity which is perceived as rigor in scientific inquiry. Striving for objectivity does not always work in medicinal plant science because, as those who partner with plants know well, plants are sentient life with which people have relationships. Those relationships sometimes include memories of years of application in numerous health conditions, healing rituals, and practices. Plant knowledge in the traditional paradigm lives in the story.

There is an old story in Chinese herbal medicine that helps illustrate a traditional paradigm of the use of herbs. It goes like this: A group of herbal students was ready for their final exam. Their teacher told them to search eight miles out on all sides of the town and bring back samples of all the plants they could find that had absolutely no medicinal value. Within a few days, all but one of the students had returned, each with a few plants. Finally, on the fifth day, the last student returned looking very sad indeed, for he was empty-handed. "Why so sad?" asked the teacher. "You are the only one qualified to pursue the herbal path."

This story illustrates traditional values related to medicinal plants. The traditional paradigm represents the "people's" cultural beliefs about plants and their rituals and habits over time. One dictionary definition of tradition is the "continuity of culture."[59] Because cultures and plant populations differ geographically, the specifics of a particular traditional plant paradigm also vary from country to country. It is beyond the scope of this book to examine each culture's herbal traditions; however, traditional and biomedical cultural traditions related to plant partnership can be compared and contrasted.

Traditional medicine as defined by the World Health Organization (WHO) is "the ways of protecting and restoring health that existed before the arrival of modern medicine … approaches to health that belong to the traditions of a country and have been handed down from generation to generation."[60] Some traditional healing with plants has been passed by word of mouth as part of folklore. The oral tradition of passing on information about herbs includes a belief system and a philosophy as well as the details of the actual virtues and applications of the healing plants. Some traditional systems such as TCM, Kampo medicine in Japan, and Ayurveda in India are highly documented, theoretically based, and researched. In addition to herbalists, WHO classifies acupuncturists, traditional birth attendants, and mental healers as traditional healers. Many countries have traditional healers who are indigenous peoples who partner with plants in their healing practices.

Indigenous people as those "who follow traditional, non-industrialized lifestyles in areas that they have occupied for generations."[61] Indigenous knowledge systems (IKS) include ways of knowing about medicines, healing, communication, art, agriculture, education, and all other cultural arenas from the views of indigenous peoples. Indigenous knowledge is local knowledge that is unique to a given culture or society. It is the foundation for decision making within a culture. A TCM practitioner in the United Kingdom, for example, although a practitioner of a traditional form of medicine, would not be considered an indigenous healer in Britain the way a Celtic person might.

Indigenous healers serve as exceptional resources about the plants growing in their regions. Their relationships with plants are strong and direct. Indigenous healers wildcraft or cultivate their herbs. They are the knowledge holders and wisdom keepers about healing plants. Indigenous peoples still hold that plants are sacred. Traditional healing practices emphasize balance and harmony between the elements, person, Earth, the universe, and all living creatures, including plants. Self-care with plants as partners can be a sacred act in which one connects with the elements of Self, Earth, universe, and all living creatures.

North American Indian, also known as First Nation, indigenous medicine healers taught European settlers how to apply local plant remedies when caring for themselves and their families.[62] Early North American medical dispensatories included plant medicines commonly valued by various Native American tribes. Yet the Native American contributions to the medical practices of North Americans have often been devalued if not grossly under-recognized.

American Indian herbal tradition is well documented.[63] Some of the knowledge of healing plants, such as corn, was transmitted along a tribe's matrilineal lines. Many indigenous peoples' beliefs include the view that plants and animals are their brothers and sisters. Animals are often thought of as ancestors. American Indians believe that it was respectful to pray to the Creator to ask for the wisdom and help of plants before harvesting them for medicine.

The term "medicine" to a North American Indian has a meaning that extends well beyond the physical remedy or treatment. Medicine is equated with the Creator, the Great Spirit within all. This book does not even begin to account for the rituals and mystical understanding held by indigenous American healers regarding plants. Indigenous knowledge of plants is often a wisdom tradition that is protected as a valuable treasure with no sharing permitted without the express permission and spiritual guidance of the tribal elders and healers. Ethnobotanical studies have revealed the richness of the healing traditions of various American Indian tribes such as the Zuni and Cheyenne, and that knowledge of traditional beliefs and customs about medicinal plant healing is diminishing. But there are some living wisdom keepers and medicine people, such as Cecilia Mitchell, an elder from Akwesasne Mohawk Country.[64] They teach, heal, and tell stories that help root their tribe's knowledge of healing plants deeply within the community so that the understanding of the plants is preserved. Cecilia also fights to preserve her herbal "apothecaries" from political and corporate land claim and other potential public developments.

I have lodged with Cecilia in her home, where five rivers meet on the border of Ontario, Canada and New York, USA. She is a wisdom holder of the legends of the people of Six Nations (Iroquois). We talk plant, take medicine walks, pray, and share medicine stories. Many times, Cecilia told me the story of the Peace Maker and the history of the *White Roots of Peace* that is one of the most important stories of the Six Nations people of the Iroquois confederacy and therefore fundamental for understanding the essence of their medicine tradition. (See Conclusion in this book) To experience the stories and legends of a people, including one's people, is the beginning of understanding medicine as fully as is possible from the perspective of traditional and indigenous healing.

In traditional ways of knowing and being, the way life is viewed is quite differently from views of the biomedical culture. Whereas the central question of those of the biomedical culture might be "What makes this plant work?" the main question of those of the traditional paradigm might simply be "What is the healing spirit of this plant?" The need for understanding the components that make up the plant before deciding whether or not it can be applied is not part of a traditional paradigm. In traditional practice, herbs are most often combined synergistically as opposed to the biomedical approach of targeting a single constituent.

In folkloric healing and domestic medicine—types of traditional practice—herbal recipes and remedies were traded freely within community communication and healing networks. These recipes were single plant simples. Apothecaries or pharmacists have been busy developing all sorts of new complex drugs from animals, vegetables, and minerals over the years when they could not make a living by selling the simples that grew freely in their customers' gardens or nearby fields or forests. Today, many pharmacies are selling large amounts of herbal preparations to people who lack knowledge of the plant, its story, or the ability to grow or harvest it themselves. From a traditional and biomedical safety perspective, partnering with one plant simple at a time is a sound Self-care plan.

Traditional practitioners also have their language for describing illness. Although the explanations about the cause for illness and rationale for knowing the virtues of a particular herb may be very different from that of the biomedical paradigm, they are similarly scientifically based. Traditional and indigenous practitioners use logic and some form of pattern recognition when describing illness. They match the pattern of disease or discomfort with an herb or herbs that bring about greater balance and health. Traditional medical knowledge is typically coded into household cooking practices, home remedies, and health prevention/maintenance beliefs and routines. It is not uncommon for people who practice traditional and folk medicine also to consider biomedical treatments and medicines. They, like many other people, are inherently integrative in their considerations of what might help them in Self-care. One American study showed that "Among the 44% of adults who said that they regularly take prescription medications, nearly 1 in 5 (18.4%) reported the concurrent use of at least one herbal product, a high-dose vitamin, or both."[65]

People choose to use traditional healing methods for many reasons. Their decisions can be quite logical and are often based on trust. People who have seen the effectiveness of plant remedies in promoting the health of their families may suspect the newest treatment introduced by the biomedical practitioner. That is human nature. It is also very logical. People also know from experience and a long history that plant medicines are gentler medicines and have not had the same adverse effects that pharmaceutical drugs do. Because many of the day-to-day health concerns are not life-threatening, many people logically turn to lifestyle issues such as diet and home remedies (e.g., plant medicines) to effect changes that can result in balance in body and peace of mind. People have a sense of timing in their healing process. Although they often prefer to provide self-care and not rely on someone else for care, they also ask for help when it is needed.

Culture clashes between the biomedical and traditional medicine paradigms often occur in private, public, hospital, or community-based health care facilities. I have seen how cultural gaps, such as how folk remedies from one culture can be misinterpreted by those who work in the biomedical culture, cause high tension in the healing relationship and environment. For example, when I was a school nurse in Minnesota, where many Hmong refugees had immigrated, I had been given some education as to Hmong cultural beliefs. One day a child came to school with small, circular burn marks along his spine. The teachers thought that the parents were abusing the small child by burning him with what looked like might have been a cigarette, but the child had been burned on specific acupuncture meridian points to heal the cold sore on his lip. I realized the burn pattern because of my background in TCM, not because of the cultural training the county had given me. Although other treatments for cold sores are less physically harmful, the Hmong parents' intent was not to harm their child with the moxibustion treatment but to heal him. We must understand the traditional paradigm and practice before making any kind of assumption about healing practices, including applications of herbs.

The tension between the herbal practices of those of the traditional paradigm and those of the biomedical paradigm is often fanned by the clashes of the two paradigms. People can learn their own and others' herbal traditions as well as the herbal knowledge of the biomedical world. Options from both paradigms, especially for chronic conditions, health promotion, and day-to-day discomfort, can be relevant to health decision-making. Biomedical practitioners who understand as much as possible about their patients' belief systems and what their traditional knowledge of plants is like can better develop healing and helping relationships with their clients when they seek help from the biomedical world. Traditional people do, as Cecilia demonstrates, often have the desire and interest in understanding biomedical knowledge of plants and thinking about how it can better inform the traditions that they pass to their children and grandchildren. As countries continue to address the concerns about health care for all, traditional/indigenous healers are becoming more valuable each day for their herbal knowledge and wisdom. In some countries, they are an active part of the community's primary health care network.

SELF-CARE PARADIGM

Over the past decades, industrialized countries, such as the United States, have moved further away from the tiered system of health care that has endured for centuries[66] to put their faith in the promises of the biomedical paradigm alone. The public demand for holistic, alternative, complementary, and integrative care is their plea for a return to an inclusive system that publicly acknowledges the value of all medical cultures to welcome Self-care along with the beliefs, knowledge, and practices of traditional and biomedical paradigms.[67]

Nurses witness this health culture diplomacy approach as a natural course of action for anyone who has endured human suffering of any significant measure themselves or with a family member. It is common sense to seek out the best solutions for care, starting with one's Self-care skill and coping strategies, which people often have faith will be enough to help them. Self-care focuses on lifestyle and diet changes, and herbal simples that promote well-being and prevent illness through that which is perceived and experienced as creating balance in body and peace of mind.

As discussed in the first chapter, Self-care is the first tier of a balanced system that welcomes the consideration of healing knowledge from all directions. If further help is needed, the second tier is to seek advice from family and friends and numerous advice books and websites that are available. Today there are so many resources that the key of the second tier is knowing how to discern what the best choices in Self-care will be. The third tier is made up of community experts such as nurses, midwives, and other healers. The fourth tier is the biomedical tier of physicians, surgeons, Advanced Practice and Registered Nurses, and pharmacists. This tier is commonly and rightfully believed to be avoided if and when possible. It is uncommon for people to want a surgery or have to endure the adverse effects from taking a drug that eases their suffering. The fourth tier is very strong medicine with known potential for extensive risk and expense. In the process of Self-care decision making, this tiered system is not necessarily perfectly tiered at all times. Nurses and their patients often find that the tiers overlap.

Yet the biomedical paradigm alone is equated with healthcare in most industrialized countries, such as the United States. It has come to monopolize education, social conversations, and the media as it is only ever represented as progress without acknowledgment of its risks or the other paradigms that have been foundational also to the ongoing evolution of healthcare and the healing arts. "So-called primitive and folk health practices have been elaborately described by anthropologists, defended through testimonials, rationalized, and codified, or criticized is dangerous, ineffective, placebo, or nuisance, (delaying seeking professional care or interfering with professional advice) ... Each system of practice has its criteria for judging effectiveness, yet the validation criteria of allopathic medicine [orthodox medicine] have been universally applied."[68] Research demonstrates that the most common health-related experiences that people deal with on a day-to-day basis: minor illness and injury, such as cold, flu, skin conditions, indigestion and the like and chronic concerns from allergies to weight problems, are best and most often treated by ones' Self or family.[69]

There are many reasons for considering a partnership with plants in Self-care. Plant therapies work well; they are usually affordable; they have a strong history of successful use; they can be fun to make, and they are, for the most part, very gentle. Describing *whole* herbs as gentle does not mean that they are not potent and active and do not need to be used wisely and safely. Herbs are gentle in how they convey their medicine to humans, especially when compared with many pharmaceutical drugs. They may have very toxic constituents in them, but the amounts are often quite small. Even a properly used purgative herb can be experienced without the significant aftereffects felt with many pharmaceutical drugs.

People need whole herb medicines and therapies as well as pharmaceutical drugs. Many times, when people don't feel well, a cup of the appropriate tea and a nap is just enough to work through the ill-feeling. Children are excellent examples of this. Children who have stomachaches will often feel better quite quickly by holding a teddy bear, having a few sips of chamomile tea, and taking a short rest. Making a cup of herbal tea with a child when they feel queasy can be an opportunity for the expression of gentleness. As children experience plant medicine, they learn to discern when they might benefit from an herbal remedy or not. Often pharmaceutical drugs, over the counter or prescription, are powerful. Sensitive people can feel the not-so-subtle differences in their bodies between taking a pharmaceutical drug and an herb. The gentleness of herbal therapies also has to do with the preparation.

When people make their herbal medicines, there can be a tremendous healing effect. Children with whom I have made medicine from plants have often commented on how much "fun it is!" A nurse researcher found that women in her study liked to take teas that they had made for themselves rather than pills they were given because, ". . . the substance that makes up the pill is a real unknown and cannot be trusted... they feel that the teas are natural and talked about the acts of handling the leaves, boiling the water, and watching the remedy brew as critical to the known therapeutics of the remedy."[70] As reported by the women in this study, we can fully trust the medicine that we make for ourselves. The next five chapters guide you in the design of your plan for making and becoming your own medicine, which is precision Self-care in which you utilize the five elements, fire, air, water, earth, and ether to create a healing environment within and without with plants as partners.

CHAPTER 4

Start Your 5 Elements of Care®
Self-care Plan

The next chapters are a step-by-step guide for designing and implementing your five Elements of Care® precision Self-care plan. Plant partners will be chosen mindfully that catalyze the changes you decide to make in one or all of the elements. Each element has its unique qualities and, together with the other elements, integrates your whole Self, fire, air, water, earth, and ether in a plan to provide balance in body and peace of mind.

The earth element is associated with the physical body. Chapter 5—Entering the Earth Element—focuses on designing the part of your precision Self-care plan that includes your physical connection with the environment, explicitly healing plants to know yourself. Topics include anatomy and physiology, the chlorophyll connection and the healing environment, green pharmacy, and wildcrafting. Chapter 6—Awakening the Air Element—is associated with the mental body and how we think and learn about the integration of healing plants in Self-care. Topics include the use of symptom-sign patterns in a process for mindful decision making and problem-solving, how to decode herbal scientific data, and knowing when to Self-refer to a health practitioner when Self-care is no longer the best choice. Chapter 7—Welcoming the Water Element—is associated with the emotional body and how we feel and experience the flow of Self-care with plants as partners. The content of this chapter focuses on techniques for making ten different kinds of herbal simples. Chapter 8—Fanning the Fire Element—is associated with the spiritual body. The spiritual Self is equated with the laws of man and the Creator that guide behavior as individuals and communities. Topics include how to evaluate the effects of the herbal Self-care solutions you choose for your precision Self-care plan, my ten best botanical Self-care practices guideline, the 5 "rights" of precision plant partnership in Self-care and putting any fears about Self-care with plants as partners into the flame. Chapter 9—Effecting the Ether Element—concerns the fifth element of Self, which is associated with the whole essence of Self. The topics of this chapter include secret recipes, plant alchemy, herbal formulation, "thinking" plants, flower remedies, and the harmony of patterns in Nature such as the golden ratio. In the Conclusion, you will discover peacemaking and the "Way of the

Thornless Rose," how to manage your Self-talk, and apply the wisdom of the elders in putting the finishing touch to your precision Self-care plan.

How you care for and comfort yourself and your family is a manifestation of the elements of your Self: body, mind, emotion, spirit, and essence. Your Self-care plan is a unique representation of the five elements of Self at a particular moment in time and space. It will change as you change and heal. The presence of all five elements of Self, form a pattern that you choose as essential to the fullest expression of your intention for better balance in body and peace of mind. It is your conscious commitment to connecting with the natural world, plants, in particular, understanding your symptom-sign patterns in terms of the five elements of Self that invite opportunities for healing. Try out every element. Engage all 5 of the EOC in starting a practice plan that has meaning for you.

—Starting a Self-care Plan—

As you read the next chapters and do the Self-studies with herbs, I recommend that you begin to write down your intentions and plans for your precision Self-care plan. For this purpose, I have created an experiential guide to accompany this book. The first element chapter is about the earth element. The earth element is an excellent place to start to root your interest in plant partnership and your creative ideas for Self-care. The process of designing a Self-care plan is just like creating a garden. Your Self-care plan is your garden plan that you can use as a guide and an organizing framework for ideas and inspirations. There is no right or wrong way to create your Self-care plan. But there is one "rule" I like to suggest for you now as I would for any creative endeavor. Do not edit or critique your ideas or design work. Turn off the critical thinker and turn on your free thinker and dreamer modes! Give yourself the luxury of time to dream your dream while you read the rest of this book and engage in the Gentle Medicine Self-studies. Know that any meaningful Self-care plan also can be inspired and aided by the most beautiful plants, flowers, and trees.

As you start your Self-care plan, begin to observe what plants come into your world— waking and dreaming. Be sure to enter them also into your Self-care plan though you may not immediately know what role they will play. Just let the images, ideas, impressions, and dreams come into being. Open the gate to the flow of creativity. This book suggests a structure, the line drawings if you will, that lend definition to the work, but only you can provide the color and meaning for your design within that definition. Begin by picking a medium for your Self-care plan. You can use the *Experiential Guide* at the end of this book and a carefully selected journal, canvas, or sketch pad. Then choose your instrument for documenting your notes: a pencil, pen, or paintbrush. You may find that you prefer to record in words or pictures. The structure provided throughout this book for the development of your precision Self-care plan is the EOC program. The Experiential Guide is organized by the five elements. You are beginning the process of manifesting your vision for plant partnership in 5 elements Self-care.

Chapter 5
Entering the Earth Element

This chapter is the first of five chapters on the five elements of the Elements of Care® program for creating a precision Self-care plan with plants as partners. As you enter the earth element, think about how much you know about your physical body, its structures, and functions. What would you say is the current state of balance and peace in your physical body?

—Know Your Self—
Anatomy, Physiology, and Pattern Science

Do you know the anatomy and physiology of the human body? Anatomy is what the body structures are, and physiology is how they work. Anatomy coloring books are an effective, engaging technique for learning more about the structures and functions of each organ and bodily system involved in various health concerns. Discerning the possible causes of everyday concerns, manifest as an uncomfortable change in the body, is an essential result of recognizing one's unique energetic symptom-sign patterns that begin with knowing anatomy and physiology.

For example, the colon is also known as the large intestine. It is an excretory organ, which means that it like the kidneys, and the skin is an organ that removes waste products from the body. The large intestine shaped like an upside down "U" connects to the end of the small intestine in the lower right quadrant of the abdomen, where there is a small tail-like part called the appendix. Whe we ingest food and fluids, they move from our mouth to our stomach, to the small intestine, and the large intestine. The purpose of the movement in the large intestine is to allow for the final absorption of certain nutrients and the excretion of waste. Peristalsis is the name for the wave-like physiological movement through the large intestine. That movement is under the control of a part of the endrocrine or hormonal system in the body called the pituitary gland. The pituitary glad is a pea-sized gland that resides in the brain.

Every day, the normal excretion of waste products is the result of the regular ingestion of food. Yet, excretion through the colon is not as easy as it might seem from studying anatomy and physiology. Over the counter and herbal laxatives are one of the most widely purchased Self-medications.

Constipation, the inability to excete through the large intestine, is one of many common everyday problems for many people. What is the best process for solving common problems such as constipation?

Nurses use a systematic problem-solving process for their own Self-care and when helping patients learn Self-care for common health concerns such as headaches, colds and flu, trouble sleeping, and constipation. This problem-solving process is a five-step process that begins with observing your health patterns. You can use the 8 Principle Patterns as a language for describing the health patterns you observe. Keen observation, using all of the senses, helps in recognizing and discerning the health patterns, the second step. The third step in the process is making choices and developing a Self-care plan that addresses the energetic imbalances observed. The plan is then implemented with gentle medicines using the five elements as a guide. The fifth and final step is evaluating the results of the Self-care plan. The process is not linear, as described, but cyclical in that evaluation leads to confirmation of discernment and pattern recognition. Knowledge of anatomy, physiology, and pattern recognition is the foundation for the systematic problem-solving process in precision Self-care.

It is essential to be systematic. For example, it is best to observe, assess, and discern health patterns and make a plan that is subject to evaluation later before implementing a solution (step 4). Perhaps you have noticed that people in social situations often offer advice without doing any of the first steps. What happens in these social situations is akin to hit or miss because the purpose is different. The purpose of offering an intervention in a social situation is often to share knowledge or to demonstrate kindness; but precision Self-care engages the problem-solving process to make the most informed choices.

It is a scientific process that is proven time and again to work as it supports learning more about Self, energetic health patterns, imbalances and how to resolve them with the most precise gentle medicines. The worst-case scenario of starting at step 4, without mindfully engaging in steps 1-3, is that the remedies could actually worsen the existing problem, requiring a tier 4 intervention. Starting at step 4 can, at the very least, lead to wasted remedies that "don't work." I have had so many clients over the years, who when they start to work with me, show me drawers of remedies that they cannot tell me "work" or "don't work." I ask them how they know if a remedy works for them, but they cannot tell me. In EOC precision Self-care, you will know if and how a remedy works or not.

The purpose of following a systematic process for problem-solving is that there are numerous reasons for common problems. Remember, the notion of one-cause, one-cure, does not typically work in common everyday health concerns. For example, person "A," who experiences a common concern of constipation, cannot move his bowels because his feces is too dry and hard. The person may feel hot quickly and is thirsty. His tongue has a thick yellow coating and is very red. The solution that would create an energetic balance is to cool and moisten the bowels. But there are others with constipation, such as person "B," who cannot move their bowels, yet the consistency is normal. Person B's bowels are sluggish, and they consistently experience bloating with indigestion and gas. They are also very fatigued, and their tongue is pale and wet with a think white coating. While both have the physiological problem of constipation, the term constipation does not tell the whole story. Constipation simply names the result of the problem; it does not recognize the energetic pattern(s).

While both might benefit from herbs that are purgatives in their physiological action, there are other qualities to consider for the most accurate herb solution. Consider the example of rhubarb root (*Rhei spp.*), which is a common purgative included in laxative formulas east and west. While rhubarb root can stimulate digestion, which suggests that it might help person B, it also stimulates peristalsis, which could benefit both persons. From a tea tasting, it is known that rhubarb root is classified energetically as bitter tasting and cold in action. It is also known that rhubarb root drains damp-heat and moves the stool.[71] Using the taste buds as our regulatory sense system, we know from tradition that bitter tastes generally have cooling and draining effects on the body. Person A would find balance and benefit from cooling herbs by draining heat, while person B would most likely become further exhausted, chilled, and their indigestion worse. They may even become dependent on the purgative to stimulate peristalsis. The herbal choice of rhubarb root most precisely matches the energetic symptom-sign patterns of person A. So let's begin with step one, observation and assessment.

—*The Chlorophyll Connection*—

Step one, observation and assessment, begins with tuning the instrument of the senses through centering. Centering is the time set aside for personal spiritual practices such as meditation (receiving), prayer (requesting), reflection, and body scanning for tensions that could impede the work. Centering time is when you make an *effort* to activate your connection with Nature and the Creator (symbolized by an ascending triangle) to create a healing environment for yourself. In this healing environment, you engage the flow of energy from the Creator that some refer to as *grace* or *blessing* (represented by a descending triangle) to start the Self-care co-creative process. ▲▼

I first learned about centering and the creation of a healing environment for myself and my clients when I worked with a German healer named Oma in the 1980s in her foot reflexology clinic in Glendale, California. Oma was very connected with Nature and plants. We always spent time before opening the clinic each morning, preparing the space. We cleaned carpets, organized treatment rooms, freshened oils, made teas, and even hosed down the outside of the building with cold water. We "demagnetized" the space with our visualizations of the brilliant white light of purity and the gentle violet fires of transmutation during our centering meditations. Oma taught me that it was the caregiver's responsibility to manage the energies in a physical space, and she was right. We taught the same to our clients as part of their Self-care.

I use those same techniques that I learned more than thirty-five years ago and more in a centering action that establishes a space that is settled and energetically clear. Why is this important? Because in observation, the first step of Self-care, the senses must be awake and the environment receptive. Clear senses begin with a clear space created by putting objects in order, throwing out the trash, and opening the windows. Regulate the temperature of the room so that what you observe about your patterns can be understood without interference. Placement of objects in a space is also essential to how the energy flows through an area. Furniture can assist or impede the flow of energy and therefore affect the ability to experience your center.

Practice letting go of the weight of the world by entering the green world. The action of partnering with plants to strip the energy from your feet in the ancient ritual of ablution is one of the best ways to leave the world outside and center in the present moment. How to do this ablution with a five elements herbal foot bath is discussed in Chapter 7. The effect of the ablution is experienced by the weight you feel in your feet. Energy can be perceived as weight. After the ablution foot bath, people invariably say that they feel "lighter."

GENTLE MEDICINE SELF-STUDY #10
ENTERING THE GREEN WORLD

Make a list of the 5 elements. Then go outside and find a representative in nature for each of the 5 elements that you can legally and ethically take into your home.

Create a healing environment in your home and position your 5 element representatives in that space. You can integrate the representatives into an existing space or create a new space.

Record your reflections. What drew you to the objects you chose? Did you choose any plants? What do the elements mean to you?

Plants are all around us in the physical space we call earth. Biology reveals the nature of the unique physiological connection that humans have with green plants. On a molecular level, plants and humans are very similar. The chlorophyll found in the leaves and stems of green plants and algae and the oxygen-carrying molecule, hemoglobin, found in human red blood cells are nearly identical in atomic design.

Heme   Chlorophyll

The most striking difference between heme and chlorophyll is that the porphyrin ring of heme is built around iron (Fe), and the porphyrin ring of chlorophyll is built around magnesium (Mg). A porphyrin consists of four pyrrole rings, each containing four carbon atoms and one nitrogen atom linked by methine (-CH) groups. These porphyrin compounds are essential in understanding human health because they absorb light. Human blood, like chlorophyll, carries light in the body. Light is the source of energy we need for increasing balance in body and peace of mind. As we understand the chlorophyll connection, we gain insight into the gentle, powerful medicine offered by the plant world.

Although science has found that heme and chlorophyll are not interchangeable, their similarity in structure and respective functions still captures our interest. Though we are deeply interconnected, plants do not depend upon us for their existence. We, however, depend upon the green world for the very oxygen we breathe. Take a deep breath and thank the plants!

Numerous studies demonstrate the health benefits of chlorophyll in humans. Many of these studies on chlorophyll were performed before 1960, and there has been little research since. I have reviewed those studies, and the findings from those studies are still relevant and useful. It is not just a story that the cartoon character Popeye's claim to strength (aka light) was related to his love of the green leafy vegetable, spinach *(Spinacia oleracea L.)*. Research has provided some data for how chlorophyll seems to help "build blood." Scientists such as Dr. Arthur Patek (1936) found, from studying patients with iron-deficiency anemia, that when patients received iron and chlorophyll treatment together rather than separately, the number of red blood cells and blood hemoglobin level increased more quickly than with iron or chlorophyll alone. I have provided this information to the obstetricians with whom I work. We have found that giving women iron and chlorophyll was much more effective than giving iron, the standard care for anemia related to blood loss.

Some animal studies have led researchers to hypothesize that chlorophyll's ability to "build blood" is related to its tendency to stimulate the bone marrow. Research also has shown that chlorophyll or its derivatives have been successful in significantly decreasing symptoms of constipation and excessive flatus, decreasing urine and fecal odors related to incontinence, and decreasing the odors associated with colostomy, ileostomy, and chronically infected skin ulcerations. It has a drying and deodorizing effect on wounds that have been shown to be superior to penicillin, and some small human trials have shown that chlorophyll can reduce symptoms of nasal and ear infections.[72]

What has happened to the prescription of chlorophyll or chlorophyllin? Although these studies seem to indicate that biomedical health practitioners no longer suggest chlorophyll for their patients as they used to, people continue to consider chlorophyll in Self-care. People continue to attest to the health benefits of eating a diet that includes green leafy vegetables. Health food stores sell chlorophyllin products in liquid or capsule forms, often referred to as "liquid sunlight," in the form of wheatgrass juice, blue-green algae, barley green, and alfalfa supplements.

Chlorophyll is a gentle medicine. It is important to note here that some animal studies with mice have shown that chlorophyll, extracted directly from Indian spinach leaves or in commercially purified form, demonstrates a strong chromosome-damaging activity. Therefore, the chlorophyll products on the market typically contain chlorophyllin, the copper-sodium salt food-grade derivative of chlorophyll, instead of chlorophyll. Many chlorophyll products are extracted from alfalfa (*Medicago sativa*), a plant known to create inflammation in the body. I recommend a liquid chlorophyll product extracted from nettles (*Urtica doica*). Nettles, also known as "stinging nettles," are traditionally eaten as a potherb like spinach; however, they must be cooked. In their natural and raw state, they sting when coming in contact with human tissues. The hairs on the fresh leaves can cause local inflammation on the skin, and therefore I have seen botanists apply them are purposefully for joint pain such as elbow pain. Ingesting chlorophyll from any plant in liquid form would not be necessary and contraindicated in those who have high red blood cell counts (hemoglobin and hematocrit).

Humans are entirely dependent on plants for their very life. Chlorophyll is involved in photosynthesis, a process that ultimately produces the oxygen fundamental to sustaining human life. The word "chlorophyll" is derived from the Greek "chloros," meaning "green," and "phyll," meaning "leaf." Chloroplasts are organelles found in the cytoplasm of the plant where light energy is transformed into food, the process of photosynthesis. When a green plant turns yellow, it merely means that the leaf has lost chlorophyll.

During the first phase of photosynthesis, the chloroplast pigments in plants gather sunlight and, in a fraction of a second, split water molecules into hydrogen and oxygen atoms. The oxygen is released into the atmosphere through pores in the leaves and the stem of the plant for the respiratory process of animals, plants such as mushrooms, and humans. During the second phase of photosynthesis, carbon dioxide unites with the sugar, ribulose diphosphate, and hydrogen from the first phase are added. Several types of sugars are produced. Numerous glucose molecules combine to form molecules of starch and cellulose. Starch is the principal food stored in plants and can be utilized later as an energy source. In contrast, cellulose is incorporated into the cell wall of the plant and usually is not decomposed.

The release of oxygen from plant photosynthesis and the absorption of carbon dioxide from the environment by plants is critical to human survival, yet how often do we think about this magical process that goes on in our presence all day long without a sound? Humans have never been able to duplicate the process of photosynthesis, which enables all cellular respiration. If it were not for plants and the exquisite process of photosynthesis, humans would have no food, clothing, shelter, or warmth, and no air to breathe.

Although plants utilize the carbon dioxide released by humans in respiration, they are not dependent upon humans for survival. The relationship between humans and plants could be characterized as one of benevolence on the part of plants. The most striking thing about our relationship with plants is that we need them for breath and, therefore, life. They do not need us in the same way. We do, on occasion, help plants. For example, we help seed them. As we walk through the woods, the seeds of a plant that may not be thriving cling to our clothes and then are dropped in a new location, thereby potentially giving the plant a better place for growth.

Biomedical science cannot fully explain why plants help as they do. Not all plants help human beings in the same ways, and this is seen most clearly in the individual healing qualities and energetics of various plants. Some plants soothe the skin; others irritate and stimulate the skin and circulation. Some plants cause the mind to hallucinate, and some plants increase the heart rate. Many cultural traditions recognize the powerful spirits or essences of plants as being the reason for how a plant helps humans.

—*Gentle Medicine Begins at Home*—

Over the years after graduating from nursing school, I have had the opportunity to practice in many different environments. I have practiced nursing in medical clinics, hospitals, infirmaries, schools, psychiatric care units, community clinics, my own office space, and in my home. I have practiced nurse-herbalism in group practice settings where I had my own office and acres of cultivated herb gardens as my laboratory. I have practiced herbalism in hospitals, in-home health care, and in private practice offices without gardens. From my action research in a private practice, speaking around the world, and from my historical research of healthcare, nursing and botanicals, I have found the most powerful medicine is that which people pick and make themselves either from a garden or the wild or even more so from their own home and gardens. In addition to serving clients herbal teas and special herbal snacks and counseling them in my home, I invite them to the gardens and the kitchen for opportunities to learn how to make their gentle medicines. I have a theory in the EOC program that when people *choose* to make their own medicine, they actually heal more easily, more thoroughly, more quickly, and often more gently, meaning that they do not have unintended adverse effects.

Gentle herbal simples, such as a cup of tea or soup, take on more meaning for a person and, therefore, more power when made at home. Participation in making medicine and the direct relationship with medicinal plants is a part of the creation of the healing environment within and without. One study by a nurse found that among women who used folk remedies such as herbs, foods, and over-the-counter medicines, the actual remedies were not as critical to the care of the person who was ill as the "meaning of the cultural memories inherent in acts of caring."[73]

Making one's own gentle medicine Self-care is a healing tradition in every culture. Before the emergence and expansion of the influence of the pharmaceutical industry in the late 19th and early 20th centuries, making one's own medicine, especially from plants from the garden and natural environment, was common and highly valued. It was the nurses of the early Shaker communities in the United States who participated in creation of an herb industry that would ultimately become the foundation for the American pharmaceutical industry.[74] The Shakers were spiritually connected to the plants and would not have understood today's industrialization of society from which comes a separation not only from Nature but also from the medicines that come directly from the earth. When others make our medicines for us, we are not only faced with issues of physical quality and safety. The energy infusing that medicine, or the prepared herbal remedy, is critical to healing too.

While we make our remedies, we are saturating a remedy with exactly the right energy, life force, qi (pronounced "chee") that our body needs. Through visualization, the remedy is infused with our healing intention and purpose. Not unlike the research on the power of prayer, this theory of gentle medicine making experience is based on spiritual as well as natural and behavioral sciences that inform the creation of the healing environment.

We are the healing environment. Physical energy is a vital element in the making of the gentle remedies and the healing environment in which those remedies are designed and created. How remedies are made and applied is as vital to the healing outcome as the remedy itself. The demonstration of caring that imbues how the herbs are prepared and applied may be of crucial importance to the overall effectiveness of the remedy, perhaps even more important than the biochemical constituents in the plant. We are connected with our gardens and the natural world through chlorophyll and energy. Your decision related to your home and garden medicine making is one way that the earth element is represented in your gentle medicine plan.

COMMUNITY ETHICS AND CANNABIS, TOBACCO, AND AMERICAN GINSENG

Think about the role you and your family currently play in your community's knowledge and understanding of medicinal plants. Start with tobacco (*Nicotiana tabacum*) or marijuana (*Cannabis sativa*) use, for example. What do you know about these plants? How do you talk about these plants? I am often asked about cannabis use and legalization. I remember first being asked my opinion about the subject in 1998 when I served on an ethics board for a hospital in Denver, Colorado. I decided at that time, which was about the same period I encountered the St. John's Wort, that I would respond *from a plant perspective*. To this day, I say that marijuana is a "loud plant," meaning that it gets a lot of attention. It is also trying to get our attention for very good reason. The plant is responsible for our emerging knowledge of the endocannabinoid system, a significant part of human physiology, that science is just beginning to explore. It is named after cannabis.

Now, 20 years later, widespread highly publicized public attention to this loud plant continues. Scientists know that knowledge of the endocannabinoid system can lead to breakthroughs in the care of many human problems, such as epilepsy. The study of the endocannabinoid system, and physiology in general, is one of the most essential tasks of entering the earth element, not just of the leaders in the scientific community. Every person demonstrates responsibility for their body by pursuing knowledge of their anatomy and physiology. The ancient Greeks demonstrated in their building of the Parthenon with architecture modeled after the human body, with its curves, *Symmetria,* and imperfections, a reverence for the human body as a model for balance, a quality highly prized in building structures. To create balance in body and peace of mind, we need to know our own

Self-structure first, which is the loud message of marijuana.

Cannabis is a hallucinogen and therefore is not appropriate for children. Because of the extraordinary potential benefits in the management of diseases such as epilepsy, it is one plant that begs pharmaceutical research to preserve its benefit but curb if not remove the hallucinogen effect so that it can be prescribed safely to children. This may or may not be possible. Some believe that the hallucinogen effect is only related to the tetrahydrocannabinol (THC). But THC is one of over 100 cannabinoids identified in marijuana. Like so many other plants, as discussed previously, identifying one plant constituent that is responsible for the "mechanism of action" of a plant is an elusive part of pharmacognosy (plant drug development). So, for now, protecting children by weighing the benefits and risks carefully before introducing them to marijuana or its constituents in any form, including cannabidiol (CBD), is a primary community health concern.

In some cultures, such as in India, cannabis has a very sacred use by the rishis or holy men. Hallucinogens are revered in many cultures as part of a sacred ritual. In the United States, however, the plant may be used repetitively but is not exactly a partner in sacred ceremony. I am always concerned about peoples' choices to partner with any plant routinely—particularly by smoking it—because of its potential harm to the lungs from the heat of the smoke. I also have questions about the partnership with plants or the use of any substance to obtain an elevated or out-of-body state that can be achieved equally through spiritual practice when a person's energy centers are prepared, and they have the attainment to be able to apply the elevated experience for service to humanity.

Tobacco, another plant that is smoked by thousands, is considered a sacred plant by indigenous peoples in America. I was taught to include it ceremonially when I worked with Cecilia Mitchell. Whenever I harvest medicine from my garden or the forest, I place a small amount of dried tobacco leaf in the earth as an expression of deep gratitude for what I am about to take for myself and my family. It is important to take only what we need. This is a principal lesson that many have learned during the COVID-19 pandemic when hoarding led to severely depleted stores.

When I moved to North Carolina, Cecilia gave me some tobacco seeds and a vision for connecting with the plants there. I never did plant the seeds, but I did work with many tobacco growers in North Carolina who wished to switch from tobacco to herb growing. It is not an easy choice to make as the growers' livelihood, and the state economy is entwined with the tobacco industry. I observed a fascinating pattern in the tobacco plants that I saw growing in the facilities I visited. As I looked out upon the plants lined up in rows upon rows for mass production and marketing of the tobacco plant, I saw the plants "chained" to their tables, still enslaved to the tobacco industry, while the human slaves who used to cultivate and harvest them were liberated decades ago!

There is an ethical responsibility that people have as members of the human community to exercise care and caution in all of our partnerships with plants. The United States, for example, is a vast country where mass marketing of plants for saving human lives is not the only consideration. Mass marketing can lead to a decrease in plant partnerships thereby posing a higher risk to humans. It also can stress the earth and plant populations. One example is the over-harvesting and poaching of American ginseng root (*Panax quinquefolium*). Laws have needed to be enacted that require people to wait ten years before harvesting the roots, so that plant populations are not wiped out. The story of American ginseng is important for understanding the community ethic surrounding plant partnerships.

In TCM, herbalists are taught that ginseng (*Panax ginseng*), also commonly known as Asian or Korean ginseng, is an incredible qi (energy) tonic but is energetically warming. Asians who understand traditional medicine and energy balance prefer a qi tonic that is more neutral to cooling. American ginseng is not Panax ginseng. It is unique and highly prized in Asia because it is cooling, not warming! Most people who seek energy tonics have interior heat patterns, so a slightly cooling herb is indicated whereas a warm herb is not.

Asia imports nearly all of the American ginseng produced in Wisconsin, for example, where it grows wild as well as is cultivated well because of the perfect growth conditions or Di Tao. They export their Asian ginseng to the United States with the sales slogan of "energy tonic." But because Americans know little to nothing of energetic health patterns (until now!), they buy the Asian ginseng instead of their own creating an imbalance in plant economy. Americans and American ginseng growers need support at home from the plants that grow outside our backdoors. It is our medicine that growers must export because the public lacks knowledge of what plants are best to create energetic balance in the body.

We are called to be mindful and just stewards of our planet. I caution communities to make sure that people think carefully about their partnerships with plants in Self-care and any ethic and risk associated with the commercialization of those partnerships. Many herb companies have, for decades, preserved the ethic of plant partnership exhibited earlier in history by the Shakers, for example, who as mentioned were one of the first American communities to produce herbal products for national and international markets. Shaker nurses made their famous rose water (*Rosa gallica*) for the care and comfort of those with pain related to migraine headaches.[75]

The mindful expansion of a community's knowledge base about herbal remedies is essential to the health care of the community as a whole. The focus on Self-care rooted in ethical partnership with plants is a significant contribution to healthcare reform in communities and the movement toward an ecocentric philosophy and becoming green.

—*Becoming Ecocentric and Green*—

An ecocentric philosophy views all life forms, including human beings, as fundamentally interrelated where the health of Earth and the health of all are reciprocal. This consciousness that Earth and its plant and animal life forms are interlinked and harmonious rather than animals and plants as separate servants of the human race is not new. In ancient healing traditions, animals, plants, Earth, and the stars and sky are all considered vital to health and life itself; therefore, they are often fully integrated into creation stories, life events, health beliefs, and healing practices. For example, Cecilia talks about Nature, such as the trees, plant medicines, and animals, as if they are family. Her connection with Nature is profound. She says:

> The amazing thing is our environment. As I get older, I tend to listen to the world, listen to our mother, like our mother the earth and the planets and the trees and the bugs and animals and everything all round me. I pay attention to what our environment says. The moon and the sun and even the wind affects us. ...Like us, us Indian people, our land is like a mother, because she gives us everything, like medicine. Anything we hold dear is sacred to us, like our land because that's where our medicine comes from. You take care of the land; it takes care of you. That's why we call it Mother Earth.[76]

Cecilia lives in Akwesasne in Mohawk country where Mother Earth's hair, the sweet grass, is fragrant and beautiful.

All peoples have ancestral traditions that show a closeness with the earth, the green world. The association between humans and the green world is demonstrated in a curious part of my Celtic tradition known as "The Green Man." This motif, while found throughout the world, is a part of the Celtic Nature tradition that is preserved in British culture, such as in the carvings found in the decorative architectural ornamentation of cathedrals. The Green Man motif is a human face emerging from the leaves, vines, or branches of plants or trees. Peoples who are close to Earth often see human-like faces emerging from the plant world, such as the "face" of a pansy or an orchid. The Green Man[77] is the archetype symbolizing a plant-person connection that is mutual rather than human dominant.

Thought leader, Dr. Larry Dossey also has written about "green" awareness as an archetype of consciousness about the plant-human connection. He suggests that it is counterproductive to "regard green medicine in a purely pragmatic, utilitarian way, to consider herbs as merely the latest tricks in our black bag."[78] We are partners, and yet so often, humans forget the reciprocal nature of this green arrangement that is also encoded on our genetic experience. Charles Lewis, renowned horticulturalist, researcher, and author of *Green Nature/Human Nature*, writes:

> A green world was our teacher at a time when the species' survival was a continuous challenge. The sight of living vegetation stimulates the neural pathways established then, so we are biologically prepared to feel a sense of connection with green environments. ... Plants possess life-enhancing qualities that encourage people to respond to them. In a judgmental world, plants are non-threatening and non-discriminating. They are living entities that respond directly to the care that is given them, not to the intellectual or physical capacities of the gardener. In short, they provide a benevolent setting in which a person can take the first steps toward confidence.[79]

The ethic of Self-care with plants as partners incorporates awareness of the inherent goodness and contribution of plants to all life. It is from the position of being the Green Man or Green Woman and being in direct partnership with the world of healing plants, that we can best understand the energetic patterns of green medicine of a plant and how to partner with it safely. As we become more attuned to the personality of plants and their unique energetic patterns, we welcome a greater insight into the creative ways to match the numerous applications of specific plants for specific health patterns.

Like the great trees that lend their shade of protection, people can also stretch in two dimensions, up with branches and leaves toward the sun and deeply into the earth with roots. In Celtic tradition, this image of a person as a tree is known as axis mundi, or the world tree. Trees represent the three realms of being. The leaves represent our spiritual dimension. The trunk of the tree represents middle Earth or this dimension of daily existence and consciousness, where we learn Nature's cycles and the patterns of all living things, including health patterns. It is in the dimension of the roots that we connect with the unconscious. Carl Jung defines the root dimension as the unconscious mind or the world of dreams, symbols, and patterns.[80] A world tree is a place where the strengths of the spirit and dream worlds are drawn toward earthly manifestation, and the energy of the earth dimension is drawn toward the spiritual. When we become the world tree, as the Green Man or Woman, we enter into an understanding of the meaning of ancient teaching of many cultures, "As Above ...So Below," in which the nexus of the human axis mundi is the heart. The heart with all of its power, wisdom, and love is the door to plant knowledge for the green man or woman who would ethically, respectfully, and safely create a Self-care green pharmacy.

PROTECTING YOUR SELF-CARE GREEN PHARMACY

Partnering with plants in Self-care requires an understanding of the source of the plant in much the same way, as prescribers are expected to understand the supplier of pharmaceutical drugs and the traditional herbalist understand the source for plants in their formulations. To be even more confident of safety and quality, traditional healers and herbalists often abide by an ethic that they grow or wildcraft (harvest from the wild) medicinal plants themselves. If they do not, the practitioner cultivates a practice in which they are highly mindful of the quality of their sources for herbs and herbal products. Herbalists often make the medicine themselves that they apply in care or teach clients how to make the medicine for themselves from available plant sources. Dosages are individualized.

A precision Self-care plan can position a person to know more than they do about over the counter or prescribed pharmaceuticals, when they grow the plant, harvest it, and prepare the medicine. If you do collect an herb, it is essential to also be aware of regulations involving wildcrafting practices for your areas. In general, plants are considered by the public as a product of Nature, which may be freely collected by anyone. It is not hard to imagine what can happen if a locally grown plant is found to be highly medicinal, and the market price skyrockets. People do trespass on private properties to gouge the earth of valuable plants. Countries in which the culture of respecting medicinal plants has been taught from generation to generation have protected the right to collect what is needed for personal use, not economic gain. For example, the right to gather wild plants anywhere is in Bavaria, Germany's Constitution. In some countries, such as Austria and Switzerland, the uprooting of plants is prohibited, and the amount of the aerial parts that can be wildcrafted is limited to five to twenty flowering stems or branches, depending on the area. In some cases, the maximum amount that can be harvested is that which can be held in the palm of one hand.

Although we may only collect what we would typically use in our Self-care or family care, we must be aware of the impact that wildcrafting herbs will have on plant populations. If wildcrafting, consider teaming up with a local botanist, who is often highly informed about local plant populations. When I was coordinating an herb program in Montana, I regularly checked in with the lead botanist associated with the Lewis and Clark National Forest. We went out on herb walks together to identify the plants in my area. It was fun and educational!

Conservation of medicinal plants is not a simple matter. Legislation protecting endangered species, although necessary, is considered inadequate. Plant habitats also must be protected to sustain the growth of medicinal plant populations. In the 1991 *Proceedings of an International Consultation* on the conservation of medicinal plants organized by WHO and others, seven points related to legislation regarding the management of medicinal plants were raised to include: prevention of over-collection, use of permits as management instruments, use of a management plan, implementation of controls on the trade of medicinal plants, collection of license fees, habitat protection, and incentives for artificial propagation.[81] Those who partner with plants in Self-care may want to consider cultivating and propagating their plants as much as possible. You can also consider sending samples of your most-common plants to laboratories for analysis if you would like further understanding of the quality of the plants.

When purchasing herbs, it is best to order organically grown plants. Pesticides and herbicides are chemical compounds that, when ingested orally or topically, also have effects, as would any drug. It is counterproductive to ingest or apply herbs topically that include chemical residues from pesticides and herbicides. Pesticides and herbicides can cause changes in health patterns. When purchasing aerial parts of plants, such as leaf and flower, it is best to buy *whole* plant versus cut and sift. Leaves and flower petals can always be chopped before application. Purchasing whole plant helps to prolong the shelf life of volatile oils, in particular. Roots are cut before drying to increase surface exposure to air drying. They can be decocted or pulverized for oral or topical applications when needed.

Create a special pharmacy space in your home. In our house, I have air-conditioned darkened rooms with a sink where I can process and dry herbs. I also have herb cabinets in my apothecary office. I regularly open packages and containers to test the crispness and dryness of the herbs. I keep bay leaf (which I have grown myself) in my herb closets to repel any potential insects or moths. The herbs in the kitchen, pantry, and apothecary are used more frequently, so I keep those herbs in jars with lids that I remove whenever I use them. My herbs for long-term storage are kept in bags with an opening so that any residual moisture can escape.

To protect medicinal plants, the environment in which they are nourished must be cared for as well. Because plants obviously do not speak out, it is up to humans to understand and provide for their needs. Plants thrive in healthy environments, just as people do. The plant itself produces its medicinal constituents in relation to its environment. For example, Indian studies on the *Ephedra sp.* plant have shown that the amount of rainfall in a particular area has a relationship with the ephedrine content of the plant. The higher the annual rainfall, the smaller the ephedrine content, and occasional heavy showers also lower the ephedrine content. Altitude affects plants too. It has a significant bearing on which plants grow in a particular area. High altitudes have different plant life than those found at sea level. People who live at different altitudes have traditionally learned to use the plants that grow in their areas for healing.

Indigenous people partner with the plants for medicine as directed by what grows in their environment; hence, they have a strong connection with the Earth and specifically the environment in which they live. More recently, increasing agricultural, mining, and lumber industries pose threats to the habitats of medicinal plants. Pollution is also a severe threat to plant life and their environments. In 1950, 30 percent of the globe was forested, but by 1975 only 12 percent of the surface of the Earth was covered by forest.

In 1995, it was reported that the tree populations in the 1990s shrank by 10,000 per minute.[82] "Transformation of local ecosystems wrought through human economic activities has been exercising severe constraints on the availability and accessibility of specific types of plants and animal species used for medicinal purposes."[83] Along with the disappearance of the forests is the disappearance of indigenous people, who not only have the expertise in partnership with medicinal plants in a particular location but who also protect the environment. With the numbers of these people who are national treasures dwindling, the habitats of many medicinal plants, the plants themselves, and the knowledge of these plants as medicine are at serious risk.

It is up to those who value medicinal plant life to speak up and protect the environments of these plants. People such as Rosita Arvigo, an American herbalist who apprenticed with Don Elijio Panti, one of the last surviving Maya traditional healers in the rainforest in Belize, help preserve the traditional healing methods and the plants of the areas in which they live. Arvigo has been an advocate for conserving the medicinal plants of the rainforest, and *Sastun*,[84] her story of her relationship with a Mayan healer, can be very inspiring to those who work with healing plants.

The WHO has produced numerous documents and guidelines regarding the importance of protecting medicinal plants in their native habitats.[85] Also, many countries have botanical gardens, even in the inner cities, where plants are preserved for the public so that they can have a place to go to connect with the plants and gain a greater awareness of how the plants that are responsible for many of their medications grow. Interacting with the plants that provide medicine or the inspiration for medicine is one way that people move into a more ecocentric paradigm and reconnect with the essence of Earth as the source of the natural beauty and abundance of unique healing plants.

Chapter 6
Awakening the Air Element

This chapter is the second of the five chapters on the five elements of the Elements of Care® program for creating a precision Self-care plan with plants as partners. As you enter the air element, wake up and think, ponder, remember, reflect and wonder. What do you think about Self-care? What do you know, and how do you know about plants as partners? What would you say is the current state of balance and peace in your mental body, your thoughts?

All life begins with the breath. Are you aware of breathing now? Are your breaths deep and full or shallow and tight? When we become stressed, our breathing can become shallow and tight. Inhalation and exhalation are similar in movement to the tides in the sea. The ease with which we breathe impacts the flow of blood, light, and qi through all of our body organs and systems. Doing a Breath and Body Scan can facilitate the flow of ideas from the mental body for this next element of your precision Self-care plan.

GENTLE MEDICINE SELF-STUDY #11
BREATH AND BODY SCAN

One of the largest muscles in the body is the diaphragm. This muscle sits under the ribs and moves in rhythm with other chest muscles and the lungs to support breathing. Begin by releasing any muscle tension you may feel around your diaphragm or chest. Do not tell your body to "relax!" This typically makes the body tense the muscles more. You may wish to massage your abdomen to help the muscles release any tightness.

4-PART BREATHING

Breathe in for a count of eight. Lift your ribs and sustain the breath for eight counts; then release fully over the count of eight as you drop your jaw and allow the breath to release with a pop of the lips (like a balloon). Continue to gently push the breath out of the lungs for the final count of eight.

Repeat the four-part breathing of eight counts each two to three times. Finish by breathing in and out and then normally. The four-part breathing can also be done with four counts instead of eight.

BODY SCAN

Close your eyes to avoid distraction. Turn your attention inward to the top of your head. Move your awareness from the top of your head to the tips of your toes as you assess where your tensions are held. When you observe tension, breathe in as if you can breathe into that part of your body, tense all muscles and release the tension into the ground. Perform a body scan before and after the 4-part breathing. Notice any effects the 4-Part breathing had on the tension in your body. Journal your results.

—*Mindful Decision-Making and Problem-Solving*—

The mind is a trickster, often casting illusions into the field of our human perceptions. Ideas and mental impressions come and go like the wind. The mind's impressions alone should not dictate choices made for a Self-care plan with plants. For example, the mind could conclude that watching a bird eat elderberries (*Sambucus nigra*) would make it "ok" for a person to do likewise. But elderberries eaten raw are toxic to humans. Or perhaps someone remembers eating "elderberries" as a child when, in fact, it was black currants (*Ribes nigrum*).

Instead, it is best to study the plants with whom you would partner and also access all of the elements of Self through the senses, providing a check and balance to the winds of the mind and mental body. Nature scientist Johann Wolfgang von Goethe once said that "the senses do not deceive; the judgment deceives."[86] Educating the mental body through study and skill development leads to the organization of thoughts and a greater orientation to detail that can lead to improved seeing, judgment, and analysis of health patterns as well as sound decision making and problem-solving. Education and study provide the platform for the grounding of intuitive promptings.

Partnering with plants spawns intuitive internal experience because plants are non-verbal living beings. Intuition is the first form of thought. In contrast to perception, which is an externalized orientation, thought content comes from within us. When partnering with plants, we access memories of the non-verbal, pre-verbal selves that we were in early life, using different ways of communicating, knowing, and being in the world that exists after the eruption of language. Intuition, as well as observation through the senses, is often the source of our knowledge. Intuition is important in making connections with and ultimately knowing our environment and ourselves. But, intuitive promptings without "roots" anchored in the mental body, thought, and intellect can lead to imbalances in body and mind.

The preparation of the mental body through the study of any subject takes time and effort. The desire for knowledge and an abiding interest in the truth about the object of study helps to ensure successful preparation. Over time we gain momentum in building awareness that sustains us when we need to engage our minds in making important decisions and solving problems. Study is especially important when one has not had a knowledge of plants cultivated in them from childhood.

In some cultures, healers are mentored their whole lives to learn to partner with plants. They learn from parents, grandparents, and elder community healers how to manage and interpret intuitive experience and then how to integrate that experience in a way that informs the knowledge that they are taught of plant medicines. I first received education on intuition during my graduate studies in nursing. Nursing programs typically teach the importance of understanding different ways of knowing, including intuition. But I learned how to keep intuition in balance with education from Oma and other healing elders who trained me in herbal care and comfort. It is the air element, and its representation in the education of the mental body and continued study, that is the antidote that can keep the trickster mind in check. Intuition without rooting in the mental body is termed a "negative psychic state"[87] in the classic work of Dr. Bendit, a Jungian psychiatrist and his wife, a clairvoyant. The psychic sense is similar to the other five senses in that it can be dull or acute. Negative psychism is uncontrolled, undifferentiated, and primitive. A person in a negative psychic state cannot differentiate the products of his mind from that which is external to it. Reactions are most often unconscious. The mechanism of action of the negative psychic state resides in the coeliac plexus, a nerve center near the center of the diaphragm. The openness to a negative psychic state can be observed as leading to an unchecked projection of thought onto others ("I know more about you than you know about yourself"), spiritual boundary violations, and physical problems.

The positive psychic state, however, is controlled and consciously directed by a person. The mechanism of action of the positive psychic state occurs in the head. It develops with maturity as the person learns to exhibit greater and greater discernment and discrimination and make deliberate choices in response to intuitive impressions. The Bendits explain that society is still very much under the influence of primitive "urges" and "only partly governed by the conscious mind."[88] The refinement of the positive psychic state informed by intuition begins when the intellect is engaged and applied in analyzing and making conscious choices about the intuitive or psychic promptings. In the case of precision Self-care in which healing plants and their powerful energy fields are routinely encountered, all intuitive promptings about plants would be informed and checked against the awareness born of experience and knowledge. Herbs should not be applied in comfort and care based on an intuitive or psychic hunch as this is not a precision Self-care approach, and the risk to Self and plant populations is too high.

Here is one of the numerous examples I have witnessed over the years of the risk associated with negative psychic states driving herbal Self-care choices. I once worked with a chiropractor who "muscle tested" his clients for herbs and essential oils, of which he had little to no knowledge. There was a client who went to him for a spinal adjustment, and later she came to my nurse-herbalist office for follow-up because he had prescribed 60 drops of tea tree (*Melaleuca alternifolia*) essential oil sublingually for her every day for her toenail fungus. He had put the bottle of tea tree oil near her body and used the science of body circuitry (aka "muscle testing") to determine that she needed 60 drops of the oil. But he did not know that essential oils should not be given orally without extensive knowledge of the oil and that the dose he intuited through muscle testing was very high. He did not factor into his decision that the oil of that plant is very cooling energetically, and his client was thin and cold with a recent history of breast cancer, which is typically a cold condition of the breast and might therefore energetically aggravate the underlying cold condition. While the science of body circuitry can be a sound method of determining the general effects of herbs on energy flows in and around the body, it is not safe to simply use muscle testing to determine which herbs should be applied in Self-care. It is a clear example of negative psychism. Fortunately, this client's common sense was still intact, and she sought an herbalist's opinion about the oral use of the drops for her toenail fungus. It was her sense of taste and smell that also brought her to the clinic as the idea of taking 60 drops of tea tree oil sublingually made her nauseous. We worked together and came up with a solution that addressed her health patterns, including the resolution of the dampness represented in the toenail fungus. She did decide to use the tea tree oil for a while, but she applied it topically.

It is not uncommon for a sensitive person to intuit a particular plant's benefit for themselves. But this chapter provides some structure for the training and organizing of the mental body experience that allows for the best decision making and problem-solving. Plants are such simple "folk." They are part of our daily lives, and therefore it often seems silly to some to think that they should be studied. If we lived in the 19th century, I would agree. Peoples in all cultures have had intimate and powerful knowledge of their healing plants. Still, people today just do not grow up in rural areas where plants grow abundantly, and they are continually bumping into plants and knowledgeable, plant-loving people. People do not have connections with the medicinal plants of their predecessors. Nor are they educated by their grandparents, parents, community healing elders, or school programs about healing plants. Self-care must include educational and mental preparation to partner with plants. Surfing the internet for facts is not sufficient. It often only produces a plethora of facts and points to yet a constant stream of more information. But how does one decide what if any of these facts and information apply or even appeal to the pursuant of Self-care? That is the problem that must really be solved.

SELF-CARE PROCESS FOR PROBLEM SOLVING IN SELF-CARE

Every question and concern in Self-care has at its roots questions to be answered and problems to be solved. There is a regular sequence to learning to adapt to changes in body, mind, emotion, and spirit. Remember that despite the best efforts of medical science and research, there is still no cure for the common cold. Therefore, the question must shift from what is the cure to what is the care during the change and transition from life before, during, and after the cold or any other health challenge? Common maladies become our perpetual teachers in life that show us what our bodies, minds, and spirits are made of, where we need to learn more as caretakers of the gift of life, and how we can take those experiences and victories we call health to serve humanity better. Health decisions and solving problems have as their goal greater energy and strength to fulfill one's life purpose. Within that time-honored frame of "man know thyself" so that one can serve others and fulfill life's purpose, we can draw much from centuries of nursing science, a human science, this problem-solving process, known as the "nursing process." The nursing process provides a historical order to health decision making and solving tough problems that characterize one of the best approaches to caregiving whether for Self or others that we encounter as part of everyday human existence. As applied in precision Self-care, the nursing process, referred to here as the "Self-care process," comprises five phases: Observations, Pattern Recognition, Planning, Reframing Self-care Interventions, and Evaluation.

OBSERVATIONS

In this phase, use all of your senses to observe yourself and identify behaviors while suspending all judgment and desire to name, analyze, or diagnose. In addition to the physical, emotional, mental, and spiritual self-observations, be sure to take in all aspects of your environment, to include the driving and restraining forces (people, issues, and things influencing the behaviors) that impact the problem and the changes that are envisioned. Return to your safe place (Gentle Medicine Self-study #9) and ask yourself these questions and take some notes for your journal:

> **"Why is this happening now?"**
> **"What plants are in my life?"**
> **"What are my dreams about?"**

Usually, people and their caregivers, especially in the biomedical world, ask the common question, "What is the cause of the problem?" and "Can I/we fix it?" These questions are focused on the past rather than the now. Problems often continue because they serve a purpose in a person's life. Reframing your problem to work toward solutions inspires hope as the cycle of habit is interrupted and redirected as an upward spiral pattern or helix rather than the downward spiral of the flow of water as in a toilet bowl.

This simple process of thinking in terms of solutions diminishes any disease-orientation absorbed in the biomedical culture. It therefore significantly reduces the risk of slipping into a mode of practicing *medicine* rather than precision Self-care. To start the solution-focused process, ask this goal-oriented assessment question, *"How will I know that I have achieved what I want?"* Set a three-month timeline and ask yourself, *"What will I be doing differently or how will I be feeling differently in three months if I am successful in my precision Self-care plan?"*

Visualize and claim your success in solving your problem! Imagine a positive outcome. You are now working backward from that vision of success, setting detailed short- and long-term goals that will end in your realization of your vision of success. Going through the process of answering these questions, will gently call to your mind those memories of what behaviors you are doing or thinking that maintains the problem.

If you have a hard time imagining a positive outcome, ask yourself what you are doing in the present time that is "working" and then create goals that encourage you to do more of that which is working. These Self-care observations are all part of a wellness strategy that can move you more quickly toward the ultimate solution of greater balance in body and peace of mind. A solution-focused precision Self-care plan identifies and organizes goals that promote your strengths, which you may not even be aware that you have.

Next, write down or draw pictures of your observations and assessments of the following health patterns:

1. Respiratory Pattern and Breathing
2. Lifestyle (Work, Play, Habits)
3. Intake (Thirst and Appetite)
4. Outflow (Urine and Feces – color, quality, smell, and consistency)
5. Thermal (Hot and Cold in the Body)
6. Pain (Location, Quality, What makes it better or worse)
7. Skin (Dryness, Itching, Color)
8. Senses
9. Sleep/ Rest (Patterns, Insomnia, Dreams)
10. Motion (Gait, Speed)
11. Speech (Speed, Pitch, Loudness, Force)
12. Tongue Coating (Color, Presence, Moisture, Thickness, Pattern)
13. Tongue Tissue (Color, Shape, Fissures)
14. Behavior and Thoughts (Moods, Interactions, Self-concept, Body Image, Ideals, Ethics)
15. Roles and Relationships (Home, Work, Environment, Global)

PATTERN RECOGNITION

Pattern recognition is the phase that follows observations and assessment. Use the 8 Principle Patterns discussed in Chapter 3 as a guide. You also can use your mind, your heart, and intuition to gather, order, and synthesize the patterns from the behaviors you have observed and create your names for the patterns of behaviors you have observed. For example, name a repeated pattern of pain in the front of the head that occurs after eating fatty food, "my fatty food front of my head - ache" rather than "migraine," which is a generic medical diagnosis. Medical diagnoses do not describe the precise behavior that needs to be changed and resolved as will your pattern name.

PLANNING

Before moving into action, reflect on your observations and patterns to ask yourself, *"What does this mean to me at this time in my life?"* Finding meaning in life's everyday health challenges and periods of change and transition helps to propel one forward. Getting stuck in repeating patterns of emotional turmoil, physical imbalance, and disturbances to one's peace of mind can lead to disease. Primary prevention begins with planning to create change that shifts any repeating patterns that drain and deplete one's energy from life purpose. In the thirty-five years I have been a nurse, one of the most life-changing caring actions I have witnessed is that of setting meaningful goals for resolving each and every health concern. The responsibility for meeting goals is yours. Remembering in Self-care to establish priorities and desired outcomes and set measurable short-term and long-term goals using all necessary and available resources is critical to the success of your precision Self-care plan. Measurable goals may be subjective or objective. An example of a measurable goal might be that your pain level will go from a 10/10 on a 1-to-10-point scale to an 9.5/10 within one to two weeks as measured by the 10-point pain scale. This is called scaling. The actions of gentle medicines such as plant remedies are often so subtle that we may not recognize the benefits. Scaling with numbers helps to give us a better perspective of the progress we make. Keeping a journal allows one to reflect on this progress.

REFRAMING SELF-CARE INTERVENTIONS

Setting goals enables you to consider the possibility of reframing all health concerns or problems as "teachers" that lead you toward Self-care solutions if you are observant and willing to learn how to change and adapt to a new situation and environment. Social psychologist Ellen Langer writes, "Changing of contexts generates imagination and creativity as well as new energy. When applied to problem-solving, it is often referred to as reframing."[89] Reframing generates innovation and creates the space for non-judgment of behaviors and pattern recognition. It is also an antidote to breaking down habits of unconscious momentums of mindlessness that do not support the goals of your Self-care plan. Langer defines that mindlessness as "automatic behavior" and "acting from a single perspective."[90] She differentiates the Eastern concept of mindfulness meditation from her work on mindfulness as the opposite of mindlessness. She writes that in Eastern mindfulness meditation, a person is encouraged to quiet the mind, whereas, in the mindfulness work that she describes in her book, the mind is actively engaged.[91]

It is a healing tradition for people to share ideas about remedies that have helped them with their health concerns. I hope that you see in this EOC program that while there may be many benefits, there are also potential risks to merely applying a remedy in Self-care. The EOC program seeks to raise the bar on the social dialog about Self-care to include more discussion of the energetics and health patterns associated with the remedies people discuss. The five elements of plant partnership and the five-phase Self-care process can be used to guide these discussions. The next chapter *Welcoming the Water Element* details numerous gentle medicines for inclusion in a precision Self-care plan that addresses imbalances in observed behaviors and patterns.

EVALUATION

This phase is about reflection and review of the pattern, changes made, and your progress toward the fulfillment of short and long-term goals. If necessary, revise your Self-care plan for change and do some further observation of behaviors. Applying the five-phase Self-care process can help in developing a new level of comfort, mastery, and precision in health decision making and problem-solving.

—*How to Decode Herbal Scientific Data*—

Western culture values the results of clinical studies of healing plants. Because so many healing plants have been used by humans as food and medicine and are so prevalent in our culture, it is less common to spend the billions of dollars necessary to validate the actions of a medicinal plant that may have been used safely and effectively for centuries. Although there are clinical trials for any number of plants, herbal scientific data also includes traditional evidence for the safe and effective application of the herb in Self-care. People gather knowledge of the plants that they choose to partner with from the evidence, information, resources, and research of plant scientists, physicians, nurses, ethnographers, and ethnobotanists, to name a few. Then the challenge begins! How can all that data be "decoded" into a precision Self-care plan? Decoding or translating herbal scientific information is not an easy task.

You do not need to have a research degree or experience to be able to decode scientific data, but it does help to have some working knowledge of the language of research, how to find and apply published studies. Data are often used in advertising and by journalists in their media reports, but they may not reflect accurately or entirely, leading to misunderstanding.

RESPONSIBLE REPORTING AND WRITING

Responsible reporting and writing about research on medicinal plants should include the following. First, a review of the literature that supports the research should consist of the botanical literature, such as is published in journals on botany, ethnobotany, phytopharmacy, and folklore. International publications should not be excluded because herbs are researched by scientists all over the globe. International references are particularly important if the plant in question is not indigenous to the researcher's or author's country of origin. Look for evidence that the person reporting accessed botanical databases such as NAPRALERT and HERBCLIPS (American Botanical Council). Book publications can be included in a literature review as plants are often most fully represented by those who have done extensive research and then published on a single plant.

Second, the data reported should include evidence of a plant perspective. The scientific name of a plant, genus, and species should accompany all common names. Scientific credibility is questionable when research is conducted or reported without clarity as to the exact plant included in the study. Whole plants should be distinguished from plant constituents, and the specific applications should be clearly identified. Third, researcher bias should be controlled. It is customary in scientific writing that investigators or authors demonstrate respect for cultural traditions and rituals. Slurring of healing traditions, plants, or peoples that use them is typically not permitted in scientific writing. Instead, it is customary to call for further research rather than seek to debunk herbs or herbalism. Gross generalizations or overstating the significance of data is best avoided.

Journalists, in particular, are prone to inflate the significance of data, such as that which is gathered through simple surveys, one of the least rigorous forms of research. They often discuss the "lack" of clinical trial evidence but neglect to consider other types of data available on healing plants. They typically report only from the standpoint of the biomedical paradigm and focus on the clinical trial method as the "gold standard." It is the gold standard of pharmaceutical research but does not always lend itself to answering the questions associated with herbal medicines. Clinical trials are not necessarily appropriate for illuminating the questions of botanical science. The WHO, for example, recognizes historical and traditional records of use as important, relevant data for the safe and effective application of herbs in human health.

Typically, herb research that is conducted by those with biomedical values strives for the most rigorous clinical trial with the intent to establish causation and predict outcomes or determine the plant's mechanism of action for a specific effect in humans. Biomedical researchers refer to herbs as "products," "drugs," and "constituents," or "constituent groups." Scientists with biomedical and traditional values may study herbs using ethnographic, historical, or folkloric methods. In the traditional paradigm, herbs may or may not be studied at all. When they are studied from a traditional perspective, herbs are viewed as whole plants or whole plant parts such as roots or flowers rather than plant constituents such as phytosterols or antioxidants.

Self-care is informed by both biomedical and traditional ways of knowing as well as how the plant has been applied historically in care and comfort. Because the herbs in Self-care are often common, it is rare that time and resources are used to study them. In industrialized nations, research is conducted to increase the knowledge and marketability of a particular product as a means to reimbursing the cost of research to further scientific knowledge. To review: This is a list of sample questions about herbs from a biomedical view.

- What makes this plant work?
- Are there any clinical trials on the use of this plant drug?
- How safe is this herbal drug for human consumption?
- How efficacious is this herbal drug in *curing* specific disease?
- What is the proper dose?
- What are the active ingredients/constituents in the crude herb-drug, and can they be synthesized and standardized?

When designing a Self-care plan, reframe the questions as plant-focused:

- What type of research questions need to be asked about plant applications, and what methodologies will best answer these questions?
- How is safety best determined with a plant medicine?
- Do plants "cure disease" or do they act in other ways?
- How are the plants best applied in Self-care, what is their history of application and what kind of dosing is best?
- What are the healing properties, energetic characteristics, and personality of the plant?

The plant-focused scientific perspective is often lacking in the research literature. There are a number of examples in which scientists, scholars, and public officials have rendered opinions on herbs publicly without any plant knowledge whatsoever. They may base their opinions on the results of a single event or research study. Some people simply do not realize that they have no knowledge of the actual plant and that this impairs their perspective. The following are examples of questions that can help decode any herbal scientific data in weighing the benefits and risks of engaging a plant as a partner:

1. Be sure to note the exact herb and/or the herbal preparation used in the study. Is the genus/species of the plant reported? Did the research focus on plant constituents or the whole plant? Whole-plant studies are rare. Is the plant preparation described in detail? Here is an example of poor reporting. Berthold et al. Garlic Oil Study – The herbal preparation is a central issue for the decoding of this study. Garlic *oil* has not been known for its effect on cholesterol levels because steam-distilled garlic oil may not contain one of the active compounds, allicin, known to affect cholesterol metabolism unless it was prepared fresh each time it was used. http://cms.herbalgram.org/press/061898press.html
2. Does the published study identify the type of study such as *in vitro* or *in vivo* – animal/human? *In vitro* studies are conducted in the laboratory. Herbal remedies from living plants are not typically applied in the laboratory environment.
3. Who are the subjects involved? Human? Animal? Cells? This is also important. How the bodies of animals metabolize herbs is not the same as in humans.
4. What are the data results and the limitations of those results? Every study has pros and cons in terms of its design and implementation. These are referred to as "limitations of the study." One example is whether or not the data from the one study can be "generalized" or applied to a larger group. There are certain parameters of scientific research that must be met for a study to be generalized. Generalizability is not so easy to establish, and yet the media often report studies on herbs and other health-related issues as if the data can be generalized to the general public.
5. Questions to ask:
    a. What data or evidence is the investigator basing their

       advice/concerns/recommendations on?
- b. What is their knowledge and experience with this herb either in their care or in client care?
- c. What are the benefits and risks of trying or not trying an herbal solution?

In general, herbal data are just data. They may have no relevance to the success of your Self-care plan. Yet, data have the potential to help or harm Self-care practices, especially when data that are shared or communicated person to person or through the media take on the energy of public health policy. The most common example of concern is when data from a single study or event surrounding a particular plant are utilized to ban the use of a plant in health and healing. One such example is in the case of ephedra (*Ephedra sinensis*) in the United States, a plant that, in formulation, has been used safely for hundreds of years in Asia. The purpose of the scientific process in herbalism is to mindfully explore questions about the plant world and generate new knowledge. The meaning of data lies in the minds and hands of the people who use it. Responsible decoding and reporting of herbal data are an essential responsibility in supporting precision Self-care with plants as partners. Four other questions you might ask yourself as you use information and resources in decision making include:

Are we talking about the same plant?
Be very careful to be sure that you are discussing the same plant. Compare plants or the packaging of a plant product. Do not assume the herb or herbal remedy is the same without clarifying the genus and species of a plant.

How long are you thinking about partnering with the plant?
In general, most herbs can be safely applied in Self-care for common everyday concerns for less than thirty days.

What is the plant's history for application in Self-care?
What is your experience with the plant? Are you trying to treat a disease (biomedicine) with plants? What is known about the application of the herb for the way you are intending to apply it in Self-care? For example, some people plan to ingest herbs in capsules that are not meant to be eaten and have historically been decocted or extracted

rather than ingested. Knowing this history, would you change your decision about the application of the herb in your Self-care plan?

Does this herb help you and make you happy?
Happiness is important, and so is familiarity with medicines. Self-care with herbs makes people happy. People tell me that making their medicines and remedies is fun and empowering! People trust the herbal remedies that have been used by their families for generations. People like to smell and taste the herbs of their family traditions that hold positive memories.

—*Referral Beyond Self-Care*—

Practitioners of herbal medicine, such as nurse-herbalists, physician-herbalists, doctors of Oriental medicine, naturopathic physicians, and clinical herbalists, have extensive education and experience in individualizing herbal therapy for their clients. If, after partnering with herbs in Self-care, you still have a concern about your health pattern or an unresolved common health concern, the most prudent action is for you to consider referring yourself to an experienced herbalist. In general, a person should self-refer or be referred to a herbal practitioner when: considering taking an herb for more than thirty days (perhaps less); taking medicinal amounts of herbs (more than beverage teas) and are pregnant, elderly, or if your family member is an infant less than 15 months old; or if considering taking pharmaceutical drugs and herbal remedies simultaneously to treat a specific biomedical condition. A guideline to follow when referring to others involves three questions about their practice:

1. What is the herbal practitioner's education and experience? Do they have a specific model for practice that they follow, such as TCM?
2. Is the practitioner a graduate of a formal education program, or does the practitioner hold a certification, if available? Educational programs require a greater level of commitment to study and, therefore, may demonstrate potential expertise as well as a commitment to knowing the state of the science.
3. Is the indigenous/traditional herbalist recognized by their community as a healer?

4. Does the practitioner to whom you are thinking about referral communicate well, and will s/he talk with you?

Seeking to learn new or different solutions to health problems and health decision making is a common part of the human experience. That is why people share recipes and remedies and contact community healers. Seeking or requesting help never means that the person does not have a solution or multiple solutions of their own. People often try many remedies before approaching another for assistance and insight. Self-care includes many types of interventions, substances, techniques, and activities. The next chapter delves more deeply into those solutions in welcoming the water element to the creation of a precision Self-care plan.

Chapter 7
Welcoming the Water Element

Symmetria, the harmonious relationship of one part of the body to another, was, for the Greeks, the definition of beauty. Their medicine, remedies, and solutions to easing discomfort in the body beautiful were drawn from the elements of Self—ether, fire, air, earth, and water. Water is a solution to many health problems. But the water element reminds us that solutions are not only found in the substance, but also in the movement or *flow* of energy within and around that substance.

The healing benefits of water are not merely due to its hydrogen and oxygen atoms. Water is the totality of its hydrogen and oxygen atoms that together flow in a unique pattern that we know as water. Without the flow of pure, clean water, there is no life. Stagnant water is harmful.

The water element is traditionally associated with the emotional self. Emotion is energy-in-motion! This chapter on the water element focuses on the development of precision Self-care solutions that include both substance and the flow of energy in motion. Flow is motion and is the "how factor" in Self-care. How we prepare an herbal simple, such as a tea, is equally as important as what herb is chosen for the tea to be included in our Self-care plan. The emotion that we put into choosing or preparing a solution guides how that solution is chosen or prepared.

Many Self-care solutions involve the use of water. Hot water bottles, one of my favorite gentle medicines, provide gentle, even-flowing heat because water is in perpetual motion. Hot water bottles can gently and deeply warm any part of the body, including joints, the feet, the back, and the abdomen. When I was a school nurse, I had a care plan for young children with tummy aches. Children would hold a hot water bottle to their abdomen while they rested lying down. I would also offer them their choice of teddy bears to help hold the water bottle too. They always felt better within a few minutes. What amazing relief from a simple hot water bottle...and a teddy bear!

Herbalism is a full body of science and healing art that offers many choices in Self-care solutions. This chapter covers some of the most enduring of healing traditions in herbal medicine making and how to create a plan of care that welcomes the water as Nature care solutions that include creative means for implementing the elements of your Self-care plan.

Many of the applications include water: the creation of herbal teas, liquid extracts, and soups, and the application of topical herbal remedies, such as baths, foot baths, steams, and compresses.

Making medicine from plants is an art, a science, and a cultural experience. For example, how people prepare and serve tea in Japan is different from how people prepare and serve tea in England. Both tea ceremonies are beautiful and diverse in their flow of expression. Individual herbs can be used in any number of different ways to make a variety of plant remedies. As you learn what plant medicines grow outside your backdoor and in your neighborhood, you will also learn how people make the best remedies from those plants to create climate change, which is to shift the flow of energy within the body and in the environment. One simple remedy, such as a teddy bear hot water bottle, holds power to accomplish change and adaptation.

The healing arts throughout history has emphasized the importance of the relationship between people and their environment. Nature care is the inclusion of natural elements in Self-care. We can think about including water, light, fresh air, and warmth in creating a healing environment within and without. Plant remedies also are included. They are accessible, inexpensive, and effective when chosen and applied for the right health patterns.

Many resources on plant medicine-making are available. Local traditional healers and herbalists are a great resource for studying plant medicines. National resources include a country's formularies, pharmacopoeia, dispensatories, and historical texts on medicine making. The plant medicine-making information in this chapter is a sample of common traditional knowledge of making simples. All remedies presented in this chapter are based on the application of whole plants or parts of plants. Pharmaceutical techniques of extraction of plant constituents are not covered. The recipes in this book for making herbal simples are organized into three areas: healing foods and oral remedies, topical applications, and simples for creating a healing environment.

— *Recipes for Making Herbal Simples* —

Plant parts from which we make medicine include the bulb, bark, twigs, flower, leaf, fruit, skin, juice, pollen, root, rhizome, tuber, and seed. The quality of plant medicine is a result of the way the plant is grown, harvested, processed, and prepared. Medicinal plants should be grown without pesticides and herbicides because the chemicals used in these products are toxic and counterproductive to a Self-care plan. There is a potential for chemical residues to remain with the plant even after processing. The plants used should be fresh. Dried herbs can maintain a fresh quality for specific periods of time, depending on the plant. Flowers and tiny leaves are more fragile and susceptible to a loss of vitality than whole roots. Using plant materials in pieces that are as whole as possible preserves freshness. Individual plant constituents, such as volatile oils, however, may deteriorate or dissipate quickly. Freshly picked herbs can spoil or lose vitality in a matter of hours or minutes. In general, fresh plants require an immediate application. In contrast, thoroughly dried plant materials are incorporated into a remedy as soon as possible but usually have a shelf life of approximately one year, again depending on the plant. Dried herbs for external use may be stored longer, depending on the plant.

Some plant medicine-makers consider how and when the plant or plant part is harvested a significant part of the process. Some herbalists and herb companies continue the tradition of planting, harvesting, and preparing remedies according to specific lunar, solar, and planetary cycles and configurations. Attention to cosmic forces is known to increase the hardiness of the medicinal plant and the potency and prevalence of medicinal components. Large European pharmaceutical companies, such as Weleda and WALA, pay close attention to how the medicinal plants are grown in relationship with the whole environment, including the flow of water near the plant, the balance of the soil, and the position of the planets.

The processing of the plant effects the quality of the medicinal plant preparation. Traditionally, plants have been said to have healing properties, but the medicine is actually within the healer. Many plant medicine-makers are aware of this and are very careful and meticulous about their preparations. Remedies are often thought to be best if harvested by hand. The purity of the menstruum (solvent) used to extract the medicinal constituents of plants, such as water (referred to as the universal solvent), alcohol, glycerine, vinegar, and oil, is very important. Some herbalists recommend using only distilled or soft water in making remedies to facilitate the extraction process because hard, well, or spring waters can foster precipitation.

HEALING FOODS AND ORAL REMEDIES

The medicinal benefits of plants are most commonly acquired through ingestion in foods and teas. Some medicinal plants, such as saw palmetto

(Serenoa repens) have a history of also being eaten as staple foods. Herbs are applied through food preparation in many cultures. Herbs such as dill (Anethum graveolens) and basil (Ocimum basilicum) are incorporated into cooking because of their supportive effects on digestion. They are included traditionally in small amounts determined by taste.

Oral ingestion of herbal remedies through teas, juices, and foods enable the person to taste the plant. Because many culinary herbs and spices come from plants that also can serve as medicines, they should be included sparingly. Taste is an excellent way to regulate oral ingestion of herbs because many medicinal plants and many plant constituents are not the most pleasurable to taste. Medicinal plants can be bitter, sour, pungent, astringent, salty, and sweet. Often, tasting a medicinal plant reveals a combination of tastes that is unique to that plant. The understanding of the importance of taste in herbal medicine is highly developed in traditional medicine systems such as TCM and the Indian system of Ayurveda.

In the Ayurvedic system, the bitter taste is thought to restore the sense of taste. In many cultures, medicinal plant bitters, (a combination of bitter plants), is used in aiding digestion. Typical bitter plants include goldenseal (Hydrastis canadensis), yarrow (Achillea millefolium), and dandelion (Taraxicum officinalis). My mother harvested dandelion flowers in the spring to make a vat of dandelion wine that was drunk with dinner to aid digestion.

Sour taste is helpful in digestion as well. Sour is experienced with lemon (Citrus limon) and other citrus fruits, as well as rosehips (Rosa canina) and hawthorn berries (Crataegus laevigata). Pungent taste increases the appetite and promotes digestion and sweating. Examples are black pepper (Piper nigrum) and onion (Allium cepa). Astringent taste is drying and constricting and is used to promote absorption and restriction of fluid. The astringent taste, associated with the tannin constituents in plants, can be found with raspberry leaf (Rubus idaeus) and witch hazel (Hamamelis virginiana L.). In addition to its effects on digestion, the salty taste found in plants such as seaweeds also promotes the body's ability to retain fluids. Sweet taste found in herbs such as licorice (Glycyrrhiza glabra L.) and psyllium (Plantago psyllium L.) is nutritive and moistening to tissues.

In TCM, practitioners taste teas made from hundreds of medicinal plants as part of their education. Plants are recognized by taste (part of the safe use system). Herbal formulas of several carefully selected herbs are prepared for each patient. TCM practitioners believe that, despite the intense and often repulsive taste of a formula, a patient will be aware of craving the formula that is designed for their health concern, if that formula is appropriate for them. TCM herbal formulas are designed for the patient with the goal of greater balance in body and peace of mind. The body is said to crave that which assists its natural tendency to seek greater balance and harmony. I have seen this happen time and again in clinical practice.

TEAS – INFUSIONS AND DECOCTIONS

Teas also called "tisanes," are aqueous or water extractions of medicinal plants. Water extractions are often hot but can be cold, especially if the plant has highly volatile active principles. *Infusions* are water extractions of the plant material that is more delicate, such as leaves and flowers. The plant material is allowed to steep in the water for some time. Fresh or dried plant can be infused, but because of the water content in the fresh plant, more plant should be used per cup of tea than with dried (approximately three teaspoons [15 g] of the fresh herb is equal to 1 teaspoon [3 to 5 g] of dried herb). The decoction method of making tea is appropriate when the plant material is hard or woody (i.e., roots or barks) because more heat is needed to release the medicinal constituents in the plant (usually the mineral salts and bitter principles). For decoction, the plant material simmers or boils for approximately fifteen minutes. In TCM practice, the formulas often contain roots and harder parts of plants, and the usual decoction time is 1 to 2 hours. If the plant material is dried, it is steeped in warm water for approximately 4 hours before simmering to allow the dried herb to absorb water and expand. Infusions and decoctions can be taken internally and used externally. External applications will be discussed in the section "topical applications."

How to Make an Infusion

Supplies:

- A china or glass teapot (for 2+ cups [500 ml]), a tea ball or net for 1 cup (Note: Do not use aluminum when making herbal teas. Tea nets made of cotton do not compact the herb as tightly as the stainless-steel tea balls and allow for greater circulation of the water around the plant material during extraction)

- Tea strainer to place in a cup when infusing loose herb (not teabags) in a teapot

- Herb of choice, usually leaf or flower, cut or ground in small but not minute pieces
- Boiling water

Method:

Boil the water and choose your herb. When using large dried flowers or leaves, break up the amount of herb needed in the pot or tea net. If using fresh herbs, cut them into pieces and bruise them with a knife so that volatile oils do not absorb into the skin of the hands. Measure the herbs for the tea. In general, use 1 to 2 rounded teaspoons (about 5 g) per cup of water. Pour the boiling water over the plant material and cover the cup or teapot to prevent the volatile oils from escaping. These oils will accumulate with water on the underside of the lid. Be sure to shake the condensation on the lid back into the tea. For fragile and tender parts of plants, steep for approximately three to five minutes. For other plant materials, steep for approximately ten minutes. Strain and drink tea hot.

These are general guidelines, and following a specific formula may be required, depending on the herb(s). Infusions are made in small quantities on an as-needed basis because they often contain constituents that spoil quite readily after hot water infusion. Beverage teas are infusions. They are usually a blend of plant leaves or flowers and are steeped so that you receive tiny amounts of any one plant's medicinal constituents. The concept of a beverage tea can be compared with the use of a blend of herbs in seasoning Italian foods, such as oregano *(Oreganum vulgare L.)*, basil *(Ocimum basilicum)*, and thyme *(Thymus vulgaris L.)*. Instead of making an infusion of thyme and using it medicinally, either drinking it or putting it in a bath, a small amount of thyme is blended with other herbs and put into a sauce for pasta. Likewise, the intent of the beverage tea infusion is for culinary purposes rather than medicinal use.

How to Make a Decoction

Supplies:

The same supplies as for making an infusion are needed, but the plant material is usually the harder part of a plant such as a root or bark. With roots, the pieces are often much more substantial than with leaves or flowers.

Method:

Use approximately 30 g (1 ounce) of herb per 750 ml (1 1/2 cups) of water. Place dried, hard herbs in a pot and cover completely with cold water. Bring water almost to the boil, cover, and remove from heat. Allow to stand at least four hours to allow dried herbs to expand. (You may eliminate this step when using fresh herbs.) After standing, the herbs are simmered in a pot (not aluminum) for approximately fifteen minutes. Volatile oils will escape during simmering. These instructions are a generalization and specific instructions (as with TCM formulas where the herbs are cooked for up to 2 hours) should be followed whenever possible. Strain the decoction *after* cooling slightly and then taken warm. Decoctions are considered more potent than infusions. Larger quantities of decoction often are made. In general, decoctions can be kept refrigerated for up to 72 hours and portions reheated, without boiling, for use during the day.

SOUPS

One very common way of receiving the benefits of small amounts of medicinal plants is to make soups or broths with herbs. Soup and broth making with herbs is a common nursing tradition that has been important to holistic care and comfort since the seventeenth-century work of the nurses who were Daughters of Charity of St. Vincent de Paul. These early nurses under guidance from their foundress, Louise de Marillac, viewed making broth as an essential intervention that strengthened the person. Broths and soups were made from meat, vegetables, and occasionally grain, such as barley. The nurses also used culinary and medicinal herbs in the preparation of their broths. The Daughters followed "Particular Rules" that included the section title "The Ordinary Diet to be Given to a Patient." The herbs that were considered best for a patient's broth were sorrel, lettuce, purslane, chicory, white beet, Chinese leaves or Chinese cabbage, and caraway. In winter, when aerial parts of herbs were not as available, the sisters used chicory, parsley root, and hulled barley.[92] They fed and healed thousands of sick poor in Paris and throughout France with broths and other herbal remedies.

Broths and soups are still an easy and effective herbal remedy to employ in the care of Self and family. You can add ginger *(Zingiber officinale)* and astragalus *(Astragalus membranicus)* to chicken soup to strengthen the stomach and spleen energy systems because many people have sluggish digestion, particularly during cold months. One of my favorite winter soups is onion and watercress *(Nasturtium officinalis)*. This soup was inspired by one of my favorite herbalists, a Swiss naturopathic physician named Dr. Alfred Vogel. The Bioforce herb company was started by Dr. Vogel, who suggested that watercress is helpful for sore throat and health patterns related to colds and flu. He stated that the watercress "boosts" the thyroid.[93]

Dr. Martha's Winter Watercress and Onion Soup recipe

- Slice two large onions and place in a 3-quart saucepan or soup pot.
- Cover with 3-4 cans organic chicken or vegetable broth (or make your own!)
- Add 1-2 cups water.
- Add Braggs Liquid Aminos to taste.

This soup should be a little on the salty side to cut the phlegm in the throat. It will also be balanced out by the sweet taste of onions after they cook. Add freshly ground pepper to taste. Bring to a boil and then cover and simmer until onions are soft. Take one tablespoon of Kudzu (*Pueraria lobata*) powder (from the macrobiotic section of the health food store) and cover with a little water. Stir to paste. Add 1/4 cup of the broth to kudzu and stir until thoroughly mixed and then add to the pot. This mixture will thicken the soup slightly. Kudzu is a cooling herb that heals the gastrointestinal lining where the viruses that cause the common cold take hold. When the onions are soft, and you are ready to eat, cut the watercress leaves gently and place 1/4 to 1/2 cup of leaves in a soup bowl. Cover with boiling soup, and by the time you get to the table, the greens will be ready to eat. They are slightly spicy. Substitute chard, kale, or other chopped green leafy vegetable if you do not have cress available.

PILLS AND CAPSULES

In industrialized countries, herbs are often sold as capsules or pills. Because many people are used to taking pills prescribed from biomedical practitioners, they usually prefer taking herbs in these easy-to-use forms as opposed to having to prepare their own medicine. It is simple to make one's own capsulated herbal medicine. The herb is crushed using a mortar and pestle, and the capsules are either filled individually or by using a capsule holder where the herb powder is spread into the open capsules, and the excess scraped away. The other half of the capsule is then applied. In terms of safety, capsules that are self-prepared from herbs you have identified may be better quality than those bought in a store. When purchasing herbs in capsule form, the consumer must instead rely on the integrity of the manufacturer and the standards of the regulatory agency of the country where they live. Because the herb is powdered, it is not easy, if nearly impossible, to identify the herb by visual inspection, smell, and sometimes taste. The risk of adulteration (the wrong plant being added to the product) also can be higher with powdered medicinal plant products.

In addition, the plant is not tasted when ingested in capsule form. In traditional medicine systems, such as Ayurveda, taste, and sensory experiences of the plant medicine, are considered the beginning of the healing process because the senses stimulate the nervous system. The person who ingests the herb in capsule form may not be getting the full benefit of the plant that they would get by tasting the herb in decoction, infusion, or liquid extraction forms. Some traditional herbalists also consider the bulking agents used in making herb capsules and tablets to be unhealthy in daily quantities. In TCM, these filler materials can be stagnating to the liver energy system, an important issue for women who often have symptoms indicative of liver stagnation before selecting their herbal remedy.

Many herbs are sold in pill or capsule form as dietary supplements. But not all herbs should be eaten as whole plants in pill or capsule forms. Traditional herbal *Materia Medica* is specific about which herbs can be eaten after decoction. Therefore, they may not be as safe or effective ingested in a supplement or pill form as when used according to tradition. For example, in the Chinese *Materia Medica*, "dong quai" *(Angelica sinensis)* is said to be edible. Many people might find the taste of "dong quai" or any other herb repugnant and therefore, may ask to take the herb in capsule or pill form. In addition, some practitioners believe that the benefit of using pills and capsules is that doses of specific plant constituents may be more easily controlled than in tea form. While this may be correct, whole plant dosages can be accurately measured out for teas. Although traditional herbalists create herbal formulas using dosage strategies with precision to 1/3 of a gram or better that meet the specific needs of a patient, some practitioners and patients are more comfortable with pills and capsules. Precision Self-care plans include the benefits and risks associated with applying herbs in these various forms.

SYRUPS

When people talk about medicine, they often do not know the critical role that syrups have played in healthcare history. Nurses have been expert syrup makers for hundreds of years. The French Daughters of Charity nurses used fruit syrups as a carrier for administering bitter-tasting herbal extracts and powders. They made syrups from peach blossoms, cherries, chickory, water lilies, and roses! In the 18th and 19th centuries, Shaker infirmary nurses documented many syrup recipes in what was called their "receipt" books. One such recipe for "Syrup for summer complaint"— a blackberry and clove syrup used for dysentery, was recorded as being "an excellent medicine; and has cured many.[95] Additionally, the Canterbury Shaker nurses' recorded a receipt for Onion Syrup which states: "Slice your onions then put them in a vessel cover them with honey make your vessel air tight then let it stew gradually till the onion is done. Strain off the liquor & it is done."[96]

To make a syrup, start with a strong herbal tea or the juice pressed from a plant such as the berries of elder *(Sambucus nigra)*. Elderberries *must* be cooked thoroughly for human consumption, and then the seeds strained from the liquid. Sugar or honey is added to the tea or juice. Then the liquid is boiled, reduced, and thickened into a syrup plant remedy. I preserve my syrups with a small amount of organic vodka or brandy. Syrups make excellent children's remedies. My young clients like my thyme (Thymus vulgaris) syrup, in particular, during cold and flu season. I do not preserve children's syrups with alcohol.

TINCTURES AND LIQUID EXTRACTS

Tinctures and liquid extracts are preparations in which alcohol extracts the medicinal components of a plant. Alcohol is an excellent menstruum (solvent) for most plant constituents, and it also serves as a preservative for the finished product. Because of the alcohol, the shelf life of an herbal tincture or liquid extract is approximately ten years. According to the 1902 International Protocol, tinctures of dried toxic or intense plants should be a 10% or 1:10 plant weight/volume of menstruum. Tinctures of the dried nontoxic plant should be a 20% or 1:5 solution, and fresh plant tinctures are 50% or 1:2 weight/volume solutions. In the marketplace, a tincture is often a 1:10 preparation, meaning one-part plant is used to ten parts of alcohol. A liquid extract is usually a preparation of one-part plant to five parts of alcohol or less. When buying alcohol preparations, it can be somewhat confusing for the consumer because the words tincture, and extract are not always used in a standard fashion by manufacturers. Understanding the preparation is essential when buying alcohol products because cost comparisons should include how much plant may actually be extracted.

Making your alcohol preparations requires some research because some plants are best used dry and some fresh. Alcohol preparations are performed by either the percolation method or maceration. Because percolation involves the use of laboratory equipment that most people do not have in their homes, maceration, a simpler and effective method, is described here.

How to Make an Alcohol Tincture or Extract

Supplies:

- Fresh or dried herb (see information following method for selecting)
- Wide-mouthed jar with lid
- Food grade ethyl alcohol (Pure grain spirits up to 190 proof [e.g., Everclear] are used for maceration.) The amount of alcohol used is discussed after method.

Method:

Maceration begins with cutting up fresh herb or powdering (coarse, not fine) dried herb and putting the plant material in a wide-mouthed jar. Pour the appropriate amount and type of menstruum over the plant material and close the lid tightly. Place the jar in an accessible but dark corner of the kitchen. Shake the jar at least twice daily so that the menstruum can thoroughly penetrate the plant material. This action is when you can really potentize the gentle medicine with the energy of your heart! Shake and store the jar for two weeks. Heat is not necessary because of the more extended maceration period. At the end of the two weeks, strain the plant material into a bowl. Use cheesecloth to press out the remaining menstruum from the plant material. Take the alcohol extract, pass it through a coffee filter, and transfer the strained liquid to dark-colored dropper bottles.

Tinctures and liquid extracts lose potency when exposed to light and therefore are prepared and stored away from light. The bottles used to store tinctures and extracts should be dark-colored glass, such as brown, and have glass droppers. Dropper bottles are necessary because the dosages for the concentrated tinctures and liquid extracts are smaller and are given in drops. Be sure to label the bottle with the name of the remedy and the preparation date.

The alcohol extraction process entails understanding the water content of the plant material used and then adding the appropriate amount of grain alcohol necessary to extract the medicinal constituents. Different amounts of alcohol are used for fresh and dried plants. Often alcohol is diluted with water for extraction—50% alcohol and 50% water, or 100 proof. A 19th century botanical medicine guide states, "Diluted alcohol or proof spirit is employed, when the substance is soluble both in alcohol and water, or when one or more of the ingredients are soluble in the one fluid, and one or more in the other, as in the case of those vegetables which contain extractive or tannin, or the native salts of the organic alkalies, or gum united with resin or essential oil. As these include the greater number of medicines from which tinctures are prepared, diluted alcohol is most frequently used."[97]

If choosing dry plant material, then the amount of menstruum to extract the plant material to make a 1:5 liquid extract is five times the weight of the plant material. Thus, if you have 500 g of dried plant, you will need 2500 ml of menstruum for the liquid extraction. If a 1:10 tincture is to be made, then ten times the weight of the dried plant or 5000 ml of menstruum is needed. Generally, the menstruum used for dried plant tinctures is 50% alcohol and 50% water, or 100 proof (vodka). If choosing fresh plants, there is already a significant amount of water present, so water rarely needs to be added. A fresh plant can have as much as three times the amount of moisture as a dried plant. The water content can be measured by moisture analysis, and then the correct amount of menstruum calculated. In *general*, for fresh plant tinctures, a 1:2 weight-to-volume calculation is made, and the plant is extracted in straight 190 proof alcohol (Everclear). For example, if 200 g of the fresh plant is collected, then 400 ml of alcohol is used for the maceration.

A NOTE ABOUT HOMEOPATHY

Many people ask what the differences are between homeopathic remedies and herbal extracts. A fresh herb tincture made by extracting one-part herb in two parts alcohol is often referred to as a "mother tincture." This mother tincture can be shaken and diluted 1:10 to give a "homeopathic" tincture with a potency known as 2X. Then that 2X tincture is shaken and diluted once again 1:10 with alcohol/water and that dilution is known as 3X. This shaking and dilution process is known as "potentization." Samuel Hahnemann, a renowned homeopathic scientist, described his observation of the effect of potentization as, "The more a substance is succussed and diluted, the greater the therapeutic effect while simultaneously nullifying the toxic effect."[98] The potentization process continues, and the potencies are recorded carefully.

Homeopathic medicine includes the use of remedies that have been diluted as many as twenty-four times (Avogadro's number), the point at which there are no detectable molecules of the original mother (herbal) tincture. Homeopathic remedies are not only derived from plants. Minerals are also used. The remedies are then taken based on the "Law of Similars" (like treats like) in which the symptoms of a condition are actually treated with a homeopathic dilution initially made from a substance, such as a plant, known to cause the same symptoms. Thus, homeopathy, although it includes plants as mother tinctures, is not the same science nor the same healing art as herbalism.

Alcohol extracts and tinctures are usually taken in a small amount of warm water, but they can be taken directly in the mouth. Taking directly in the mouth is an important choice when quick action is required, such as an allergic response. Before rubbing one's eyes, taking a liquid extract of nettles (*Urtica doica*) can affect itching, an early allergic response pattern. Non-synthetic vegetable glycerin also can be used for the maceration of plants. Glycerin is a type of alcohol that also is known as glycerol or glyceric alcohol. Glycerin is not as effective as alcohol in preserving plants, so some plant medicines include a greater volume of glycerin or are a mixture of glycerin and alcohol. Glycerin also is more effective than water but less effective than alcohol in extracting resinous and oily plant constituents. Glycerites are often used with children so that they do not have to experience alcohol. Glycerites are also for those who are sensitive or opposed to alcohol, but tea is often a better choice. People who are sensitive to alcohol can be carbohydrate sensitive and do not do well with simple sugars, carbohydrates, or alcohol, which are metabolized quickly. Standardized extracts are not the same as liquid extracts or tinctures. As discussed in a previous chapter, standardized extracts are plant preparations in which some plant constituent, an active ingredient, has been adjusted to ensure that the potency of the product is standardized.

TOPICAL APPLICATIONS

Topical applications are a common part of Self-care plans. You may already be familiar with the use of creams, salves, lotions, liniments, packs, and other remedies to the exterior of the body. Although the whole body can be affected by topical applications, the skin and the nervous system are most particularly affected. The skin, as the largest organ of the body and the peripheral nervous system, both have a connection with the whole body. Topical remedies are used not only in skincare, such as care of a localized wound (an application called a vulnerary in herbalism), but also are used to address systemic discomfort and imbalances affecting body, mind, emotions, and spirit.

Herbal topical applications are powerful but gentle medicine. They soothe the nervous system, which in ancient Vedic texts is likened to a tree called the "triple tree." Yogananda, who many years ago introduced yoga in the west, wrote of the origin of the triple tree that, "The two trees of nerves and the life force are condensed out of the tree of human consciousness, the elemental ideas in the causal body, which in turn emanate from Cosmic Consciousness."[99] As we access the triple tree of nerves, consciousness, and life force through the five buds of sensation (sight, hearing, smell, taste, and touch), we contact the elements of Self with a capital "S."

The topical application of plant remedies to the skin allows a physical-chemical reaction to occur and also creates a healing moment when you focus your attention on that part of your body receiving the external application. Use the moment to go to your safe place, ask your body what it needs for healing, and then intuit the answer. Applications to the skin and nervous systems provide a comforting way to stay aware of your body and fully engage in the healing process. Remedies can be applied to the skin in the form of poultices, plasters, compresses, salves, ointments, lotions, and more. Herbal medicine also emphasizes the art and science of applying these topical applications as well. As discussed previously, the water element suggests that how the topical application is applied to the skin and nervous system is as vital as what herbal simple is applied. Consider the importance of what you feel emotionally as you apply the following herbal simples.

COMPRESSES

A compress, also called a "fomentation" or "stupe," is a folded piece of material, made of natural fiber, that is applied moist to a part of the body so that it presses against that body part. Applying a compress combines the knowledge of the external use of herbs and the science of hydrotherapy or the use of water. Natural fiber cloths such as wool, cotton, silk, and linen are used because they are more absorbent and allow the skin to sweat and breathe during the compress. A compress can be applied hot, warm, or cool, and is made with an infusion, decoction, tincture, or herbal oil. The size of the cloth chosen should be the correct size to fit the area of application. For example, a compress for the eyes will be smaller than a compress for the kidneys. Some examples of compresses that can be used in patient care are arnica infused oil *(Arnica montana)* compresses for a sprained ankle, witch hazel liniment *(Hamamelis virginiana)* compresses for puffy eyes, and lemon *(Citrus limon)* infusion compresses for fever or heat in the head, back, abdomen, or thighs.

How to Make a Compress

Supplies:

- Natural fiber cloths cut to the size and shape of the body part to be covered
- Cold, warm, or hot herbal infusion, decoction, or tincture to be used
- Bowl to soak the compress
- Bath and hand towels for warm/hot compress

Method:

Cool compresses are made by dipping the cloth into the infusion, decoction, or tincture, wringing out the cloth and applying it to the body part. In the case of fever, it is unnecessary to cover because the compress will be changed frequently as the body warms it. With warm and hot compresses, your goal is to keep the compress as warm as possible. The cloth is dipped in the hot or warm infusion or decoction and is placed in a wringing towel so that you do not have to touch the steaming compress directly, and it can be wrung out thoroughly.

Hot compresses are not applied wet and drippy because they cool too quickly. After wringing, the compress temperature is tested against your arm and if tolerable to the skin is applied as hot as possible to your skin. After the compress is applied, it is completely covered with another cloth and then a wool cloth or towel to keep in the heat. Each successive cloth covers the previous one by a few centimeters to be sure to seal in the heat. The compress remains in place for about 20 minutes. Some people use a piece of plastic, like a plastic bag, to seal in the heat of a compress. If the compress turns cold, you will become uncomfortable, and it should be removed and replaced with a warm one. You may find that you relax deeply and fall asleep. Set the alarm so that if this happens, you will awaken to remove the compress after 20 minutes. Compresses that are secured and worn for longer periods are kept moist by adding a small amount of the infusion, decoction, tincture, or oil at intervals throughout the day. For certain conditions, hot and cold compresses using different herbs may be alternated.

Examples of Cold and Hot Compresses

Use witch hazel *(Hamamelis virginiana)* infusion or tincture. Dip cotton bandaging cut to the size of the eyes in the infusion or tincture and squeeze out the excess. Apply to the outside of the eyes to relieve puffiness. For an example of a hot compress see Gentle Medicine Self-study #12

Gentle Medicine Self-Study #12: Comforting Ginger Compress

Grate 4 to 5 ounces (150 g) of fresh ginger root. Put the ginger into a small cloth bag and add it to 1-gallon (3.8 liters) of simmering (not boiling) water. Allow the decoction to steep gently for five minutes. Holding both ends of a hand towel, dip the middle into the ginger water. Wring it out and fold it to the size of your mid-back where the kidneys are. Take care in applying the hot compress, making sure that the skin does not burn because of the heat. The compress should be applied as hot as is tolerated. Place a dry towel over the compress and a blanket over the towel, tucking each layer around your body so that air does not enter the compress and cool it. Prepare a second compress as the first. Replace the first compress after three to four minutes. Remove the blanket and dry towel. Place the second hot compress on top of the first and flip the compress over, making sure that the temperature is tolerated. This technique ensures that the connection with the ginger and moist heat is maintained.

The compresses should be flipped every three to four minutes for twenty minutes. The ginger compress will create increased circulation of blood and body fluids and move qi and blood stagnation that usually manifests as pain, inflammation, swelling, or stiffness. Many people with chronic pain benefit from ginger compresses to the kidneys as a systemic remedy rather than applying the compress to individual joints. Ginger compresses should not be used when high fever is present (too warming), on the head area, on the abdomen in pregnancy, for infants or the very old (too stimulating), or on an area of the body experiencing infection (heat) such as chest/lung area during pneumonia. I taught this compress to teenage women who were preparing to go to nursing school. They were taking NSAIDS every day for "pain." They were so surprised and happy to experience such pain relief with the ginger compress to the kidneys. They asked me if the effect was due to "the ginger, the hot water compress, or the loving kindness with which they had applied the compress?" I asked them what they thought was the answer. They said, "All three!" Yes, the ginger is warming and stimulating as is the hot water. But the feelings of love with which the ginger compress is applied is just as important to the connection through comfort that can be made between you and the plant.

To apply herbs in wraps, packs, and compresses, you must first learn the preparation of the plant infusion, decoction, tincture, or oil used in the topical application. Think about the flow and rhythm of applying compresses. Learning topical applications is similar to learning to make a bed. A well-made bed is associated with comfort. The sheets should not be wrinkled because that can affect the health or your skin. A compress or wrap should not be wrinkled and should be tucked in to ensure that it does not move or fall off. The compress or wrap should be a comforting temperature.

How to Make and Use an Oil Compress

Herbal oils, such as castor oil *(Racinus communis)* can be applied as healing compresses too. I learned the benefits of a warm, soothing castor oil pack or compress from a healer who had been affiliated with the Edgar Cayce Foundation in Virginia Beach, Virginia. Edgar Cayce (1877–1945) was a medical clairvoyant for 43 years whose work includes the use of numerous plant remedies. Cayce recommended castor oil packs in cases of impaired lymph flow; inflammation; congestion; constipation; gallbladder, liver, kidney and pelvic disorders; muscle spasms, and back pain.[100] Castor oil is very thick compared with other oils and, when placed on the skin, provides a protective coating that subsequently penetrates the tissues very deeply. With the assistance of heat, the oil is taken up readily by the skin and tissues and provides a deep healing and soothing effect.

Supplies:
- Cotton flannel cloth (two swatches a size that when doubled will completely cover the body part)
- Castor oil—warmed
- One large thin hand towel and one large bath towel for each body part treated
- Hot water bottle filled and burped

Method for Castor Oil Pack to Your Feet

Try applying a castor oil pack to your own feet! There are two ways of doing a castor oil pack to your feet or any part of your body. The Cayce method is to thoroughly soak the flannel with the warmed castor oil and apply it to the feet or body part. These packs are reusable if refrigerated. For personal use and in clinical practice, I use another method that is not reusable. I use significantly less oil by applying the oil directly to the feet or body part and then applying the flannel soaked in very hot water. Either way, the pack is applied warm and moist to facilitate the update of the oil. A piece of thin plastic can be used to protect the heat of the pack. For the feet, large plastic baggies are put easily over the foot after the compress is applied and squeezed next to the foot so that all air escapes. After the plastic is applied, the small hand towel is wrapped around the foot in a way to keep air from entering the pack. After both feet are wrapped and tucked in, place them at the center edge of a larger towel, and the hot water bottle at the bottom of the feet outside the small towels. The edge of the large towel away from the patient is folded up over the bottle and pack. Then the towel ends are wrapped up and around the feet, securing the bottle in place and keeping the warmth in. Cover yourself with warm blankets and keep the castor pack in place for up to an hour. After the castor oil pack is removed be sure to keep the body part treated with the pack, warm.

POULTICES AND PLASTERS

Herbal poultices, also known as cataplasms, are similar to compresses, except that instead of putting the cloth in an infusion, decoction, tincture, or oil, the cloth is used to hold a slurry or softened paste of the plant material, which is then applied to the skin. Herbs commonly applied as poultices and plasters include flaxseed, onion, or hops. They can be used as a therapeutic measure for lung congestion, to relieve distention in the abdomen, and for painful, inflamed, and infected wounds. Oats, cornmeal, arrowroot, carrots, and charcoal were also common for poultices. With the advent of germ theory, the poultice fell into disuse by many clinicians because it was thought that the poultice might introduce bacteria. In many countries, people continue to use the poultice, prepared fresh, with appropriate attention to hygiene and the possibility of introducing bacteria and infection.

How to Make a Poultice

Supplies:

- Linen, cheesecloth, or a light natural fiber fabric cut to size
- Cut or chopped herb chosen for poultice. May be raw and cut or mashed or may be lightly sautéed

Method:

Prepare the herb of choice. Place the slurry of the raw or cooked herb in the center of the cheesecloth or fabric and fold the fabric to enclose the herb. The poultice should be a size that fits the body part to be treated. The poultice is left in place for a certain amount of time determined by the energetic quality of the herb and the amount of moisture in the poultice. Drier poultices can be secured with a bandage and left in place for hours if comfortable whereas a moister poultice such as an onion slurry poultice applied to the chest might be removed after 15 – 30 minutes.

Plasters are a type of poultice in which the plant material is applied directly to the skin or through a thin cloth, but the plaster is often made of a plant powder that has been mixed into a thick paste. Common examples of plasters are green cabbage *(Brassica oleracea L.)* leaf plasters to the breast in cases of engorgement during breastfeeding and aloe vera leaf plasters on first- and second-degree burns.

INFUSED OILS, LINIMENTS, SALVES, AND OINTMENTS

Herbal oils (also called oil infusions to distinguish them from essential oils) are made by saturating fresh plant material with a fixed oil such as olive, sunflower, or canola oil. The oil is massaged into the skin for various reasons, depending on the plant used. For example, the flowers of *Arnica montana* are infused in oil and massaged into sprains and sore muscles.

How to Make an Herbal Oil

Supplies:
- Use fresh or dried plant material, depending on which plants are best used as oils and whether they must be prepared from fresh or dried herb. You may need to do some research to answer these questions. Some plants such as St. John's wort must be used fresh.
- Wide mouth glass jar
- Cheesecloth
- Oil (Olive, Sunflower, Canola)

Method:

An oil of the flowers and tiny leaves of the St. John's wort *(Hypericum perforatum)* plant are used as an example here. St. John's wort oil is applied to first- and second-degree burns and is used in wound healing and for muscle and trigger point pain. I prefer the solar method for making herbal oils. The aerial parts of the *fresh* plant (flowers and small leaves) are collected, and left out to wilt slightly. Then the plant is chopped, and placed in a wide-mouthed jar. Do not use dried St. John's wort. A little oil (preferably olive) is added to the plant material, and then the flowers are crushed again with the back of a spoon. Then more oil is added to cover the plant material completely. The jar is shaken and placed in a warm location for two weeks.

The oil must be approximately 37.7°C or 100°F during the infusion time. St. John's wort oil turns red due to a plant constituent known as hypericin. After the oil infusion is completed, the plant material is strained out of the oil. The residual oil can be pressed out of the plant material with cheesecloth. Because fresh material is used, some water may still be in the herbal oil especially if pressed. Keep separate and use it first. The residual water in the pressed oil can cause it to go rancid over time. It is best to let the strained oil sit for one to two weeks undisturbed. The oil will rise above any water remaining and can be decanted off into brown glass storage bottles.

If dried plant material is used to make an herbal oil (herbs other than St. John's wort), grind the dried herb to a powder when you are ready to make the oil. Wet the herb thoroughly with oil and stir. Add oil so that the level is a few centimeters above the herb powder. Cap the jar tightly and put in a warm place. The same method is followed except dried herbs absorb the oil. The oil level must be checked after the first twenty-four hours, and more oil is added if needed.

Liniments are lighter topical remedies than oils and are usually alcohol or camphor based for quick absorption by the skin. Liniments have been used traditionally to warm and stimulate muscles and ligaments. They rapidly evaporate so that nothing remains on the skin as with herbal oils. Liniments are often applied before physical exercise to warm up the body, but they also can be used for local inflammation after exertion. Liniments are applied to specific areas of the body, not for full body massage. The herbs traditionally used as liniments are the more warming herbs like cayenne (*Capsicum frutescens*) and lobelia (*Lobelia inflata*). One of my favorite liniments is a camphor-based liniment with lobelia that is massaged into the temples for discomfort related to headache, migraine, and eyestrain. The camphor, as with all alcohol-based liniments, is cooling, while the herb is warming. Liniments feel initially cool on the skin and then quickly begin to warm. They cause a beneficial exchange of the blood in a specific area through this cooling and warming action.

Herbal salves and ointments are semisolid plant preparations that are absorbed into the skin. The base for an herbal salve or ointment is the herbal oil (already prepared) and a natural wax such as beeswax.

How to Make an Herbal Salve

Supplies:

- Herbal infused oil already prepared or plain oil can be used (Plain vegetable oil is used when drops of essential oils are to be used.)
- Beeswax (approximately 28 g per 250 ml oil or 1-ounce wax per 1 cup oil)
- Tincture of benzoin (1 drop per 30 ml or 1 ounce of oil) as a preservative

Method:

This is a basic process for making a salve. The ingredients must be adjusted based on the herbs used and the consistency desired. The oil and shaved beeswax are placed in the top of a double boiler to melt the wax. Test the consistency by pouring a small amount of the salve into a jar. It should harden quickly and be the consistency that you want. Add more oil if you want the salve to be softer and more wax if you want it harder, depending on the nature of the application. For example, in the care of an open wound, a hard salve would not be used because applying it takes a little more rubbing, which is not helpful when the wound is healing. A softer salve would be needed that can be applied on the wound easily. When the consistency of the salve is right, add the tincture of benzoin as a preservative.

Aromatic essential oils also can be used in making oils, liniments, salves, and ointments for topical applications. Essential oils are extracted from aromatic plants. They make up a tiny amount of the whole plant. Essential oils evaporate readily and therefore, once extracted, must be kept in sealed bottles. They are sold in small amounts because they are a highly concentrated plant constituent. For medicinal purposes, they must be used in pure form. Aromatic oils often are considered precious and valuable and are used in small amounts. Like perfume, essential oils should be included in amounts that do not overpower the sense of smell. Some essential oils are lighter in fragrance than others. For example, lemon verbena is less intense than cinnamon. Herbal oils, often used for massage, are made with drops of essential oils in a light, carrier oil such as sweet almond oil, which has no fragrance. Use a 2% to 3% dilution (10 to 12 drops per 1 ounce/30 ml of vegetable oil) and a 1% dilution (5 drops per 1 ounce/30 ml oil) for pregnant women, people with illness, and children. For a liniment, use essential oils of ginger, eucalyptus, and peppermint. You should always choose your aromatic massage oil or liniment because fragrance preference is very personal. Essential oils also can be blended for specific medicinal effects related to the absorption of the properties of the oil through the skin and the inhalation of the scent. Through their unique fragrances and their visual beauty, healing plants contribute to the creation of a healing environment.

SIMPLES FOR CREATING A HEALING ENVIRONMENT

The personality or medicine of a plant is not only ingested or felt through contact with the skin. Plant medicine can be experienced through environmental interaction. It can be inhaled with the air as aromatherapy, steams, and inhalations, absorbed with water through herbal baths, "taken in" through vision, and experienced by direct interaction through a garden experience. The creation of a healing environment is a vital part of your precision Self-care plan. The healing environment you create can sustain the action of your Self-care plan while you go about your daily life.

AROMATHERAPY, INHALATIONS, AND STEAMS

Aromatherapy, like homeopathy, is a plant-related science and healing art. But it is very different from herbalism because the essential oils used in aromatherapy are extracted as single constituents from whole plants. In that sense, essential oil is more like a pharmaceutical drug or standardized extract, and therefore, should be treated with greater caution that accompanies single constituent products, even those that are from natural sources as are essential oils. It is best to apply essential oils externally or inhale them through the air. Do not take essential oils internally.

The essential oils breathed in from aromatic plants can affect the health of the body, mind, emotions, and spirit. The human sense of smell is one direct connection with the environment. The olfactory cells are the only place in the human body where the central nervous system comes in direct contact with the external environment. Plants are ready providers for that sensory experience. Throughout history, perfumers have known of the medicinal benefits of the volatile aromatic fragrances they used. Religious rituals continue to include the aromatic use of plants as incense, such as frankincense *(Boswellia carterii)*. Studies of the essential oils from plants used in aromatherapy often show antibacterial, antiviral, and antifungal effects of essential oils in the human body. Studies also have demonstrated other significant effects on moods, alertness, and learning behaviors.

In addition to aromatherapy with extracted essential oils, other medicinal qualities of herbs also are taken in with the air through the modalities of smoking and steaming. Herbs such as mullein leaf *(Verbascum spp.)* are smoked for their healing effect upon the lungs. The herb is smoked in much the same way a tobacco cigar or cigarette is smoked. Herbal steam inhalations are often used in the healing of the sinuses. Chamomile inhalations are one example.

How to Make an Herbal Steam Inhalation

Supplies:

- Plant material to be infused—usually an aromatic herb such as chamomile *(Matricaria chamomilla)* or lemon balm *(Melissa officinalis)*
- Large bowl
- 1 large and 1 small towel

- Hot water bottle

Method:
Prepare a warm room and sit next to a table. Dress warmly, with socks on, and rest your feet on a hot water bottle. Place the herb in the bowl and pour boiling water over the plant material. Cover your head and shoulders with the large towel and place the towel over the bowl so that the vapors (essential oils) do not escape. Breathe in the vapors for ten to fifteen minutes (no more for chamomile). Dry your head and cover yourself with a dry towel to prevent chilling.

HERBAL BATHS

Some people may consider herbal full-body baths a luxury. They are a necessity. Hippocrates, the father of modern medicine, is well known for having stated that the key to good health rested on having a daily aromatic bath and scented massage. During an herbal bath, the plant medicine surrounds your body, allowing for the intermingling of plants and humans in a profoundly healing experience. Many herbs, such as lavender *(Lavendula officinalis)* are considered for their aromatic and other healing effects. Lavender also can be healing to the skin.

How to Make an Herbal Bath

Supplies:
- Herbal infusion (i.e., a strong water extraction that can be diluted in the bath)
- Tub or sitz basin
- Towels

Method:
To prepare an herbal bath infusion, use one handful of cut herb per liter or quart of water. For a full-body tub, make 3 quarts/L; use less for smaller basins. Steep the herbs in cold water for a few hours or overnight and then heat almost to boiling, cover and allow the herbs to steep for ten minutes. Strain the infusion and pour into tub or basin filled with warm water. Adjust the temperature and submerge. Baths should last at least twenty

minutes because that is the amount of time the pores take to open fully. After the bath, the body should be wrapped warmly in towels and allowed to perspire for a short time. Dry the body and put on fresh clothing. Some essential oils, such as rose, eucalyptus, and rosemary, can be used instead of herbal infusions in a bath. Start with three drops of pure essential oil per large tub or footbath.

FIVE ELEMENT FOOT BATH

Senior nurses will remember the importance of the footbath. Hospitalized patients were given footbaths as part of daily AM and/or PM care. Footbaths are an enduring treatment in nursing science for common health concerns from tension and stress to headaches, insomnia, gastrointestinal problems and more. Herbal foot baths are the simplest way to integrate all five elements in your precision Self-care plan! The soothing effects of the herbal applications to the nerve endings in the feet representing the entirety of the body[101] potentiates the possibility of clearing the negative effects of stress that helps to manage the kidneys' bank account in addition to the flow of energy. The soles of the feet have a high concentration of pores. Helping the pores of the feet to open not only clears waste from the feet but can also support the health of the entire excretory system of the body, including the kidneys where the body's stress is registered. The gravitational pull on the body can promote the accumulation of wastes or metabolic substances such as uric acid in the feet. It is possible that over time a buildup of these substances can make the feet toxic or inflamed, so it is best to open the pores and let them be drawn gently out of the feet. The footbaths facilitate this very effectively and restore vital energy to the body as a whole.

While a footbath is essentially a water element application, any or all of the five elements can be represented in the choices of herbal remedies that are added to the water for the footbath: infusions/decoctions (water), aromatic bath oils (air), bath salt (earth), flowers/leaves (ether), invocation/prayer (fire). The creative choice of herbal remedies is based on your knowledge of herbs and your assessment of your health patterns. Modify your footbath to match your need for a cooling or a warming environmental experience.

Supplies:
- Foot Bath Basin. For this, I suggest that you get a recyclable plastic basin typically sold as a "dishpan." The dimensions of the bottom of

the basin are approximately 12x10 inches by 4 to 5 inches high. You can use the electric footbaths that vibrate and produce heat but remember that this will change the energy field of the feet. Be sure to disinfect the basin after a footbath. Scrub it with hot soapy water and rinse with warm water and followed by a cold bleach water solution.

- One cotton bath towel. Use cotton towels, as they are absorbent.
- Two cotton hand towels. These should be thin rather than plush as they will be used to wrap the feet later on; plush towels are harder to stretch and tuck around the foot.
- Herbal bath infusion, oil, salt
- Comfortable chair.
- Blanket for shoulders.

Method:

Take off your shoes and socks or hose and roll up your pant legs above the mid-calf area. Choose the remedies to include in the footbath. Plain water is healing, too, but the reason for considering a five-element footbath has to do, once again, with anatomy and physiology and the opportunity to absorb and release through the large pores in the soles of the feet. During a warm footbath, those pores open and can readily absorb the healing effects of herbal and other remedies through the feet.

Fill the basin two-thirds full. Make sure that the temperature of the water is hot enough (approximately 92 degrees F) to produce a relaxation response. In the summer, I often use cool footbaths when feet are hot, sore, and swollen from walking in the heat. If you work in air conditioning, you may still have very cold feet even in summer so that the hot footbath can be used all year. Put the basin in front of your feet on a bath towel the long way. Your feet are longer than they are wide and therefore fit more comfortably in the basin placed in the long direction. Fold two hand towels in half the long way and then in half again and position them on the bath towel next to the basin with the folded edge toward you. Have your towels ready to use quickly after the feet have been in the bath to retain the warmth of the feet. Put any remedies you have chosen into the basin and swirl the water with your hand using a figure-eight motion. This pattern, known as "water coursing," reflects the same movement found in Nature, which can purify water.[102] While your feet are in the water, you can enter your safe place, meditate, pray, or center yourself during the footbath. When you take your feet out of the water, be sure to cover your feet with the small towels immediately and dry them so that they do not get cold. Put on some warm socks and shoes. Reflect on how your feet feel before and after the five-element footbath. Take some time to journal your experience.

HEALING GARDENS

Experiences in Nature can promote balance in body and peace of mind. A stroll through a meadow, a walk in the woods, and gardening too can decrease stress levels and cultivate a positive outlook on life. Landscape architects and artists have created gardens in healing institutions where patients can have the opportunity to interact with Nature. Cancer patients can see the plants that inspired the drugs they take in the hospital's botanical gardens where they go to for treatment. Gardens and gardening provide a connection with the earth, the soil, and the life that springs forth from it. Watching a plant grow gives a sense of the continuation of life. Watching a plant go by or a tree lose its leaves in the winter provides reassurance that all life, not just human life, is impermanent and has a season. When people become sick, they can feel isolated and afraid. Being part of Nature can reconnect people with the broader processes and cycles present in Nature of which we are all a part. Reestablishing a connection with Nature can be comforting and healing. Even *viewing* pictures of bright, colorful Nature scenes has been shown to improve health outcomes.

Horticultural therapy is a specific modality that is described as one of the oldest healing arts. The horticultural therapist is concerned with how people interact in the horticultural environment and how people partner with plants, often viewed as non-threatening gentle medicine. People are given an opportunity to pot plants or seeds either individually to improve hand-eye coordination or attention skills, or with others to improve their socialization skills. There are a growing number of horticultural therapy programs in hospitals, community centers, and botanical gardens that offer people an opportunity to dig in the dirt, plant a seed, and be part of the nurturing of life in plants.

The staff at botanical gardens are great resources for learning about how to grow medicinal plants. Start by picking just one plant to study. Learn about its growth cycle, its personality, and its medicinal properties. A garden does not have to be extensive. It can be as simple as a small window box on a sunny windowsill. The size does not matter. It is the opportunity to experience the tending of plant life, harvesting, and making your own plant medicine that is most important.

The care expressed in the harvesting and processing of the plant is vital to the potency of the resulting medicine. How a nurse applies an herbal oil to the skin, prepares a bath, and serves tea are essential parts of the healing experience with a plant as a partner. As you grow in your understanding of herbal simples and medicine making, consider sharing your experiences with others. This sharing of experiences heart to heart has historically been the way to promote healthcare reform. Reform that is the reintegration of Self-care with plants as partners, the first tier of any system of care, can be instrumental in bringing about balance in body and peace of mind that can connect us with our roots in the flow of the five-element universe.

Chapter 8
Fanning the Fire Element

Herbal interventions, such as teas, poultices, alcohol extracts, soups, and other remedies made from healing plants, initiate a gentle but powerful action that catalyzes, or initiates change in body, mind, emotion, and spirit. Herbal interventions have a power to create change in a manner that is quite different from the interventions of the biomedical world, such as surgery, pharmaceutical drugs, and radiological treatments. All employ energy, the fire element, but how that fire is utilized is a matter of scale. Irradiating a tumor with a machine is a bigger dose of the "fire" element than saying a prayer. Evaluating which is more potent or more effective is hard to say until observed and tried.

Biomedical interventions are often very powerful, sometimes overwhelming a person with their chemical or energetic intensity. This power is often observed in the body as heat or fire. Herbs, as one example of gentle medicine, provide different energy or fire than biomedical treatments. However, like the treatments of the biomedical world, herbal remedies are powerful, and their effects can be evaluated and measured in some fashion.

This chapter examines the fire element represented in such manifestations in Nature as the spiritual fire of the human heart, the warmth of the sun, and the growth of plants. As the last part of the Self-care process, this chapter focuses on the review and evaluation of the catalyzing powers in the body, the life force, that when harnessed, begin to produce desired changes. It also identifies the principles that guide safe and effective precision Self-care practices.

Throughout history, people have requested strong medicines to overcome their ailments. Some examples are chemotherapy and radiation treatments of the 20th century and calomel (mercury chloride) and bloodletting of the 19th century. Some of the most pervasive health beliefs in society have included the notion that to heal serious illness, one needs first to take remedies that will propel one to the brink of death where the body must then overcome the illness and rise like a phoenix bird. But in the 19th century, the people, with the support of many nurses and physicians, began to reject such notions of "heroic" medicines as they were called that sometimes harmed more than they healed. Critics of heroics had found a home even in sophisticated medical circles where physicians began to favor the gentler healing power of Nature. There have been periods in history where our health beliefs changed, and we no longer thought of healing as a need to pass our body through a fire. Heat, power, and fire are a matter of degree. While some herbs such as mustard (Brassica alba) and cayenne (Capsicum frutescens) certainly can scorch the body inside and out, the power of herbal remedies is, in general, gentler than the calomel and radiation heroics of the biomedical world.

Gentle is defined as "kind and delicate."[103] Is it possible for effective medicine and treatments to be kind and gentle, and yes, even fun? Or is it customary that in our psyche, we must have medicine that heroically damages us in the process of healing? Is it possible that the delicate expression of Symmetria and beauty in the plant world is, at the same time, powerful and heroic? Colors, shapes, and structures are often intensely engaging. Tasting a plant too can be a powerful experience. The gentleness of a healing plant's presence and its healing action is its gift. Herbal medicine, a gift from Nature, is living medicine. Each plant contributes its gentle, powerful gift or essence to the healing relationship. People are often well aware of the healing powers of plants. Yet the gentle but powerful properties of plants sometimes elude those in biomedical science. Only 10-15% of the 250,000 species of flowering plants on the planet have been considered for medicine.[104] Healing plants often defy human demands for better and more drug development. To appreciate the healing power of plants, their *fire*, one must enter their gentle, subtle world.

Plants, like humans, are all unique. The face of one pansy (Viola tricolor) is not the same as another. The exquisite violet buds of the paw-paw tree (Asimina triloba) are shaped differently than the buds of the fig (Ficus carica). How fortunate we are to have such partners who, like the St. John's Wort, are not only ready to help and heal but actively seek the opportunity to connect with the human world. Seeds ride on our pant legs. Flowers appear in our dreams. The roses let us know that the most etheric beauty in the plant world often requires protection by thorns in this dimension. *Urtica doica*, commonly known as "stinging" nettle, is a plant that reminds us that receiving the fire—the benefits of a medicinal plant—is still a mystery to scientists and comes with a price that, in the case of nettle, is a sting to remember. If we are to receive the chlorophyll, carotene, and vitamin C stored in the nettle leaf and experience its antihistamine action, we must know how to approach it, how to handle its stinging leaves, and how to make medicine with it.

The price for partnering with nettle and all healing plants is knowledge and a caring heart. We must know the plants with which we partner and a caring heart that desires to use that knowledge for the healing of humanity. Knowledge and a caring heart are the keys that open the door to plant partnerships and the release of energy for healing. Plant knowledge may seem like a simple commonsense maxim. Still, the stark reality is that people, particularly those who live in industrialized rural and urban society, often think that they know the healing properties of a plant when, in fact, all they have is access to that plant. That access may be a description of someone else's knowledge of a plant documented in a book, journal, or podcast. It may be a ground-up leaf stuffed into a capsule. A person can have access or an invitation to ingesting and applying herbs in many forms and in many ways, some of which have no connection whatsoever to traditional, time-honored application. A person may never have gone into the woods, been stung by a nettle, or grown their own plant medicine to receive some healing benefit from the green world. Greater access to herbs potentially means lesser knowledge of the healing plant itself. It is the responsibility of each person who would ensure the inclusion of the fire element, to seek conscious awareness as well as knowledge of the living plant.

The fiery dimension of precision Self-care begins with the development of knowledge and a caring heart that would use plant knowledge for healing Self safely and efficaciously. To have knowledge of a plant means that you know a plant's botanical and common names, where it grows, its physical and energetic characteristics, its smell and taste, how and when it is harvested, and how it is best applied in precision Self-care, orally, topically, environmentally, or a combination. Partnering with a plant includes being with the plant in its habitat in the wild or the garden. Medicine is made when you develop your first-hand knowledge and heart connection with the plant with which you have chosen to partner. This is *best* precision Self-care *practice*.

—*Evaluating Best Precision Self-care Practice*—

Best precision Self-care practice is identified through consistent and thorough evaluation over time. Evaluation is the fifth step in the Self-care process in which you will compare the change or transformation of behavior against the stated goals of your precision Self-care plan. If the result of your herbal gentle medicine intervention does not measure up, you make a change to the plan and keep working to solve the problem. Goals and interventions are adapted based on your evaluation, so be honest. If something works, it works. But if you cannot tell if something works, then stop and rethink what you are doing. People often pay for herbal remedies, supplements, and gentler treatments because they are natural and perceived as gentle. Yet they may have been given no instruction as to how to tell if the remedy is helping. The EOC precision Self-care program shows how to utilize energetic health patterns as well as evidence to be able to evaluate if and when and how an herbal remedy or any other gentle medicine is working or not.

Glean plant knowledge from many sources, herbal publications, and classes with plant science specialists, such as pharmacognosists, ethnobotanists, traditional healers, and herbalists. The herbalist, now sometimes referred to interchangeably as either a clinical or medical herbalist, studies some of the same theories of plant medicine as physicians and other scientists. Although some herbalists' roles in a community may be similar to that of a shaman or traditional healer, many herbalists study medicinal plants both from the perspective of the science of the time and the cultural traditions of a particular medicinal plant. They often make clinical decisions based on both viewpoints. For example, the *Materia Medica* of the traditional Chinese herbalist contains information not only about the energetic qualities of the herb, such as whether the herb moves "qi" or drains dampness, but also includes information on laboratory data, such as the antibacterial or antifungal activity of an herb and what type of organism is affected by its activity *in vitro*.

Pharmacognosy is a pharmacology science that deals with crude drugs and simples. It is the study of natural drugs and their constituents. Pharmacognosists focus on plants as a source for the development of pharmaceutical drugs. They attempt to identify and isolate a single active principle from which a synthetic copy can be replicated. Some pharmacognosists also cross-train in ethnobotany.

The ethnobotanist studies the relationships between people and plants. Ethnobotanists research the ways people incorporate plants into their cultural traditions, religions, and views of the universe, which leads to a greater understanding of the people themselves. Ethnobotanists often study indigenous peoples' relationship with medicinal plants. One of the oldest forms of ethnobotanical research is the search for new drugs among the plants found in traditional practices. In the United States, Canada, and

Western Europe, there is a "one in four chance that medicine contains an active ingredient derived from a plant. ... Eighty-nine plant-derived drugs currently prescribed in the industrialized world were discovered by studying folk knowledge."[105] Ethnobotanists are key players in the conservation of plant biodiversity and the preservation of indigenous plant wisdom.

Since early history, ethnobotanists of many cultures have recorded the purposes of healing plants. Historical writings and recordings such as the Ebers papyrus of the Egyptians, the *Shen Nung* of the Chinese, and the *Caraka Samhita* (the Sanskrit medical writing of India) have been results of the work of ethnobotanists of the day. Today, in addition to their observation and recording skills, ethnobotanists use the modern techniques and technology of the molecular biologist and the chemist to answer questions related to the behavior of plants, the human behavioral response to plants, and the relationship of people and plants. Many of the drugs prescribed today, such as aspirin *(Filipendula ulmaria)*, codeine *(Papaver somniferum)*, quinine *(Cinchona pubescens)*, and vincristine *(Catharanthus roseus)*, exist as a result of the tremendous successes of ethnobotanical researchers. Ethnobotanists go beyond simple observation in the charting of the various plants used in a particular culture and search for what people can take from the plant world in the form of drugs. They are scientists who "walk" between both the biomedical world and the world of the people and their traditional healers, often serving as translators for both realms.

When I first began to formalize my practice of nurse-herbalism in 1989, I was working as a nurse in what today would be identified as an integrative care group practice. One of my roles was to work with horticulturalists to oversee the growth and harvesting of herbs grown on the farm. We had fields strewn with red clover and row-cropped areas of valerian *(Valeriana officinalis)*, borage *(Borago officinalis)*, and calendula *(Calendula officinalis)*. We also had a large greenhouse and a formal landscaped garden in the shape of a clock in which our "mother" herb plants were grown on one of the twelve clock segments associated with twelve astrological signs. Placement of the plants was chosen per Culpeper's classification of the herb according to the astrological sign. I also oversaw the production of herb processing in the farm's food processing plant. I studied the science and art of high-volume herb production. My favorite memory was harvesting rows of valerian root on a rainy day when I had no staff but still had to meet a production deadline. It was just me and two long rows of valerian.

Valerian taught me that fresh root is energetically sweet and a little spicy.

I smelled it all day through the gentle rain because it is that powerful. I also felt its sedating effects after a few hours of handling and smelling the roots and flowers. But, like its stalks that were quite straight and tall, I had no problem staying upright. I was gently sedated, calm, and also somewhat nauseated from the heavy sweetness of the smell. A few years later, when I was a hotline service director at the Herb Research Foundation in Colorado, people would call the hotline stating that they were worried that their valerian capsules had gone "bad." They reported, as is well known in the herbal community that dried valerian root smells like dirty socks. But my valerian from my solo harvest never did and never has smelled like dirty socks. I hypothesize that valerian harvested in the gentle rain may release its sweetness for more extended periods of time than that harvested in the drying sun. I have no scientific or clinical evidence, but I do have some dried roots that still smell beautiful and inviting that I do not need to put in capsules.

Valerian[106] is also quite warming energetically. People who ingest the herb biomedically as a supplement often do so because they cannot sleep, but they might do better to try a cooling plant like chamomile. The inability to sleep is often caused by heat (imbalance) patterns that a warming plant would aggravate. In many herbalists' experience, including my own, some clients report that valerian causes a paradoxical effect in that it seems to act as a stimulant instead of a relaxant. The stimulant effect would be due to the warmth of the root. It usually poses no health threat, just minor discomfort similar to strong coffee. Some traditional texts do identify valerian as a cerebral stimulant, even while recognizing its sedative effects.[107] As we partner with valerian and other healing plants, we become aware of the complexity of living medicine. People can respond to herbal remedies differently because of what they bring to the partnership as their energetic patterns. Also, the climate, soil conditions, altitude, and other growing conditions can significantly influence the power of the herbal remedy. The *consciousness* or awareness of the grower, harvester, and producer also affects the quality of plant medicine. Some plants, like valerian, have a long history of highly attentive growers who consider the plant unique and treat it as sacred during growth, harvest, and medicine making cycles.

Spikenard, a precious aromatic oil used in Egyptian and Eastern civilizations in spiritual practices such as anointing, comes from a plant *(Nardstachys jatamansi)* that is a close relative of valerian. According to legend, valerian was discovered by St. Panteleimon and has been revered in Russia for its calming properties for two thousand years.[108] The root was highly regarded for its healing properties by ancient Greeks and Romans, who considered it a powerful sedative. One of valerian's many uses in European folklore has been as a homemade cough syrup in which the root is boiled with licorice, raisins, and aniseed. This expectorant is for those that are short-winded and have a cough. It helps to open the passages and to expectorate phlegm easily. In addition to being taken as a single herb, valerian works synergistically with chamomile *(Matricaria recutita)*, hops *(Humulus lupulus)*, and lemon balm *(Melissa officinalis)* to produce a calming effect. Valerian preparations are still a widely purchased nonprescription hypnotic and daytime sedative. It does not promote addiction and is applied during withdrawal from benzodiazepines with the guidance of knowledgeable Advanced Practice Registered Nurses.

Consciousness and carefulness lead to the development of knowledge and a caring heart and nurture the insights that can emerge from entering into the complexity of the living world of plant medicines. Herbal remedies may be gentle and simple chalices for healing energy in their whole forms as teas and topicals, but they should not be construed as simplistic. All changes and transformations from partnerships with plants such as valerian are evaluated in a person within the fiery context of consciousness, carefulness, and complexity. It is from within this context that I have developed the following 10-point guideline for best precision Self-care plans.

—Guideline for Best Precision Self-care Plans—

1. Know the plant. It is best to grow the plant with which you partner or have observed it and harvested it in its natural habitat during all seasons for a year. It is best to have someone introduce you to a plant and share their understanding and experience partnering with the plant.
2. Use simples first. Start with culinary herbs. Tiny amounts of herbs are considered for cooking and beverage teas. Culinary herbs are common and familiar, yet the public rarely notices their medicinal applications. How a plant is applied is what distinguishes it as "medicine" from food..
3. Know the cultural context for any traditional herb use, such as whole-plant applications.
4. If an herb or its constituents are considered for partnership following a biomedical world view, know the research on the whole plant

or its constituents and follow the instructions for decoding herbal data in Chapter 6.
5. Seek to integrate evidence from traditional and biomedical/clinical paradigms and your family history when deciding how, when, where, and why to partner with a plant in your precision Self-care plan.
6. Learn to make whole-plant simples.
7. Start with the first step of learning herbal formulations by exploring each plant one by one listed in any formula.
8. Exercise caution when considering herbal supplements that you cannot taste or apply on the skin.
9. Organically grown herbs are best.
10. Be mindful and scientific and be sure to document your plan with stated goals, observations, and evaluations.

Plant partnership in precision Self-care is rooted in knowledge developed over many centuries of observation, trial, and evaluation. Gentle medicine Self-care is an art and science for which some best practices and standards have been derived from common sense, knowledge, experience, and wisdom over time. The abilities of plants like stinging nettle and valerian to heal time and again when applied in specific ways are evaluated within a safety framework referred to here as *Five Rights*.

—*Five Rights of Precision Plant Partnership Self-care*—

The rest of the chapter is organized into five sections and directed to thinking of safety, the fire element, according to five "rights" of plant partnership in Self-care. Nurses in practice use a five or six rights framework for safety in drug administration and it helps. That familiar practice has been adapted here to the five rights of plant partnership in precision Self-care: Right Herb, Right Application, Right Time, Right Dose, and Right Person. These five rights are used to evaluate your conscious, careful precision Self-care plan.

The five rights seek to promote a depth of knowledge and safety that leads to a "fire" of Self-care plan precision. My definition of quality Self-care is *precision*. There is nothing more gratifying than experiencing positive change such as balance in body and peace of mind due to choosing the right plant, at the right time, in the exact right amount, and the right choice of application or combination of applications. I am a minimalist and find great pleasure in preserving plant populations by identifying the precise, that is, the smallest amount of herb, the fewest herbs, the most infrequent applications, and the shortest length of time for that application that must be done to achieve the goals that have been outlined in the plan. Precision can lead to cost savings, plant conservation, fewer potential adverse effects, and improved connection with the plant world and our inner healer. It is the gift of fire and spirit, that of our inner healer, the flame of love in the heart, and a dedicated vision of precision in manifesting the five rights that supports the possibility of the best Self-care plan at any moment of time and space.

It is the fire element that energizes Self-care with a capital S. Yet, the fire element is often under-represented and under-utilized in Self-care. It is easy to become satisfied with plant understanding associated with the first three elements: earth-physical, air-mental, and water-emotional. We can create beautiful healing environments, welcome the plants, learn about herbs, and apply them with caring hands and thoughtful communication. But to bring the fire element into practice and heal through transformation and transmutation with plants as partners, we must cultivate the fire of the spirit, the fire of consciousness, the fire of the love of the heart that would infuse all gentle medicine and Self-care with a special flame that is uniquely ours.

Helena Roerich, an early 20th century spiritual writer and founder of the Agni Yoga Society,[109] wrote of *Agni*, a Sanskrit word meaning fire, that:

> The element of Fire, the most all-pervading, the most creative, the most life-bearing, is least observed and esteemed. The human consciousness concerns itself with a multitude of empty and insignificant considerations, but the most wonderful of all escapes it. ...Much that has been told about the heart must also be applied to the Fiery World, but with particular acuteness. The impetus of Fire is as strong as the structure of a crystal. ...Live embers are needed for the purification of the consciousness; the rainbow flame affirms the striving of the spirit. A multitude of applications of the work of Fire reveal themselves as the most striking conditions of existence. Beginning with the ordinary light formations visible to the open eye, up to the complex fires of the heart, we are led into the realm of the Fiery World.[110]

The fire element is reflected in our consciousness and awareness of thoughts and actions. The fire element and consciousness are *demonstrated* in Self-care in the precision of our plant partnerships, in attention to detail, energetics, courtesy, and kindness when creating and applying herbal applications. In the way, we demonstrate love for Self, others, and the plants that allow us to heal and serve humanity in a greater capacity.

RIGHT PLANT

Many factors affect health patterns. To identify the "rightness" or effectiveness of an herb, you must be able to consciously connect the herb to a change in energetic pattern or behavior. Data from all five rights converge to create an understanding of changes in the pattern. One way to evaluate the rightness of a plant is to introduce the herb and use scaling to document a change in pattern. For example, you might try a cup of cool peppermint tea when experiencing heat in your head, such as from a fever. The heat you feel before drinking the tea is a 10 out of 10 on a scale of 10, with 10 being very hot. If after drinking the tea, you feel that the heat is a three and the discomfort "manageable," you have evidence that peppermint tea does clear heat (fever) indeed from your head, just as traditional evidence suggests that it might. If you continue to drink peppermint tea during the fever with similar results, then you could conclude that the peppermint seems to be the "right" herb for you.

Another way to evaluate the rightness of an herb is to remove that herb. In the example of the fever, you might substitute plain water for a few hours instead of peppermint tea and note any change in fever. Over many years, I have scientifically confirmed that people who experience fever in their head feel better when drinking peppermint tea. But not everyone likes peppermint tea. Despite my evidence, I still practice according to the EOC. When practitioners, scientists, or the public call into question the validity of traditional evidence related to herbs such as peppermint tea, I often suggest that they try a cup of tea the next time they have a fever. The potential benefit of simple herbal applications often outweighs any risk.

WEIGHING BENEFITS AND RISKS

Health decisions are made through an evaluative process of weighing the benefits and risks of action. People's decisions to employ means other than biomedical interventions in the care and comfort of themselves and their families are rarely the result of a lack of education or comprehension or ignorance of orthodox medicine as the "best" care. Research shows that this assumption about people's decisions to do their Self-care is not rooted in ignorance. Studies demonstrate that even people who have access to and knowledge of biomedical interventions often choose to take care of themselves or explore therapies other than biomedicine for as long as they can.[111] My research shows that people throughout choose herbs for many reasons, but in general, they choose herbs because they have weighed the benefits and risks of different interventions. They prefer to use a simple, "least invasive" treatment first. The simplest, least invasive medicine or treatment is perceived to be gentle medicine. Herbal medicines are just that.

People's needs for more straightforward, less invasive solutions are understandable. They do not want to do more harm in the process of solving their health problems. It is almost instinctual for people to want to bring about greater balance in their bodies and peace of mind. What supports the decision-making process is herbal opportunities that encourage informed choices in Self-care based upon the fullest understanding possible of the benefits and the risks of considering Self-care or not considering Self-care.

Safety is a concept that can be oversimplified, leading to gross generalizations. The EOC program offers precision Self-care education that cultivates the 5 Ps, primary prevention, perspectives on energetic health patterns, plants, and peace, all skills that the public does not necessarily have anymore. We find that herbs are not without risk. All Self-care gentle medicines are considered carefully, and the benefits and risks of partnering with plants put in the context of the health patterns. Here is an example of a patient who did not consider the benefits and risks of Self-care. I once had a community client who cut her finger. She worked in a vegetarian restaurant and knew about the healing as well as the nutritional qualities of seaweeds (*Laminaria spp.*). She knew that seaweeds could help stop bleeding. When she cut her finger, she wrapped it in seaweed. Unfortunately, the cut was very severe, and she did not apply direct pressure or elevate her hand, the recommended first aid treatment. The blood pooled and coagulated under the seaweed as expected due to its constituents that are like glue, but, without pressure, the skin did not knit together at all. After many hours, she sought nursing care. The wound could not be sutured right away because there were so many tiny pieces of seaweed in the wound that we were concerned about infection. Infection is a significant concern with a hand injury because the risk of any potential disability due to infection is high. We weighed the benefits and risks of care with her and decided to soak off the seaweed bandage so that the laceration could be sutured as much as possible.

Although the woman's understanding of seaweed's action was correct—that is, she was not ignorant or uneducated about herbs—she did not, in our estimation, realize the seriousness of her hand laceration. Herbs were not the best first choice in this acute-care scenario. I have hundreds of examples of clients with acute and chronic illness, pain, and general discomforts in which herbs have been extremely valuable and safe, especially when compared to the risks associated with long-term use of pharmaceutical drugs or invasive surgeries. As stated previously, one can best weigh the benefits and risks of Self-care with plants as partners by first knowing basic anatomy and physiology and knowing how to triage common everyday concerns such as a laceration or fever. The books *Take Care of Yourself and Take Care of Your Child* are very helpful in weighing benefits and risks to Self-care. I worked with Dr. Vickery, one of the authors of these books, in his company called Health Decisions in the 1990s. Dr. Vickery was a physician-researcher on self-care at the National Institutes of Health Center for Disease Prevention and Health Promotion. He was expert in teaching the public about benefits and risks related to health decisions without instilling fear.

Some subscribe to the fear tactics about herbs or any therapy, including drugs and surgeries. Instead, it is person-centered and safer to provide an inclusive pluralistic approach to care that recognizes that given the benefits and risks of a specific situation, any of these treatments may be best practice at a particular point in time. The guidelines in the EOC program, including the five rights, can promote peace of mind in choosing gentle medicines with the most significant benefit and least risk.

Biomedical and traditional healers alike are resources of cautionary information related to the use of plants. For example, a nurse or physician might warn that excessive ingestion of comfrey *(Symphytum officinale)* can potentially lead to hepatotoxicity because of the amount of pyrrolizidine alkaloids, a constituent within the plant. A traditional healer might recommend that a particular healing plant be harvested only in a special area. Because plants and their specific cautionary issues vary significantly from place to place, any of the cautions presented here are general guidelines related to those plant applications. Safety cannot be ensured entirely, even under the best of circumstances. Children of responsible parents still run out in the road; campfires get out of control, and, despite safety strategies put in place by communities and the good intentions of well-meaning people, properly prescribed medicines still cause illness and death.

People and practitioners who partner with plants responsibly must be aware of safety considerations and the benefits and risks associated with an herb. The regulation of tobacco (Nicotiana tabacum) products is just one example of why we must not rely solely upon external safety standards, guidelines, and agencies to direct health care decisions. Biomedicine may have evidence of a particular plant substance being helpful in laboratory studies, but this does not mean that a human being will benefit from the plant. The response of a person to any healing intervention or modality, such as herbs, is unique. Laboratory and clinical studies provide general information, but the public and practitioners must always be mindful of the potential for an individual response to an herbal application. Caution with healing plants allows us to access our inner wisdom, insight, and common sense in choosing the right plant partners.

As a healing modality, plant therapies have been shown through scientific study and hundreds of years of traditional use to be quite safe. "Based on published reports, side effects or toxic reactions associated with herbal medicines in any form are rare. ...Clearly, then, herbal medicines do not present any more of a problem with respect to acting as potential allergenic agents following human ingestion than any other class of widely used foods or drugs."[112] Herb safety is related, however, to the plant application and the person's knowledge base. The public, scientists, practitioners, and legislators often debate how extensive regulations should be on plants. Should all stinging nettle be exterminated because of its potential to sting a hiker in the woods? How do communities and governments make decisions to protect the public from the potential harm from plants, and how significant is the risk from plants, really? It is the responsibility of every individual partnering with a plant as medicine and therapy to exercise prudent care that includes using a commonsense approach to herbal medicine and understanding that the complexity of whole plants is an important safety feature. Whole-herb applications have a history of few to no adverse effects when applied according to tradition.

The purpose of legal regulation, (more fire element), is to promote the safest Self-care with a substance as possible. It has been proposed that legislative decisions about the safety of a medicinal plant not be judged based on information from one source. Nor should they overreach and deny the public the right and responsibility for their own Self-care choices. Each year, for example, several poisonings in which children have ingested the leaves of a house plant are reported to poison control centers; yet, there are no regulations banning people from acquiring house plants. Instead, pediatric health practitioners inform parents of the potential safety issues with house plants so that they are more aware and can put the plants out of the reach of little explorers.

Some of the guidelines presented by WHO regarding the regulation of herbal medicines have to do with the assessment of herbs and herbal products, evaluation of manufacturing procedures and product labeling, assessment and evaluation of toxic plant materials, and the establishment of a government agency to keep records on herbal medicines commonly applied in Self-care.[113] The regulation of herbal medicines varies from country to country. Some countries exempt herbal and traditional medicines from regulatory requirements; some are subject to all requirements. Some countries exempt herbal medicines regarding registration and marketing authorization, and some require registration. Canada, for instance, has a system whereby the Health Protection Branch of Health Canada regulates plant medicines under its Food and Drug protectorates. It assigns drug identification numbers to an herb based on the therapeutic claims. The American Botanical Council in the United States is an example of an excellent public resource on a country's regulations regarding the safety of herbal medicines in Self-care.

One area of caution that I am aware of as a nurse is the known interactions of herbal medicines and anesthetic drugs. This is not a new concern. In 1998, a report published in the *British Medical Journal* stated that solanaceous glycoalkaloids found in potatoes, tomatoes, and aubergines [eggplant] might slow the metabolism of muscle relaxants and anesthetic agents such as suxamethonium and cocaine.[114] Thus the person may take five to ten hours recovering from anesthesia rather than the expected forty to ninety minutes. These are foods, but there is a similar concern with herbal medicines.

While nurses and other perioperative health care team members have begun to ask about the herbs that people may be taking before surgery, what nurses and health care team members should do with the information they gather is not clear. If a person is taking an herb in Self-care or prescribed by a traditional healer, does the clinician tell the person to stop taking the herbs, and if so, what effect might that have on the outcome of the surgery? Should patients be told to stop taking their herbal remedies used in Self-care two weeks before surgery? Will that take care of the potential problem? These kinds of questions present nurses and perioperative team members with an opportunity to consider all benefits and risks with their patients. The ethics of do-no-harm would suggest that a practitioner would not tell a client to stop taking an herb. The herb may have significant meaning to the person's balance in body and peace of mind. The benefits and risks and the timing of all interventions, surgeries, herbs, and other gentle medicine Self-care discussions need to be open and diplomatic.

RIGHT APPLICATION

The second right has to do with the discernment of the best gentle medicine application, such as is discussed in Chapter 7 Welcoming the Water Element on making herbal simples. When choosing an application, think of precision as speed and specificity. Herbs are catalysts for change. Ask yourself how quickly you want the herb to catalyze change and where you want the change to occur. At the start, consider all applications equally from sublingual drops of alcohol extract (rapid catalyst) to steeping and drinking a cup of tea, to preparing and soaking in a footbath. People generally discuss herbs as if they *should* be taken orally. In culinary use, this is true but not so for purposes of gentle medicine. There are many effective routes for applying healing plants that will promote balance in a health pattern and peace of mind.

The reason people discuss the oral application of herbs is because that is what they see on the market. The herb industry produces oral remedies for the most part. There are some topical salves and a few inhalants and ear oils. One company sells castor oil with the pack materials to apply the remedy as an oil compress, but, for the most part, the industry sells capsules, pills, and liquid extracts. Part of this has to do with the influence of patent law on production choices. It also has to do with the fact that industrialized societies prefer herbs in pill form like pharmaceutical drugs. Many people want herbs to be alternatives to pharmaceutical medications. Therefore, thinking of herbal simples as "gentle medicine" does not always address the psychological need to have a substitute for drugs that will achieve the same result as a drug, look like a drug, be taken as a drug, and yet not have the adverse effects of the drug. However, the wrong application can, over time, lead to adverse effects, not unlike pharmaceutical drugs. A case in point is the improper use of ephedra (*Ephedra sinensis*).

Ephedra is a plant that has been in the Chinese *Materia Medica* for centuries. It is called Má Huáng and is classified as an herb that "releases the exterior." When a person has asthma symptoms, for example, they are unable to exhale. Ephedra opens the pores, releases the exterior, and facilitates the movement of the lung qi, allowing for the breath to descend. The person can exhale with the assistance of ephedra. However, ephedra is rarely, if ever, used as a simple or single herb in Chinese herbal medicine tradition. It is decocted (as tea) in formulation with the other herbs. The media reports that there have been adverse effects of ephedra. But none of these reports over the years has ever been about any harmful effects of ephedra applied according to tradition. The reports have been about ephedra taken as weight loss pills or capsules.

In some cases, the herbal dietary supplements taken did not have whole-plant ephedra in them at all, even though that was what was reported as being the culprit of the adverse effect. The supplement contained ephedrine, a constituent of the plant known to cause specific disturbing adverse effects as well as the speeding up of metabolism, which is the reason manufacturers have put the herb in their weight loss products. Few people have any idea of ephedra's important centuries-old safe use. But the media and the public called for its removal from the market, stating that the plant was "unsafe" when it was the people's applications that were unsafe. They were not using the right application.

Considering the right application for an herbal simple is part of your risk and benefit analysis. Oral doses of a plant are more invasive and therefore carry a more significant potential for risk to your safety. Herbs that are applied topically are, for the most part, slower acting because they must enter the dermal barriers and therefore are typically not considered as high risk. However, technology over the past few years has led to the invention of chemical and energetic means of creating windows in the skin that allow for more rapid uptake of drugs. Some of this topical application technology has been trickling into the supplement industry as well.

Seek the least invasive application that carries the least risk but will achieve the benefit you seek. Even within the category of oral remedies, some carry more risk. A tea poses less risk than does a standardized extract in a capsule for two reasons. First, the tea is tasted. Often teas prepared for medicinal applications do not taste like beverage teas. They are often more bitter, sour, pungent, and just downright strange when we compare a simple or tea formulation with the teas sold in restaurants and grocery stores. There is an adage in Chinese herbal medicine that if the tea formula for a person is correct, they will crave that formula despite its repugnant taste. In more than 20 years of practice, I have witnessed this to be precisely the case. Tea application is one of the safety features of herbal Self-care. If a person does not like the taste, they will be more inclined to question the herbs they are ingesting. Our five senses and our common sense dictate the right application to be considered.

Gentle Medicine Self-study #13: Home Garden Medicine

Onion (Allium cepa) is often easy to grow. Here is a simple but powerful remedy for Onion Syrup that can be made from your own garden and in your own home.

Slice 1 to 2 large yellow or white onions thinly. (Experience the onion's effects on your tear ducts!) Measure ¾ to 1 cup (180 to 360 ml) of honey (or any sugar). In a large container, alternately layer the onion slices and then the honey. Let it stand for three days in a dark corner of the kitchen and then strain the syrup into a colored glass bottle. Store in the refrigerator. The syrup can be taken in spoonfuls just like any cough syrup or can be added to a tea. Rest well after taking.

COMMON SENSE AND COMPLEXITY

Having common sense is a very important component of one's ability to be cautious. Common sense is unsophisticated judgment. Extensive formal herbal education is not required to be able to reason about the right herbal application. Common sense, if it is not repressed, can help determine the right herb, the right application, and the right dose. Common sense is demonstrated as intuition or insight related to a particular experience. As discussed previously, if someone decided to eat cayenne pepper *(Capsicum frutescens)* according to traditional evidence to improve circulation, but they took it in capsule form, they could block one way that commonly has been used to affirm right herb and right dose—taste. Taste and other sensory experiences can activate one's common sense. If a person eats whole cayenne peppers and experiences the hot spicy taste of the herb, they would, at some point, say: "I think I've had enough." Common sense works best when the plant is experienced fully by the senses. Taste, smell, vision, and tactile sensation are all critical to the proper identification of an herb and its safety. Common sense is our personal "regulatory agency."

Complexity is one reason that traditional herbal applications, such as teas and topicals, have had such a long history of safe use. Plants have many different biochemical constituents. Applied in whole form, whether decocted as tea or used as an extract or salve, the plant's action is more complex. Most of the chemical constituents occur in tiny amounts. When we apply herbs, we are using small doses of particular substances. These substances are in a natural, not synthetic, state and are in a formulation as they occur in Nature. Many herbal remedies have been taken in their natural complex form over a long period without toxicity or unhealthy effects. A safe partnership with a plant does not necessarily mean that it is effective, however. Safety and efficacy are separate issues. Continuing to apply an herb in a particular fashion when it is not effective is a waste of plant resources as well as a risk. The right application is evaluated in relationship to the goals that you establish. The effectiveness of each application is evaluated over time.

RIGHT TIME

People know to be aware of the right time for taking pharmaceutical drugs. They know that some drugs are best taken with meals, and some are best taken on an empty stomach, for example. Taking foods at certain times in relation to meals is also done to reduce gastric distress. Foods, as in the case of ginger (*Zingiberis officinale*), also can potentially alter the absorption and metabolism of certain medications, making it more challenging to regulate the dosage of drugs. Herbs, too, can potentially impact food and drug absorption and metabolism.

Determining the best time for an herbal application depends upon the herb and its constituents, as well as your energetic health patterns. A simple example of the importance of personalizing the timing of an herbal intervention is coffee (*Coffea arabica*) decoction. Coffee is a stimulant for most people, so many people drink the decoction of the beans in the morning. Some people drink it anytime. My grandparents drank coffee with milk in the evening after dinner and slept better for it. Every person is different; but, initially, you assign the herbal application to a specific time based upon your knowledge of the herb and your health patterns. After you try an herbal simple, review the effect of the remedy in the context of time. Some herbal simples and formulas are taken with food, and others are not. Some are applied before bed, others upon awakening. I have a bay leaf (*Laurus nobilis*) cordial extract I have made that is best taken before bed to inspire sweet dreams. The timing of a remedy is part of your recipe for catalyzing the changes you have envisioned.

Make a plan for applying your herbal simple that complements your daily routine and diet. Herbal remedies are best introduced in a way that is harmonious with your lifestyle and other gentle medicines and biomedical treatments that are included in your health regime. In recent years, questions about a timing issue, drug-drug, and drug-food interactions have become a very hot topic of discussion in the biomedical world. Although herbs have centuries of traditional application, questions and concerns also are being raised about drug-herb interactions. All herbs and foods effect change in body, mind, and spirit. The environment in which you live effects change in and around you. Therefore, given the concern, I recommend that you partner with plants with the simple premise that *everything that you do when caring for yourself interacts in some way.* Your responsibility in precision Self-care is to understand how anything interacts in your body and respond by adjusting the timing of an application when possible.

INTERACTIONS AND REACTIONS

Herbs interact with everything. Therefore, the most inclusive question related to the evaluation of the right time either before or after the herbal intervention is, "*How* does this herb interact with my drugs, foods, environment. and lifestyle?" The concern is about potential or actual risks associated with interactions. It is just not feasible for scientists to study every possible combination of drug-food, drug-drug, or drug-herb interaction. Most information is, therefore, theoretical. For example, conclusions about whole herb-drug interactions may be made with knowledge about a single constituent in the herb.

There are numerous sources of information that state that anyone under biomedical care should not use herbs because of the risk of herb-drug interactions. However, this is a *potential* risk. In reality, people have always used herbs and drugs during the same illness or about the same time. I remember when the research on grapefruit juice *(Citrus paradisi)* came out stating that it "interacted" with drugs such as felodipine, nifedipine, verapamil, cyclosporin, and triazolam. Human studies have shown that the plant psoralens and possibly the flavonoid naringenin in grapefruit diminish the first-pass metabolism of the drugs by suppressing a cytochrome P-450 enzyme in the small intestine and thereby increasing drug concentrations.[115] How many years did doctors and nurses prescribe or administer these drugs with grapefruit juice, never mentioning the potential effect on drug metabolism? I never remember hearing or reading of terrible results from the drugs. They have been on the market because they have been effective even though grapefruit juice is also on the market. There just seems to be an inordinate amount of fear about drug-herb interactions and little expression of scientific interest in herb-drug or herb-herb *synergy* in the timing of applications.

There are known benefits of interactions, particularly of herbs with herbs. While many herbs are applied singly in cooking, beverage teas, and as medicinal simples, others provide more significant benefit when used in combination with other herbs. Plants and their constituents have been shown throughout history to have a synergistic effect, an ability for the total impact to be greater than the sum of the individual effects. In TCM, for instance, certain herbs, such as Dong quai (*Angelica sinensis*) and Bai shao (*Paeonia lactiflora*), are almost always used in formulation together because of their synergistic effect. Sections of the Chinese *Materia Medica* explain which herbs can best be put together in a formula and which herbs should not be. This information from China of herb-herb interactions is the result of hundreds of years of use and scientific observation of the right time for herbs.

I developed a program for a cancer center, whose physicians and nurses respected the fact that patients, particularly Asian patients, were ingesting and applying their traditional herbal remedies often daily. I consulted on many cases in which we determined what herbs the client was taking that had helped and made plans of care that were inclusive of those remedies. For example, the pharmacists knew the half-life of the chemotherapeutic agents, and we worked the plan of care to be mindful of the client's need for the highest benefit of the drugs. We might suggest that the client stop their herbs while taking chemotherapy drugs and for forty-eight to seventy-two hours after the chemotherapy was administered. Often, because the client was taking the herbs every day, they were okay with stopping the herbs for a few days so that clinicians could have a clear understanding of their body's response to treatment and also to better ensure that the drug would enter their liver pathways as desired.

Cytochrome P-450 is the principal member of the class of enzymes primarily localized in the liver that is involved in the metabolism of many medications. Certain drugs and substances, such as cigarette smoke and estrogens, can *induce* the P-450 system and therefore detoxify chemical substances. Certain drugs, such as cimetidine and acute alcohol ingestion, *inhibit* cytochrome P-450 and therefore, may potentiate other chemical substances, including drugs.[116] The individuality of the person also exists on the molecular level in the cytochrome P-450 system. The range of responses to drugs and herbs is wide. Factors that influence the individual expression of the cytochrome P-450 system include gender, age, race, genetics, and liver condition. Just because an herb is shown in in vitro studies to affect P-450 in some way does not necessarily mean that the herb will affect all people in the same way at all times.

It is also interesting to find that although plants, such as St. John's Wort (*Hypericum perforatum*), may *induce* the P-450 system (inducing CYP3A4 in hepatocyte cells), many plants, including St. John's Wort, also contain the bioflavonoid quercetin, which does the opposite. It is a 3A4 *inhibitor*. What happens in the body when both inhibitors and inducers enter the body at the same time because they are both present in the same herb? Dosage, environmental, and individual factors must be taken into account. Because of the complexity of plant remedies, there may be no problems in taking herbs with certain drugs. It may also be possible that the body can sort out all the chemical interactions and produce the response it needs for greater health. However, it may also be possible that certain herbs and drugs should not be taken simultaneously by the same individual.

It is not possible for a drug in clinical trials to be tested against every food and herb there is, so there will be gaps in drug-food and drug-herb interaction information. From a traditional Chinese medicine perspective, all drugs, herbs, and foods are potentially interactive and/or synergistic. Some biomedical practitioners would have their client believe that there is no choice regarding the integrative use of medications and herbs or foods that may interact— the client must have their medication and therefore, should avoid a specific food or herb. This seems easy, but in reality, it does not work. People want information and choice.

Not every person will consider herbs for health and illness; some people have absolutely no interest in partnership with plants. Herbal Self-care is really a matter of personal choice. Many do prefer to try gentle medicine and herbs before pharmaceutical drugs for fundamental reasons—timing being one of those reasons. They weigh the benefits and risks as to whether or not an herbal remedy will be effective for their concern, and when they look at timing, realize that they do not have to go with a more potent medication right away, they choose herbs first. Timing is an essential factor in health decision making.

RIGHT DOSE

Most of the chemical constituents in plants occur in tiny amounts. When people partner with plants, they are taking small doses of particular substances. These substances are in a natural, not synthetic, state and are in formulation as they occur in Nature. If people have been shown to take herbs in their natural complex form over a long period without toxicity or unhealthy effects, then the herb is considered relatively safe. Some people believe that because a plant remedy is natural that it is inherently safe, but even the most natural of elements, water, can be toxic when taken in the wrong dose. There are benefits and risks associated with every plant use. Often, as Paracelsus is quoted as having said, "the only difference between medicine and poison is the dose."

The word "toxic" is taken from the Greek word "toxikon," meaning "poison for arrows." Many cultures have described the use of plants as poison, and not just from the tips of arrows. Socrates (469–399 B.C.E.), drank poison hemlock *(Conium maculatum)* and died after being convicted of corrupting youth and interfering with the religion of the city of Athens. Although some plants can be deadly, a plant is not labeled toxic or poisonous just because it contains a specific toxic constituent. Botanist John M. Kingsbury writes:

> In order for a plant to be functionally poisonous, however, it must not only contain a toxic secondary compound but also possess effective means of presenting that compound to an animal in sufficient concentration, and the secondary compound must be capable of overcoming whatever physiological or biochemical defenses the animal may possess against it. Thus, the presence of a known poison principle, even in toxicologically significant amounts, in a plant does not automatically mean that either man or a given species of animal will ever be effectively poisoned by that plant.[117]

Establishing toxicity is not a simple matter. The toxicology of any substance is based on many variables, such as the chemistry of the substance, the dose, and the biochemical nature of the person applying the substance. Like timing, the right dose and toxicity are best determined in context. To put toxicity in perspective, in 1998 in America, "about 100 people died after ingesting common, ordinary nuts. In the same period, fewer than

100 Americans died after consuming an herb in some form, and more than 90% of these people were intentionally abusing certain of the more potent members of our herbal pharmacy."[118]

One way to determine the toxicity of a chemical constituent of a plant is by studying the amount (mg/kg) of the substance needed to kill 50 percent of the mice in a particular population. The result of the study is stated as the median lethal dose (LD50). These numbers are not given to complex substances such as those found in whole plants, so they are often not helpful in herbal medicine. But, to establish perspective about the toxicity of plant substances, it is often helpful to know that the LD50 of caffeine, a substance many people take into their bodies every day, is 192 mg/kg and the LD50 of carotatoxin (a substance found in garden carrot *Daucus carota*) is 100 mg/kg. For a 50-kg person to be poisoned from the caffeine in a cup of coffee containing 48 mg of caffeine, the person would need to drink 200 cups of coffee. The LD50 of 192 or 100 is quite low. Many plant constituents found in medicinal plants have significantly higher median lethal doses. To clarify, a higher LD50 means that it takes more of the substance to become toxic and a lower LD50 means that it takes less of the substance to become toxic. Many people ingest caffeine-containing beverages all the time, and although it may not be the healthiest practice, deaths are rarely if ever reported.

Another source of toxicity data is the list that botanists and the FDA use of those plants that are generally recognized as safe (GRAS), generally recognized as food (GRAF), and generally recognized as poisonous (GRAP). There are certain limitations to the usefulness of this classification system. A plant may have constituents that are each classified differently. "There are probably carcinogens, mutagens, and poisons, as well as anticarcinogens, antimutagens, and antidotes in all GRAF, GRAP, and GRAS species. ... Apples are GRAF, and their extracts are GRAS but the cyanide in the seeds are GRAP."[119] Because of the complexity of plants, this system may not really be helpful to people making regulatory decisions based on a specific classification system. But this safety information adds perspective to any sweeping statements of fear regarding safety of medicinal plants for Self-care.

Establishing toxicity of all medicinal plants used by humans is not a simple matter, scientifically speaking. Numerous specialists, including botanists and clinical toxicologists, would be needed to accomplish the task. Practically speaking, it is debatable whether establishing toxicity of plants is vital data anyway. A plant may contain a specific toxin that does not cause any problem to a human when ingested. "Toxicity is rarely an all-or-none phenomenon. Species of plants vary in their content of toxic compounds owing to unpredictable extrinsic and genetic factors. Vertebrate species and individual animals vary in susceptibility."[120] Toxicity often comes down to a matter of right dose and common sense.

So often, practitioners write that herbs are horribly understudied, completely unregulated, and have serious potential for toxicity. This is just not the case. The track records of herbal medicines have been evaluated by leading botanical scientists quoted here, such as Pharmacognosist Dr. Norman Farnsworth, who have had long distinguished careers. They have been found to "not present a major problem with regard to toxicity. ... In fact, of all classes of substances reported to cause toxicities of sufficient magnitude to be reported in the United States, plants are the least problematic."[121] There is a vast body of literature on medicinal plants as well as centuries of use in health care systems. Herbs also are regulated in many countries; however, *they may not be regulated in the same way as pharmaceutical drugs.*

Although many health practitioners in the biomedical paradigm may believe that the system of pharmaceutical drug regulation is the gold standard in ensuring safety with herbal products, the literature does not support this. In the United States, where pharmaceutical drugs are highly regulated, researched, and monitored for safe use, adverse drug reactions and deaths in the thousands are found to result from properly prescribed drugs making it reported as the fourth leading cause of death in the United States. Now with the opioid crisis, drugs are the leading cause of death surpassing injuries.

Although some claim that herbs are under-regulated in the United States and therefore potentially unsafe, the Food and Drug Administration (FDA) and the herb and supplement industry have been very active in promoting the proper marketing and regulation of herbs. One of the roles of the FDA is to evaluate reports of adverse reactions to foods, drugs, and herbs, along with other products marketed for human consumption. Some have suggested that adverse reactions to herbs are underreported. Therefore, the FDA has set up an online reporting system. The data collected and used by the FDA have been called unreliable and unsubstantiated by the U.S. General Accounting Office. Linking any reaction to a specific substance is not always as easy as it appears.

The purpose of regulation is to promote the safest use of the substance as possible. Dr. Farnsworth and his colleagues proposed that the safety of a medicinal plant not be judged based on information from one source.

"Safety or efficacy of a particular drug can rarely be based upon the results of a single study. In contrast, a combination of information indicating that a specific plant has been used in a local health care system for centuries, together with efficacy and toxicity data can help in deciding whether it should be considered acceptable for medicinal use."[122] The World Health Organization (WHO) recommends that member states adopt some form of regulation of herbal medicines to address issues of quality, safety, and efficacy. Regulation can be established for educational purposes. It does not have to be for purposes of controlling people's choices.

RIGHT PERSON

The right person in precision Self-care refers to the question of personal choice. Each person has a right, if not the freedom and responsibility to choose the type of medicine or treatment that is best for them. Think about the ramifications of a law that would place limits on your opportunities to partner with the plants of your choice. Can a regulatory body know best about a person's energetic health patterns that may change throughout a given day and the precision gentle medicine Self-care choices made to adapt to those frequent changes?

Each country has its way of seeking to protect public safety concerning herbs and herbal supplements. The government document regulating herbs and supplements in the United States is called the Dietary Supplement Health and Education Act (DSHEA). It currently protects each citizen's right to choose. The media often misquote the DSHEA, government officials, health officials, practitioners, science editors, and educators. The law can be read online at the following URL:

https://ods.od.nih.gov/About/DSHEA_Wording.aspx

The following URL is a link to the department within the FDA that implements the law:

http://www.fda.gov/food/dietarysupplements/default.htm

The DSHEA is an education act first implemented to ensure public access to dietary supplements in the United States. It is the opinion of the herb industry that DSHEA has adequate authority to deal with any problems in the industry. Physicians have often petitioned in their journals for greater control over herbs, including requirements that herbal supplements be registered with the FDA and pre-market approval of evidence be obtained, showing that the supplement poses no risk of injury to the public.[123] However, they are essentially calling for greater controls over substances that have documented lesser risk when they have yet to find solutions to the problems in their own profession caused by drugs that have a known significant risk to health and that are already regulated by the FDA.

There are certainly herb companies that do not produce the best products. I remember finding an herb product in 1989, before DSHEA, that was labeled "Echinacea" but was, in fact, according to the small print, *Parthenium integrifolium*. It was clear to me that I was responsible for ensuring my clients and I did not receive adulterated products. At that time, I was in the process of harvesting echinacea (*Echinacea purpurea*) root that had been in the ground for five years. One dried root yielded 0.16 grams of herb. I learned first-hand that it is not easy to grow herbs for industry-level production. It is the best safe practice for each person to cultivate and harvest their herbal medicines when possible. When buying herbs and herbal products, research some basics about the herb company's:

1. Commitment to their country's Good Manufacturing Practices;
2. Sources for whole herbs used in products;
3. Designation as Organic or at least free from pesticides and herbicides;
4. Attention to traditional use and preparations that contribute to a strong record of safety.

In addition:

5. Buy herbs in whole-plant form that allows for the inspection and verification of the proper product.
6. Learn the art and science of simples first rather than purchasing formulations. This also holds for essential oil products. Purchase single essential oils and blend them according to your personal preference rather than purchasing someone else's formulations.
7. Very few local stores stock whole herbs anymore. Develop a relationship with a local pharmacy or health food store and partner to ensure product quality and availability.

—*Putting Fear into the Flame*—

Plants are ready partners in the five rights of precision Self-care. How and where they grow, their role in the broader environment and ecosystem, their medicinal constituents, tastes and fragrance, and their natural beauty inspire the soul, stimulate the mind, and catalyze physical changes that lead to healing and cures. Yet with all the power they hold, they go about their "work" quietly, subtly, and gently. In their natural environment, they are easily trampled and are highly subject to human will and consumption. They need our conscious attention and protection if they are to continue to be a ready source for healing remedies. Despite their vulnerability, beauty, and beneficence, there is a steady stream of reports citing public and health professional concerns about the safety of herbal remedies.

It seems as if many have simply forgotten their roots. Plants were our medicines for centuries, so what is the fear really about? Consider that there may very well be some in your family and neighborhood who would question the wisdom of your Self-care plan to partner with plants. How will you explain to people the safety, not to mention the joy that can come from really knowing precision Self-care with healing plants? For many years, I have shared with people the balance and peace that I feel when I am interacting with plants and making medicines that I know will help me and the people I love. I will say it again and again into a world often fraught with fears. Growing and making medicine makes my heart sing! It can make your heart sing too! When our hearts sing, there is no fear at all. I wonder if the fear of plants that some people put forward is just a product of their not having ever experienced their heart singing from the joy of partnering with plants.

Out of fear, we can spend so much effort seeking to assure that a plant will not harm us that we can miss the delight and the promise of healing that comes when entering the green world. Would we "ooh" and "ah" over herbs used in culinary treats, but then suspect the worst from the herbs that would catalyze us to greater balance in body and peace of mind? Agni, the fire element of Self engaged in care, can be a joyful uplifting experience for the spirit. Fire heats water to create an infusion. The fire of the sun gently warms the herbs in a jar of oil to extract the medicinal constituents of the plants. We turn up the fire on the stove to reduce the juice of an onion into syrup. Into the infusion, oil, and syrup, we also add our consciousness as we prepare and cook. We permeate each remedy with our thoughts, feelings, and beliefs about Self and healing. When we partner with healing plants, make our simple, gentle medicines while engaging the fire element, the fire of our consciousness transforms every herb into a gentle medicine.

The act of making medicine is a loving one. It accesses the heart's desire for healing and creates the chalice for the wisdom of the inner healer to manifest. Try it! Don't just believe it. Pick a plant and try it. In our partnership with plants, it is possible to strike a balance when making Self-care decisions, between caution and curiosity, common sense and scientific evidence, safety, and experience. Plants are of the same elements of matter as we are—they are air, water, earth, and fire. We are taught as children to respect the fire. Through gentle medicine making, we can as adults come to enjoy the fire.

Chapter 9
Effecting the Ether Element

"Until man duplicates a blade of grass, Nature can laugh at his so-called scientific knowledge. "—Thomas Edison

Thank you for caring enough about your Self-care plan to have read and worked on the first four elements, earth, air, water, and fire. There is, however, the fifth element, that is another dimension, another gear if you will, to precision Self-care to which I would like to introduce you. The ether element is more challenging to write about as it is of an esoteric dimension associated with consciousness—the transformation of Self, the true nature. This chapter, *Effecting the Ether Element*, is about the development of Self *as* medicine. I have wondered if I should write this chapter. Esoteric subjects, when written down on a two-dimensional page, run the risk of sounding hokey. I have already told stories of the plants such as St. John's Wort that have introduced the notion of the consciousness of plants and opportunities for spiritual experiences within the human-plant connection. This chapter contains suggestions for putting that awareness of plant consciousness and connection into action.

In partnership with plants, we become the students of Mother Nature, the powerful life force for creativity on the planet. The focus of our study is making medicine. In my heart of hearts, I know that the best medicine makers are those who perpetually experience gratitude and awe as to the power, wisdom, and love that can be found in the center of Nature everywhere. Medicine is the healing energy we carry within us in balance and peace despite what is going on around us. Medicine is our nature connected in harmony with the elements of Mother Nature. It is also the remedies and interventions that we create to contain the healing energy we would apply in Self-care and comfort of others. These remedies are the materialization of the elements fire, air, water, earth, and ether.

In the healing arts and science in general, there is often a greater focus on the basic four elements: earth, water, air, and fire. The fifth element ether is quite elusive and therefore challenging to discuss. It has been called "infinite substance"[124] in texts on the ancient wisdom traditions. Ether is essence or life force, also referred to in alchemy as quintessence, that which binds together the four other elements. Ether is essential in healing work. It is an essence discoverable and observable through the alchemical process in which the *effect* of herbal interventions is the transformation of substances in the material plane and of consciousness. The verb *effect* means to "bring into being often by surmounting obstacles."[125] There are many obstacles within and without that oppose any creative process, including the transformation of matter and spirit in Self-care.

One obstacle to surmount in Self-care as in all other dimensions of the healing arts is what to discuss. The healing process—creating and maintaining balance and peace of mind—is often quite delicate. You may have heard the expression that "life hangs by a thread." Nurses can witness to the truth of this statement. Nurses see people's healing process thwarted in the twinkling of an eye by unkind words, improper lifestyle choices, and sudden injury or trauma. As you study your health patterns carefully, notice any effects from interactions with the environment on your healing process, body, mind, emotion, spirit, or consciousness. Healers often teach people not to discuss the details of their healing process to protect the delicate presence of the ether element.

There are some aspects of herbal medicine not typically discussed in a public forum such as a book. Many healers in indigenous cultures will never write down their herbal recipes and remedies. Some say it is because they do not want the information stolen or the plant populations harmed by too many users. But another important reason is that manifesting the ether element dimension of herbalism is a spiritual experience and, therefore, sacred. I am referring primarily to the human-plant connection that people and herbalists alike make.

I decided to share some of my thoughts and stories about the sacred ether element of nurse-herbalism when that field of St. John's Wort appeared behind the hospital. I do so because I know that the experience I have had with the consciousness of plants are a gift that is meant to be shared. Those who have ears will hear. The insights in this ether chapter will help you to weave together of all parts of your precision Self-care plan, a sacred offering of the potential for balance in body and peace of mind. Please know that if you choose not to read this chapter, I fully understand. It may be a bit presumptuous of me to try to give words to the formless and that which should, in essence, remain formless. But I have made my decision to write this ether chapter for your consideration. The choice and the response are yours. We begin with alchemy as the possibility for Self-transformation available to those who practice precision Self-care.

—*Alchemy and the Secret Essence of Lemon Bread*—

Alchemy is an important term from ancient history for anyone to know about who is interested in the more in-depth study of herbalism as a healing art that leads to the transformation of Self. Alchemy is a form of chemistry and a philosophy that was practiced in the Middle Ages and during the Renaissance. Outwardly alchemical methods were discussed in terms of refining the process of transmuting baser metals into gold. Alchemists were also known to be concerned with finding a universal solvent and the ultimate panacea or elixir of life. One of the most renowned alchemists was Paracelsus.

Paracelsus applied alchemical principles in the development of a practice of medicine that stressed the importance of clients' thoughts and emotions. He applied the Hermetic philosophy of *The Emerald Tablet* of the connection of mind and matter in the holistic care of people. Although today Paracelsus might be revered as a holistic physician, during his time, he—like many creative scientists and alchemists—was persecuted. Paracelsus and many other scientists who have studied the ancient scientific writings such as *The Emerald Tablet* knew that life is not only substance but also spirit or essence. Nature, too, is also essence and substance. The Hermetic teachings applied in alchemy describe the concept this way: "That which is above, is as that which is below; And that which is below, is as that which is above." Spirit infuses all matter, and matter becomes spirit. Actively engaging this principle, we can observe that there is a strong connection between the health of the body and consciousness. People talk about the body-mind relationship, but body-consciousness is more than body-mind.

Consciousness is the quintessence, that which binds or integrates all elements in the process of Self-transformation as above so below and as below so above. The mind does not do that. Mind is the air element. It is represented in thought, belief, and reflection. Meditation and prayer can also be conducted from the level of the mind. Consciousness, prayer, meditation, and expressing praise to the Creator are all examples of the manifestation of the ether element and quintessence. According to Hermes Trismegistus, ether essence, which the Greeks referred to as "pneuma," is the "instrument or medium by which all are produced."[126] It is always present where life is, but it is intangible. Hildegard von Bingen, a twelfth-century nurse philosopher, referred to life force as "viriditas," translated as greenness, the principle of life transmitted from God into plants, animals, and gems.[127] This life force, essence, and greenness are what the great alchemists attempt to harness in their healing elixirs.

Herbalists also hold that the real medicine of any plant is in its essence, life force, or greenness. It is the plant's essence that catalyzes a particular type of change and transformation in humans. That essence might also be described as the plant's consciousness. I have also found this underlying philosophy demonstrated most clearly by traditional and indigenous peoples who have a deep respect for all life forms, including plants. They assign names to plants as a way of conveying their understanding of the consciousness of a plant and our connection with it. For example, herbalists among the Delaware (Native American) people refer to tobacco (*Nicotiana tabacum*), a sacred plant, in their medicine gathering prayer as "Grandfather."[128]

Many cultures have records of accessing the consciousness of plants. In recent times, however, these records most often have to do with the experiences that occur in relation to the psychoactive principles of plants, a relationship often described as magical or shamanistic rather than natural or scientific. The crossover between science and spirit worlds is often blurred by certain spiritual and health beliefs or the lack thereof. Scientists and healers, such as Hildegard von Bingen, have identified numerous ways in which plants affect consciousness. Their natural beauty, their fragrance, their action in the body lift our spirits, change our perceptions, and heal us. Yet, some plants are also capable of altering our state of consciousness to the degree that Self-awareness becomes lost. While I respect the choices of those who engage in such plant relationships, I want to be clear as I was earlier in this book when I discussed the negative and positive psychic states that the practices in plant-partnership of which I write stem from a relationship with plants that is fully conscious and aware, amazing but not necessarily magical. The spiritual connection with plants leads to greater insight into their nature that can also be discovered, explained, and integrated by a human partner who is willing to delve into a study that creates a parallel and balanced evolution in botanical understanding. Botanical study takes many forms.

One of my first lessons in effecting ether in herbal medicine making came from my mother. This is not surprising because, as I mentioned earlier, my Cornish Celtic roots through my mother and her father have been the source of plant inspiration throughout my life. Every year, at the Christmas holiday in December, my mother made "Lemon Bread." Lemon Bread is a delicious cake that is baked in a loaf pan like bread. For those who have tasted pound cake, it is similar to a pound cake in consistency, but those who have tasted pound cake quickly recognize that it is not a pound cake. Lemon Bread is exquisitely delicious and in a class all by itself! In fact, it is so special that it is a secret family recipe. I watched my mother make it every year for seventeen years, and on my eighteenth birthday received a recipe card with the instructions printed out by my mother. She swore me to secrecy that auspicious day and threatened "terrible things" would happen should I ever leak the recipe to a non-family member!

What makes Lemon Bread so delicious is its taste and consistency. What makes it so unique is that the recipe should not work from the perspective of culinary science. I find it most interesting to watch the transformation of the batter while I prepare it carefully according to the recipe. I am not typically a cook who follows recipes to the letter because I have enough experience to know how to achieve in the kitchen what I envision. But Lemon Bread is different. I follow the recipe. When making Lemon Bread, adding the ingredients in a particular order is part of the alchemy that ensures the transformation of the batter. You see, when the lemon (*Citrus limon*) is added to the batter, it changes consistency before my eyes. The whole process of learning to make Lemon Bread and now continuing the tradition is an experience in alchemy. My mother never told me about alchemy per se. She simply said to me that the recipe was a secret passed down through family tradition from my great-great-grandmother from New Brunswick, Canada, and Europe before that. But every year, when I begin the ritual of making Lemon Bread, I am aware of the transformation that has occurred in the batter as well as within and around me.

Herbs like lemon are catalysts for change. Many of those changes that occur in Nature are yet to be fully understood. Lemon has a powerful effect on the Lemon Bread recipe. Healing plants each have an effect. They catalyze changes in the environment, in the body, and in medicines that we make—sometimes in ways that may be observed but not always explained. Such is the case with our family Lemon Bread. It remains a secret recipe for which my siblings, cousins, and I are stewards. Some who would try to coerce us to tell the recipe have said we are not stewards but controllers. But the name-calling that occurs is just playful banter. In my experience, people enjoy a good game; they love the challenge of seeking to discover Nature's secrets. Life, like Lemon Bread, is full of secrets. Opportunity for alchemy is everywhere; that is, the opportunity for transformation and transmutation is everywhere.

Experiences and observations in people, plants, and Nature beginning with my childhood interactions with lemon and the secret recipe Lemon Bread laid the perfect foundation for inquiry beyond the substance or chemical constituents of medicinal plants and into their essence. Essence and the fifth element, ether, somehow creates Lemon Bread. Oranges (*Citrus sinensis*) do not. I know because I have tried. Each plant, like each human and animal, has its essence. That essence is vital to making plant medicines that are more than just plant concoctions of constituents. The ancient science of making medicines with plants that transform and transmute includes the ancient knowledge of drawing upon the essence of plants in simples and formulations.

—*Plant Alchemy*—

Spagyrics is the term that refers to plant alchemy. The word spagyria is derived from two Greek words meaning to draw out and to bind together. Paracelsus wrote, "Therefore, learn Alchimiam, otherwise called Spagyria, which teaches you to separate the false from the true."[129] Plant alchemists expand upon the basic science of extraction to remove the essence of philosophical principles of plants through separation, then purification, and finally recombination. In the Spagyrists view these actions lead to an increase and a release of certain curative powers in the plant. A spagyric preparation opens the plant to liberate its stronger curative power. Spagyric preparations always contain the salts obtained through incineration and calcination of the plant residue. Albrecht von Herzeele, a 19th century scientist who wrote *The Origin of Inorganic Substances*, showed that living plants are continuously *creating* matter in that they "transmute phosphorus into sulfur, calcium into phosphorus, magnesium into calcium, carbonic acid into magnesium, and nitrogen into potassium.[130]

Animals also create matter in their bodies. Louis Kervan began preparing for his career as a scientist when he noticed as a young boy that chickens ate mica in their yard, but no trace of mica could be found in them when they were slaughtered. However, the chickens produced eggs with calcareous shells even though they had not ingested calcium from land lacking in limestone. He realized later that the birds were transmuting one element into another. Antoine Laurent Lavoisier, the father of modern chemistry, stated the principle that in the universe, "nothing is lost, nothing is created, everything is transformed." Spanish moss can grow on a copper wire without soil, and seaweeds (*Laminaria spp.*) manufacture iodine. It is this etheric power that accounts for the fact that some plants germinate only in spring regardless of the amount of heat and water applied to them at other times of the year.

Like plants, the human body has a way of transmuting elements. Kervan noticed that laborers sweat potassium even though they had eaten salt. Kervan also did not give calcium supplements to those needing calcium. He knew that to increase calcium in the body, one would provide organic (not mineral) silicic acid, such as is found in plants rich in silicon. The body did the transformation of silicic acid to calcium. One plant used in silicic-calcium alchemy is horsetail (*Equisetum arvense*). Herbalists can often readily apply alchemical principles like this in practice because they work with plants rather than single chemical constituents as is the case with pharmaceutical drugs. By introducing the etheric and alchemical dimensions to precision Self-care, we open up a realm of possibilities for medicine making and healing not only in humans but also the worn-out and damaged soils of the earth's environment as well.

Scientific analysis is an important way of knowing. Learning about the constituents of medicinal plants is one of many perspectives that form integrative insights. But ultimately, the goal of scientific exploration of anything in Nature, in our case healing plants, is to understand the whole, which is greater than the sum of the parts. Scientist Johann Wolfgang von Goethe, whose focus was our experience and perception of the living world and its spiritual as well as material basis, wrote:

> In observing objects of Nature, especially those that are alive, we often think the best way of gaining insight into the relationship between their inner nature and the effects they produce is to divide them into their constitutional parts. Such an approach may, in fact, bring us a long way toward our goal. In a word, those familiar with science can recall what chemistry and anatomy have contributed toward an understanding and overview of Nature. But these attempts at division also produce many adverse effects when carried to an extreme. ...Thus observation

of Nature is limitless, whether we make distinctions among the least particles or pursue the whole by following the trail far and wide.[131]

All material and spiritual healing action in Self-care begins with touching plants. Plants come in contact with the body through the senses: tasting through the tongue, touching through the skin, and smelling through the nose. The person preparing a remedy effects the medicine or essence within that remedy. Many cultures know this and therefore have specific rules about the preparation of remedies so that the medicine of the plant is conveyed as fully as possible to the person in need. For example, in some European cultures, plants are harvested by hand only when specific planets are in certain positions in the sky. In the Mohawk tradition, medicine women, for example, are not allowed to prepare remedies when they are menstruating because it is known that the healing energy of the plants will enter their own bodies rather than stay within the remedy being prepared for someone else.

When we touch plants with both of our hands, we can deliver a wholeness current from our heart, alpha to omega. That wholeness current infuses into the remedy as an energy that can be experienced when the remedy is applied. This flow of energy is initiated in the heart as an expression of power, wisdom, and love and then flows out through the hands. The heart is situated in the nexus of the energy centers in the body where matter and spirit meet. Spirit and matter are not opposites; they are in polarity. At the center of polarity is unity. The material universe is the negative polarity and the spiritual the positive polarity. Matter (*mater*) is mother or yin. Matter (yin energy) provides the chalice for the anchoring and evolution of spiritual (yang) energy in the physical plane. Embracing the energy of the spiral of cosmic return, mater returns to spirit. This cycle of cosmic creation, known in Sanskrit as the Maha Kalpa, is the path of wholeness in which we realize all matter as spiritual essence. Through the nexus of the heart, we find the power, wisdom, and love to unify science, art, and spirituality in the creation of a healing garden and medicine kitchen where we can touch plants on a daily basis.

FORMULATION

Formulating herbal remedies that involve multiple plants rather than simples is another dimension of precision Self-care that evolves with increasing experience and study of individual plants, botanical science, and the wisdom tradition (including alchemy) surrounding medicine making. Formulation is a specific skill often under-represented in the herbal marketplace. True formulation is not "everything but the kitchen sink" mentality. Some product formulators demonstrate their lack of botanical knowledge by putting every herb with a specific known action into a product, ergo the kitchen sink. Instead, formulations are a synergistic combination of herbs that represent different but complementary contributions of the energetic, biological, chemical, and spiritual aspects of the plants that move you toward balance in body and peace of mind.

Formulations typically refer to the herbal remedy designed for a specific person. They should be differentiated from beverage teas, which are formulations, but each herb is represented in such as the small amount and drunk so sporadically rather than consistently that the tea is considered culinary rather than medicinal. In TCM and nurse-herbalist practice, the formulation is most typically a whole-herb tea. The formulator also takes into account the spirit (energetics) and matter of all of the person's Self-care and prescribed health promotion activities. The person's environment and historical connection with plants are also considered during the process of formulation. The transformative healing action of the entire formulation is greater than the sum of the parts—the herbs and health promotion activities, as they would be applied individually.

Manifesting the power of prescription in formulation does require additional mastery in health pattern recognition and botanical knowledge. The foundation for the formulation is knowledge of the character as well as the chemistry of a plant. By plant character, I mean the botany and energetics of the plant, its history, and growth patterns. Getting to know a plant's character is similar to getting to know a person. Relationships with healing plants grow through tea tastings, and herb walks, visits to botanical gardens, gardening, and making herbal simples. Many of the simples discussed throughout this book support the lifestyle and dietary changes that should, according to many traditions, including nursing, be the first interventions introduced to bring about tremendous levels of healing transformation, leaving the application of formulas to very specific circumstances. Formulations are applied in precision Self-care according to the five rights just as is done with simples.

One of the observations that I as well as many of my herbal–teacher colleagues have made for many years now is that while we used to formulate regularly, we seem to be now able to affect the desired result with the least invasive means. We don't seem to need to apply as many herbs in care. Focusing even more specifically on the ancient tradition of suggesting lifestyle and diet changes first[132] with the support of simple herbal remedies, many of us have found formulations less necessary. There is rarely a need to rush to formulation when the benefits of working with the client and developing their connection with the plant world over a few weeks or months before formulation are more than evident case after case.

Working according to tradition allows for the most evident recognition of the moment in time when an herbal formulation is needed. That clear moment emerges as an understanding of a person's overall health pattern as a combination of patterns that are best treated simultaneously so that the energy is transmuted rather than displaced. Often with herbal simples, healing is affected by moving or displacing energy that is stuck or stagnant. Nature then affects the cure because energy is in motion. But with more serious or chronic health concerns, patterns become more interwoven and the imbalances in body, mind, emotion, and/or spirit more deeply entrenched. There are instances when a formula is needed to move energy in multiple directions at one time. That formula must be specific, and this is when you would want to consider Self-referral to an herbalist formulator for assistance with this dimension of Self-care.

Each formula has a leader, an herb that provides the focus and structure for the actions of the other herbs. It is in the assignment of the herb that will take the lead position and the herbs that will support it that knowledge of physiology as well as plant energetic characteristics becomes essential. As noted earlier, I have found the TCM to be the most precise in terms of identifying and delineating plants' energetic characteristics and therefore makes it easier to create balanced formulations that address all patterns at once. Like flower arranging, an odd number of herbs is typically assigned to a formula. Herbal teas made from dried or fresh whole herbs or cut pieces in some cases such as roots and barks, allow the greatest access to alchemical complementation of a person's health pattern(s). Children and adults love to learn to recognize each herb in their tea formula. They often comment that they "see themselves" in the formula much the way a person looking at a work of art might say the same. A personalized tea formulation is a work of art that a person then creatively engages within the act of cooking and tasting. It is inspired by health patterns and a deep desire for the wisdom that can be earned by experiencing the lessons of healing and change.

Change of any kind can be disconcerting. To begin thinking and accepting that plants can be healing, a person must be able to explore plants with an open mind. Comparing a pharmaceutical drug to an herb is like comparing a bowl of crystallized fructose to an apple. It just is not the same thing, both biologically and energetically. The concept of energy, especially as it relates to healing, is not new. Throughout history, people know the importance of conserving energy, preserving energy, building up their energy, and restoring energy. In Self-care, we cultivate our energy or vital power, so that we can apply that energy very precisely in healing. Herbs are energetically different from pharmaceutical drugs because they are plant life forms, and therefore, they have a completely different action that transcends the physical biochemistry of the plant's substance.

Plants, like humans, are energy fields, that emit or radiate energy that is measurable through such instrumentation as time-lapse and Kirlian photography, optical pulse recorders, and galvanometers. They are affected by energy that surrounds them in the soil, the air, and the light. They transform and store energy. Plants respond to and interact within the environment just as humans and animals do, although they do it in different ways. When people partner with plants in precision Self-care, they receive not only the plant's chemical constituents but also the life force or energy of the plant's response to the environment that helps to catalyze their own inner ability to adapt to change and transition.

—*Adaptogen Action and Thinking Plants*—

Within every plant and every human is a seed of potential. Within every baby is a matrix for an adult, and within every acorn is the matrix for the great oak. Humans and plants, although very different in presentation, are very similar conceptually when it comes to energy potential. One manifestation of this energy potential is the ability of plants and humans to adapt to their environment. Humans are marvelous in that they can adapt to changes in the environment by reasoning solutions that ultimately ensure the continued evolution of the species. Plants, too, have been shown to have the ability to adapt to environmental changes. Plants contain signatures for adaptation within an ever-changing environment. They have their coping mechanisms, such as scent, and movement patterns, such as petal closing at night, that keep predators away.

What happens when humans and plants come together and share their adaptation responses is one of the most fascinating and possibly elusive parts of plant medicine science. Several herbs, such as eleuthero (*Eleutherococcus senticosus*) are known as "adaptogens" or plants that seemingly assist the human body in adapting to environmental stressors. Dr. Farnsworth, who researched the adaptogenic effects of eleuthero in humans, said to me once back on 2001 that, "The term adaptogen is used loosely. Some use it to describe a 'tonic' effect, and some use the term to describe a stimulant action to the immune system. The adaptogen effect of medicinal plants is related to the secretion of corticosteroids and the anti-stress effect, but there are probably other effects as well that are not completely understood."

This exchange of adaptation potential or adaptation information is not static. Some people who take ginseng (*Panax ginseng*) experience an increase in blood pressure, while others experience a decrease, depending on *their needs*. Dr. John Christopher called lobelia (*Lobelia inflata*), an herb used for many health concerns including threatened miscarriage, a "thinking herb." Lobelia also demonstrates its ability to think, an adaptogen action. "Where the baby is strong, the lobelia seems to know to assist in healing a tearing and bleeding condition and stopping the bleeding."[133] Numerous herbal medicine practitioners, healers, and plant scientists have made observations of this phenomenon. Dr. James Duke taught me his theory that "All herbs are adaptogenic in giving your homeostatic body a whole menu of phytochemicals, and exposed to a choice, the homeostatic human body grabs those it needs, excluding to a degree those it doesn't need."

Other examples of "thinking" plants with an adaptogen action are black cohosh (*Cimicifuga recemosa*) and angelica (*Angelica sinensis*), which contain phytosterols. Clinical experience has demonstrated to me that these plants affect female reproductive symptoms similarly to exogenous hormone replacement but without the side effects. Because of the similarity in action, biomedical practitioners understandably question the safety of the use of herbal remedies in the same way they examine the drugs they have used for years. However, what they do not know is that research has shown that plant phytoestrogens can "think." "Phytoestrogens are weaker than the body's own estrogen. In premenopausal women, phytoestrogens compete with women's own, more potent estrogen, reducing the total effects of estrogen. As women's estrogen production falls, phytoestrogens supplement this hormone.

When women have too much biological estrogen, phytoestrogens lower the burden; when they have too little, phytoestrogens pinch-hit."[134] What seems to be involved in the thinking process during the human-herb connection is the lock and key phenomenon in which receptor sites on specific cells seem to be able to determine the effect of the herb needed to help the body adapt or restore balance.

Although the adaptogen action of plant medicines remains somewhat of a mystery, researchers may be opening the door to a new "world" of science that might apply to the adaptogen phenomena. Dr. Candace Pert describes her research with ligands, natural or human-made substances that selectively bind to a specific receptor on a cell. Ligands include neurotransmitters, steroids, and peptides. Pert recognized in her research that drugs that are nearly identical in molecular structure can fit the same receptor but have opposite effects. "Both agonist and antagonist were believed to bind to the same opiate receptor, but somehow their 'intrinsic activity'—the effect they had on the cell—was different."[135] Although this is not precisely the same scenario as with the identical herb causing opposite reactions depending on the body's need, it does point to the importance of the "receptor."

In nursing practice, it is clearly understood that no two people respond to the same intervention in the same way. Similarly, no one person responds to the same intervention in the same way at different times. People constantly change, inside and out. We are in a constant state of adaptation. A person adapts at both the level of a whole being and at the cellular level—the world within. Herbal medicines seem to affect both levels. They may present the body with tens if not hundreds of phytochemicals, but something else happens. The body has to choose whether or not it is receptive to those substances. As with the lock and key phenomenon, if there is no lock for the key, then nothing happens, and vice versa.

—Bach Flower Remedies—

One scientist and physician who studied the adaptogenic effects of plants, flowers of plants, and trees, in particular, was English physician Dr. Edward Bach (1886–1936) (pronounced "Batch"). After a career as a noted infectious disease physician in London, in particular as a researcher of intestinal toxemia, Dr. Bach found his purpose in life during a serious illness and took a post at the London Homeopathic Hospital. This hospital continues to serve patients to this day. He studied the works of homeopath, Samuel Hahnemann, and pursued his vision of simple remedies from plants and trees that would heal more so than homeopathy. Dr. Bach found a way of potentizing the flowers from thirty-eight plants and trees using the rays of the sun. Through observational research, Dr. Bach discovered an approach of treating, not a disease, but the personality of the patient. He developed a Self-care system of 38 "healers" or flower essence remedies, known as the Bach Flower Remedies. Dr. Bach found that "Disease of the body itself is nothing but the result of the disharmony between soul and mind.... Any disease, however serious, however long-standing, will be cured by restoring to the patient happiness, and desire to carry on with his work in life."[136] This philosophy is foundational to restoring balance in body and peace of mind.

The Bach flowers are used at the London Homeopathic Hospital and around the world. The dew from the plants, carrying the essence of the plants studied by Bach, is preserved in a small amount of brandy. A few drops of the mother tincture are then placed on 1 to 2 ounces of pure water, and then a dropperful is taken under the tongue. The remedies have been shown to assist adaptation by helping the patient move through emotions and mental states that block happiness and fulfillment in carrying out one's purpose in life. Bach wrote of the system, "The action of these remedies is to raise our vibrations and open up our channels for the reception of our Spiritual Self, to flood our natures with the particular virtue we need, and wash out from us the fault which is causing harm. They are able like beautiful music . . . to raise our very natures, and bring us nearer to our Souls...They cure not by attacking disease, but by flooding our bodies with the beautiful vibrations of our Higher Nature, in the presence of which disease melts as snow in the sunshine."[137]

I have used Bach flower remedies for years with patients and watched with amazement the adaptation that occurs in the life of the individual patient as they take the remedies. When people experience feelings that get "stuck" or stagnant, they are at risk of developing pathology. The solution is moving energy and restoring and refreshing a sense of one's purpose in life.

The Bach Flower Remedies move a person through a stuck emotion. For example, Rescue Remedy is a combination of flowers that Bach recommended for trauma and stressful situations. In one holistic group practice, we routinely offered the remedy to patients undergoing stressful procedures.

For example, children needing suturing were offered the "flower water." In many instances, I observed that after taking the Rescue remedy, the child's need for the parents to stand by them and comfort them was still present, but the child stopped screaming and could listen to the parents and nurse who were helping them through the procedure.

When you are exposed to any kind of excessive stress and start to feel stuck, consider taking Rescue Remedy in your water. There are three other Bach flowers to consider for excessive stress. Walnut is a remedy that affords protection during periods of great stress, such as transition and change. Elm is for when you start to feel overwhelmed. The pattern suggesting White Chestnut is when you have persistent unwanted thoughts that go around in your head that cause mental torture. In all cases, three drops of the mother tincture are taken in a one-ounce dropper bottle of water. Mix and take one dropperful under the tongue three times a day or as the spirit moves you.

—*Remember the Harmony—*
of the Golden Ratio

When interacting with plants, such as tending them, touching them, or applying them in healing, we experience how plants live, adapt, and heal. We also learn more about human life and human healing through interaction with healing plants. When learning and experiencing the science and art of the world of healing plants, we can learn more about what it means to be human as well. Walking in the woods, standing beneath the fragrant pines, or strolling through a garden and stopping to smell the roses, we can learn through our sensory experience more about who and what we are and where and why we exist. As we scan the towering trees of the forest with our eyes, we experience the beauty of Nature. Being able to behold beauty is key to healing, for beauty, especially in natural form, instills balance in body and peace of mind. We find in the geometric leaf and flower patterns the expression of harmony in Nature.

The golden ratio (also known as the golden mean or by its Greek name [and symbol], phi [F]), the mathematical proportion numerically approximated 1.618034 . . . ad infinitum, is, as Nature demonstrates, the foundation of organic harmony, beauty, balance, and peace. Many artists, philosophers, scientists, mathematicians, and architects consider the golden ratio an essential component of beauty, if not life itself. Ancient Egyptians knew the importance of phi in Nature and built the pyramids that still stand today. Leonardo Fibonacci, a thirteenth-century mathematician, found the numerical sequence generated by the golden ratio. The sequence of numbers consists of terms that are the sum of the two preceding terms (1, 1, 2, 3, 5, 8, 13 ...). The plant *Achillea ptarmica*, also known as sneezewort, has a leaf pattern that conforms exactly to the Fibonacci sequence.

Cosmos, from the Greek "kosmos" meaning an orderly, harmonious systematic universe is governed by phi. Flowers blossom into pentagonal shapes, exhibiting phi angles. Sunflower heads and daisies have two interwoven petal patterns that follow the geometric pattern known as the golden ratio spiral. The golden ratio spiral is found throughout Nature, such as in the shell of the chambered nautilus and can be seen in traditional Chinese medicine as the T'ai chi, or symbol of life. Inanimate forms like snowflakes and crystals are governed by other mathematical principles, but the golden ratio describes with geometry and numbers a universal pattern or formula for growth that is found only inanimate forms.

We find in the beauty of design in the plant kingdom and, in all of Nature a connection among life forms. The shell of the nautilus has the same spiraling design as the inner ear of a human being. Science and mathematics clarify the essence of that common denominator or point of familiarity that people may not be aware of at conscious levels. Healing plants contain designs familiar to human genes and human memory. Familiarity is essential in the healing process. As we look out on the garden, walk in the fields or woods, or swim among the sea vegetation and stop for a moment to consider the harvest, we may find that we remember. We not only remember what herbs bring balance to our body's health patterns and peace of mind; we remember our connection with Earth, our beautiful home.

Conclusion
The Way of the Thornless Rose

Roses do not have to wear thorns. I learned this first in the dream world, and then while I was living in *Thorn*ton, Colorado! We had a marvelous rose bush growing up the side of the house. In the center of the bush was a large stalk of 7 long-stem thornless roses. Their stems were so smooth to the touch. I have heard that there are people who can "talk" roses into releasing their thorns. Luther Burbank grew thornless cacti, too, at his laboratory garden in California. What might compel a rose bush to relinquish its thorns? Thorns are protection that is no longer necessary when the environment and the people in it are expressing gentleness and peace.

People seek peace of mind as well as balance in body. This book on the Elements of Care® has provided a step-by-step program for you to create your precision Self-care plan with plants as partners for balance in body and peace of mind. When we feel balanced and peaceful, we are more likely to act peacefully. A precision Self-care plan utilizing all five elements is a formula for peace. The last two Self-care studies may be more challenging as you complete your Self-care plan. The first involves observing your Self-talk and the way that plants might be barometers for the energy that you express as thoughts, feelings, and intentions. This Self-study came to me a few years ago at the prompting of an African violet.

—Self-talk—

This Self-study requires some background. When I was studying to be a nurse psychotherapist, I was tasked with the assignment to observe, monitor, and document my self-talk. Self-talk is the thoughts that enter the mind sometimes due to mindless habits. I was walking down the stairs in my home and passed by a table with one of my African violets on it. I heard my self-talk, and I did not like what I heard or how it was directed to the plant. I heard, "Where are your flowers, and why are you not flowering anymore?" The tone projected upon this violet was very judgmental and condemning too. So, I went to a craft store and bought some faux African violet flowers and gave them to my plant as a peace offering. Within a week, she was flowering again! That was quite a lesson in plant communication and how plants are barometers for our consciousness.

Plants absorb the energy of our thoughts, feelings, and intentions, just as they drink in the energy from the sun and nutrients from the soil. They can manage human energy the size of a small seed to the largest of trees. Plants and humans can communicate harmoniously. Partnering with plants and the act of making gentle medicines is a committed peace offering that impacts Self, others, and plants in the environment.

Gentle Medicine Self-study #14 Self-Talk

As you work the process of creating plant partnerships, notice and journal your self-talk. Observe any thoughts that you have about the plants in your home and environment. Notice if you have any plants with thorns, prickles, and stingers. Can you discern a message in the pattern of these plants?

What peace offering might you give to the plants? Be patient and keep observing.

Journal what you learn.

—*Wisdom of Elders*—

Our insights about Self-care are built on experiences, observation, and study. Over time, those insights accumulate and are formed into wisdom under the guidance of our elders. Hildegard von Bingen wrote that wisdom was less about thinking than about tasting. In Latin, the words wisdom (sapientia) and taste (sapere) come from the same root word. In gentle medicine, we know herbal remedies often by their taste as well as through the other senses. Wisdom and the ability to gain insight into the plant world are acquired through the experiences of the senses. Self-care involves growing, handling, harvesting, washing, and cooking plants. It is a wisdom tradition as well as knowledge of Self-care and the five elements that have evolved and have been passed down from generation to generation. It includes ladling out bowls of healing soup, massaging a painful body with herbal oil, taking a cup of tea, bathing in floral waters, and so much more. The history and tradition continue by our choice to engage plants as partners.

With the expansion of technology-based healthcare, particularly in highly industrialized nations, there has been significantly less interest and investment in Self-care with or without plants. My hypothesis for why this has been occurring is due to memory loss of the ability referred to by Cherokee elder Dhyani Ywahoo as the "turtle mind." In the elder's own words:

> It's just thought regenerating, bringing together the left, right and the middle brain. We call that snake or turtle mind. That's very important. That is the balance of our whole nature. In the creation process, we say it's the emptiness that everything comes from, and it manifests through three fires. One is will. One is wisdom. The other is active intelligence. [It] is for the human being to rebuild—the rebuilding of the rainbow bridges to make the connection between those hemispheres of the brain. ...It is the seat of survival."[138]

Some who have studied the human brain knows that the hemispheres of the brain have very different functions. Still, together, they work as an integrated whole organ, which some scientists describe as holographic in that it has a dimension of functionality yet is virtually unexplored. That dimension is where integration occurs as the conjunction of seemingly opposing forces. Ancient Hermetic as well as twenty-first-century Mayan tradition, suggest that enlightenment is the result of that conjunction or integration of opposing forces or thought. If this is the case, as the wisdom of the elders suggests, then the integration or conjunction of technology and tradition or Nature could affect the healing and survival of the planet and her inhabitants. A focus on welcoming seeming opposites in thought provides a platform for peace of mind and peace in communities as well.

Peace is promoted through cultural expression and exchange. The healing arts are a vital part of the peaceful culture in communities. As people prepare their Self-care plans, they find ways to experience balance and peace, and as they seek peace, communities experience healing. Communities are like a forest of redwood trees. The redwoods' roots are very shallow, but they grow into some of the largest trees on the planet because of their power in community connection. Redwoods rely on each other for growth. Trees serve as symbols for life force and power in Nature.

Gentle Medicine Self-Study #15: Power Object

This is an experiment in Peacemaking begins with understanding how you feel about power.

1. Choose an object that represents your personal power. Study it carefully and write down how you came to choose the object.

2. Make a list of the qualities of your personal power object.

3. Make a separate list of what power qualities you believe are your strengths.

4. Make another list of the qualities of power you need to fulfill as you pursue your Self-care plan.

5. Compare and contrast your lists.

6. Go to your safe place and ask the question, "What is the What is the first step I can take to develop the qualities of power and peacemaking that I need for fulfilling my Self-care plan?"

Trees, as well as plants, often hold revered positions in indigenous peoples' creation stories and legends of healing. One of the most famous in America is the story of the Tree of Peace of the Peacemaker and Hiawatha. The Peacemaker and his spokesman Hiawatha effectively stopped the warring between the tribes of the Five Nations that ultimately became the Iroquois Confederacy: the Oneida, Mohawk, Seneca, Onondaga, Cayuga, and the sixth nation Tuscarora (adopted). They did this by establishing the Longhouse (Kannonsionni) where peace was law and sacred endeavor. In the thoughts of the people of the Iroquois Confederacy to this day, "peace is inseparable from the life of man. ...Peace is a way of life, characterized by wisdom and graciousness."[139] The Tree of Peace was given to the Iroquois people by The Peacemaker as the symbol that represented the shelter under which the Iroquois people gathered in peace and the wisdom that emerged since the establishment of the Longhouse.

Just as health is more than the mere absence of disease, peace for the Iroquois people is more than the absence of conflict and war. Peace as the law is righteousness in action. Right action is ethic. The Peacemaker helped the warring tribes of the Iroquois Nation find their ethic in unity. They realized their strength in unity was grounded not in the notion of *E Pluribus Unum* but in *Ex Uno Pluria*,[140] defined as out of one, many instead of out of many, one. The strength of the whole is made safe through the individuality of the members. The fires of each of the individual nations burn under the canopy of the Longhouse. The Peacemaker gave the Five Nations the symbol of fire, around which they sat together, as well as the Tree of Peace. He also gave Hiawatha and the Nations the symbol of the bundle of five arrows, a symbol of strength through a union. He taught them that while a single arrow can be broken, in unity, as in a bundle, it cannot. The purpose of the union in the Longhouse was to "provide a strength that casts out fear."[141] The Peacemaker established peace through alchemy in the community using all five elements to transform war and bring all nations to the central fire in the Longhouse. Within this legend of the Five Nations, there is a simple model for an ethic to guide the actions of any person who would cultivate peace within Self and community:

1. Begin with a prayer of thanksgiving to the Creator.
2. Chiefs (leaders) need to have courage, patience, and honesty most of all.
3. Think not so much of the present advantage as of the future welfare of the people.

4. Each separate group discusses (delegation) issues within their group, and then one person speaks to others with one voice.
5. Next, the tribes on each of the two sides of the fire compare with their brother so that each side of the fire speaks with one voice in the Longhouse.
6. In the Longhouse, all people are represented. Each tribe passes its decision to the Atotarho, or leader, of all Nations.

This model represents both practical and spiritual aspects of peacemaking and peacekeeping. It suggests ideas for structuring dialog so that all can be heard and represented before the fire of transformation. Communication, dialog, and diplomacy are fundamental skills for building caring communities that provide support for Self-care with plants as partners that would bring hope for balance in body and peace of mind to all.

— *Learning from the Lemon Balm Lawn*—

To conclude this book on *Gentle Medicine for Balance in Body and Peace of Mind*, I have chosen to partner with a very special plant. When you think about precision Self-care with plants as partners, remember lemon balm (*Melissa officinalis*). In the language of herbs and flowers, lemon balm represents "memories."[142] The very name of this plant, "balm," suggests a way of healing that is gentle. Remember that herbs are gentle medicine. The message of lemon balm is embedded in the story of one of my most recent encounters with the plant.

A few years ago, after selling our medicine house, we rented a townhouse in the Chicago area. I chose lemon balm and only lemon balm to plant in the tiny garden space allotted by the owner of the property. It grew beautifully, was fragrant and a wonderful addition to my summer beverage teas. I dried the leaves for sound sleep tea in winter and put the fresh leaves in my bathwater. One year, the lawn around the dog fence turned brown in the winter. That was unusual. We were planning to replace the areas of the lawn where there had been discoloration until I realized that the lemon balm had moved into the bare spots. At first, we decided that it might be okay to have a lemon balm lawn! Then we decided that we had best replace the lawn, until something beautiful happened. The lemon balm started pulling in the grass. As we watched over two weeks, the lemon balm reseeded the lawn for us and moved back into her original place in the garden! It really was quite amazing and helpful to us.

The takeaway lessons from the lemon balm lawn are:
1. Choosing one plant as a partner can be enough for all of your needs. There is no need to stress about learning numerous plants.
2. Be patient and observant, and the plants may surprise you and even save you money and time...if not, your life!

—Simples for Turning the Dial—

Partnering with plants can inspire changes in your life, your rhythm, and your vibration. Consider that dealing with excessive stress may only require a "turning of the dial" in your vibration to get your energy moving in a positive spiral that reaffirms your life purpose and raises your joyful spirit. The Bach flowers mentioned previously can help move through the emotions related to stress: Rescue Remedy, Walnut, Elm, and White Chestnut. The Five Element Foot Bath in chapter 7 is one of the most thorough and all-encompassing healing remedies on the planet that clears and moves energy in body, mind, emotion, and spirit. Get in a full body bath with Epsom salts and your favorite herbs to clear your energy field of all negativity. Clear all negativity and irritability known as *imperil*[143] by also putting cotton in your ears with a drop of mullein flower ear oil on it while you sip 7 drops of valerian extract in a half cup of warm water. Consider taking time out with your friends and family daily for tea to change the overall vibration of your home and community. Partner with plants to create change where you are. Protect your Self and protect your peace!

As you transition to a life of balance in body and peace of mind through precision Self-care with plants as your partners, remember to "stop and smell the roses" or the lemon balm! Remember that a time of transition follows a change. Change is not transition. Transition is the time that it takes for the adaptation to and manifestation of the changes you have decided to make in your life. Change is a spark, and transition is fire; change is a breath, and transition is wind; change is a dewdrop and transition is river; change is an acorn and transition is an oak tree. The energy of a fiery transition can range between that of a warming blaze in a fireplace on a cold winter night or a wildfire out of control in a treasured national park. The energy of wind or air transition can be a simple as taking a deep breath as one stretches when getting out of bed in the morning or as chaotic as a tornado. Water transition may be seemingly still as the dewdrop suspended on the blade of grass or powerfully gushing over rocks and carving through a ravine in Colorado's Rocky Mountains. Earth transition can be the simple seed touching the earth, waiting for the rain to soften its outer surface and release its potential into the soil or the plant or tree reaching upward and spreading its leaves to receive the warmth and nourishment of the sun. Transitions are dynamic fire, air, water, and earth patterns that express our humanity, the way in which we live our lives and serve others.

Animals and plants, as well as human beings, experience change and transition as a daily occurrence. Within each person, plant, and animal is the potential for embracing change and transition as a means to growth and evolution of consciousness that is progress towards a harmonious life of peace, the way of the thornless rose. As is the Peacemaker's vision, you can find ways to permit your arrow of 5 elements to be bundled with others who would pursue strength in union. Your individual spark can be part of humanity's bonfire of spiritual change. Each breath you take can join the winds of changing perceptions. Each drop of water you make in your body can flow with the rain-to-ocean cycle. Every cell of skin and drop of sweat or blood you shed returns to the earth.

Your five-element Self-care plan does make a difference. Do not underestimate the power of simples that you make with beautiful intentions. Share your knowledge with others and remember the children most, especially those who need your Self-care wisdom.

Consider what the role of Self-care with plants as partners will be in the future. It may be difficult to predict at this time, but one thing is clear. The time is now to make decisions about primary prevention, plants, peace, and patterns that individually and collectively as members of caring communities support our children and grandchildren as they navigate climate change within and without. They need the simple hope of knowing that we are fully committed to forging a future that will welcome the way of the thornless rose and nurturing balance in body and peace of mind for all.

Invitation to Plant New Seeds and Take the Next Step

Welcome to the Self-care Institute at Golden Apple Healing Arts.

Please visit the Golden Apple website:
www.GoldenAppleHealingArts.com
- Access 100s of Self-care Resources and Videos
- Join the Self-Care League – Free Monthly Webinars with Dr. Martha and Guests
- Educational Programs and Retreats
- Become Certified in the Elements of Care® Program
- Virtual and In Person Bamboo Bridge Global Tea Houses
- And more...!

Personal Growth with Dr. Martha
www.DrMarthaLibster.com.

Endnotes

1. Martha Libster, *Herbal Diplomats: The Contribution of Early American Nurses (1830-1860) to Nineteenth Century Healthcare Reform and the Botanical Medical Movement* (Wauwatosa, WI: Golden Apple Publications, 2004), 59.
2. Martha Libster and Betty Ann McNeil, Enlightened Charity: The holistic nursing care, education, and *Advices Concerning the Sick* of Sister Matilda Coskery, 1799 – 1870. (Wauwatosa, WI: Golden Apple Publications, 2009)
3. Richard Louv, *Last Child in the Woods: Saving Our Children from Nature-Deficit Disorder* (Chapel Hill, North Carolina: Algonquin Books of Chapel Hill, 2005).
4. Norman Farnsworth et al., "Medicinal Plants in Therapy.," *Bulletin of the World Health Organization* 63, no. 6 (1985).
5. Merriam-Webster, *Merriam-Webster's Collegiate Dictionary*, 10th ed. (Springfield, Massachusetts: Merriam-Webster, 1999).
6. Martha Libster and Betty Ann McNeil, *Enlightened Charity: The Holistic Nursing Care, Education and Advices Concerning the Sick of Sister Matilda Coskery*, (1799-1870). (Wauwatosa, WI: Golden Apple Publications, 2009), 178-79.
7. Martha Libster, *Herbal Diplomats: The Contribution of Early American Nurses (1830-1860) to Nineteenth Century Healthcare Reform and the Botanical Medical Movement* (Wauwatosa, WI: Golden Apple Publications, 2004).
8. James Fries and Donald Vickery, Take Care of Yourself., (Boston, MA: Da Capo Press, 2017). 6275.
9. Jacob Bigelow, "On Self-Limited Diseases: A Discourse Delivered before the Massachusetts Medical Society at Their Annual Meeting, May 27, 1835," in *Nature in Disease: Illustrated in Various Discourses and Essays* (Boston: Phillips, Sampson, and Company, 1859).
10. Florence Nightingale, *Notes on Nursing: What It Is and What It Is Not* (Edinburgh, Scotland: Churchill Livingstone, 1980, Originally published 1859), 110.
11. Libster, *Herbal Diplomats: The Contribution of Early American Nurses (1830-1860) to Nineteenth Century Healthcare Reform and the Botanical Medical Movement*.
12. Ibid.
13. Lowell S Levin and Ellen L Idler, *The Hidden Health Care System* (Wauwatosa, WI: Golden Apple Publications, 2010).
14. Dorothea Orem, *Nursing Concepts of Practice.*, 6 ed. (St. Louis, MO: Mosby, 2001); Levin and Idler, *The Hidden Health Care System*
15. Martha Libster, *Herbal Diplomats: The Contribution of Early American Nurses (1830-1860) to Nineteenth-Century Health Care Reform and the Botanical Medical Movement* (Wauwatosa, WI: Golden Apple Publications, 2004).
16. Merriam-Webster, *Merriam-Webster's Collegiate Dictionary*.
17. Peter Tompkins and Christopher Bird, *The Secret Life of Plants* (New York: Harper & Row, 1973).
18. Ibid., xiii.
19. Martha Libster, "Elements of Care: Nursing Environmental Theory in Historical Context," *Holistic Nursing Practice* 22, no. 3 (2008).
20. Merriam-Webster, *Merriam-Webster's Collegiate Dictionary*.
21. Martha Libster, *Demonstrating Care: The Art of Integrative Nursing* (Albany, New York: Delmar Thomson Learning, 2001).

22. Fritjof Capra, *The Tao of Physics* (New York: Bantam Books, 1975), 117.
23. Ibid.
24. Johann Wolfgang Goethe, *The Metamorphosis of Plants* (Cambridge, Massachusetts: MIT Press, 2009), 112.
25. William Bridges and Susan Bridges, *Managing Transitions: Making the Most of Change* (Philadelphia, PA: DaCapo Press, 2016).
26. A substance that increases overall, nonspecific resistance to stress.
27. A substance that improves overall general health.
28. A substance that soothes by providing a protective coating and relieving inflammation of the membranes.
29. A substance that gradually changes the metabolism and elimination in the body to improve general health. Formerly known as blood cleansers.
30. A substance that expels parasites from the body.
31. A substance that promotes wound healing.
32. Juan Mascaro, *The Upanishads: Translations from the Sanskrit with an Introduction by Juan Mascaro.* (New York: Penguin Books, 1965).
33. An herbal is a collection of descriptions of medicinal plants that typically includes common and scientific botanical names, growth patterns, medicinal and culinary properties and applications, toxicity, and history.
34. W. A. Brown, "The Placebo Effect," *Scientific American* 278, no. 1 (1998).
35. Merriam-Webster, *Merriam-Webster's Collegiate Dictionary*.
36. Margaret Fuller, "Woman in the Nineteenth Century," https://archive.vcu.edu/english/engweb/transcendentalism/authors/fuller/woman1.html.
37. Dennis Hauck, *The Emerald Tablet: Alchemy for Personal Transformation* (New York: Penguin Putnam Inc., 1999).
38. Michael Calabria, *Florence Nightingale in Egypt and Greece* (New York: State University of New York Press, 1997).
39. John Matthews, *Drinking from the Sacred Well* (New York: Harper Collins, 1998).
40. Mascaro, *The Upanishads: Translations from the Sanskrit with an Introduction by Juan Mascaro.*
41. Priyadaranjan Ray and Hirendra Gupta, *Caraka Samhita: A Scientific Synopsis* (New Delhi: Indian National Science Academy, 1965).
42. Jean Maveric, *Hermetic Herbalism: The Art of Extracting Spagyric Essences* (Rochester, Vermont: Inner Traditions, 2020).
43. Orem, *Nursing Concepts of Practice*.
44. Margaret Newman, *Health as Expanding Consciousness* (New York: National League for Nursing Press, 1994).
45. Rupert Sheldrake, *The Presence of the Past: Morphic Resonance and the Habits of Nature* (Rochester, Vermont: Park Street Press, 1995), 113.
46. Ibid., 367.
47. Barbara Griggs, *Green Pharmacy* (Rochester, VT: Healing Arts Press, 1991), 97.
48. Biodynamic Association, "What Is Biodynamics?," https://www.biodynamics.com/what-is-biodynamics.
49. Bob Flaws, *The Tao of Healthy Eating : Dietary Wisdom According to Traditional Chinese Medicine* (Boulder, CO: Blue Poppy Press, 1998).
50. Martha Mathews Libster, "The Tao of Integrative Nursing Assessment (TINA): An East-West Model for Precision, Complementarity, and Inclusion in Relationship-Centered Care," *Holistic Nursing Practice*, no. (In press) (2022).

51. Merriam-Webster, *Merriam-Webster's Collegiate Dictionary*.
52. Ibid.
53. Shigeaki Baba, Olayiwola Akerele, and Yuji Kawaguchi, "Natural Resources and Human Health: Plants of Medicinal and Nutritional Value. Proceedings of the 1st Who Symposium on Plants and Health for All: Scientific Advancement, Kobe, Japan. August 1991.," (Amsterdam: Elsevier, 1992), 87.
54. Lawrence Kincheloe, "Herbal Medicines Can Reduce the Costs in Hmo.," *Herbalgram* 41 (1997).
55. Richard Ondrizek et al., "An Alternative Medicine Study of Herbal Effects on the Penetration of Zona-Free Hamster Oocytes and the Integrity of Sperm Deoxyribonucleic Acid," *Fertility and Sterility* 71, no. 3 (1999).
56. Albert Leung and Steven Foster, *Encyclopedia of Common Natural Ingredients Used in Food, Drugs, and Cosmetics*, 2nd ed. (New York: John Wiley & Sons, 1996), xv.
57. Varro Tyler and Steven Foster, *Tyler's Honest Herbal*, 4th ed. (New York: Haworth Herbal Press, 1999).
58. Bonnie O'Connor, *Healing Traditions: Alternative Medicine and the Health Professions* (Philadelphia: University of Pennsylvania Press, 1995); Sally Thorne, "Health Belief Systems in Perspective," *Journal of Advanced Nursing* 18, no. 12 (1993).
59. Merriam-Webster, *Merriam-Webster's Collegiate Dictionary*.
60. World Health Organization, "Fact Sheet No. 134 Traditional Medicine," (Geneva, Switzerland: W.H.O., 2003), 1.
61. Michael Balick and Paul Alan Cox, *Plants, People, and Culture the Science of Ethnobotany* (New York: Scientific American Library, 1996), 5.
62. Libster, *Herbal Diplomats: The Contribution of Early American Nurses (1830-1860) to Nineteenth Century Healthcare Reform and the Botanical Medical Movement*.
63. Daniel E Moerman, *Native American Ethnobotany* (Portland, Or: Timber Press, 1998).
64. Steve Wall, *Wisdom's Daughters: Conversations with Women Elders of Native America* (New York: Harper Perennial, 1993).
65. David Eisenberg et al., "Trends in Alternative Medicine Use in the United States, 1990-1997: Results of a Follow-up National Survey," *JAMA* 280, no. 18 (1998): 1572.
66. Libster, *Herbal Diplomats: The Contribution of Early American Nurses (1830-1860) to Nineteenth Century Healthcare Reform and the Botanical Medical Movement*, 248-50.
67. "Cultural Diplomacy: Demonstrating Person-Centered Care and Coaching " *Perspectives on Cultural Diplomacy* Vol. 1 (2015).
68. Levin and Idler, *The Hidden Health Care System* 72.
69. Ibid.; Fries and Vickery, *Take Care of Yourself*.
70. Ruth Davis, "Understanding Ethnic Women's Experiences with Pharmacopeia.," *Health Care for Women International* 18 (1997): 433.
71. Dan Bensky and Andrew Gamble, *Chinese Herbal Medicine: Materia Medica* (Seattle, Washington: Eastland Press, 1993).
72. W. Bowers, "Chlorophyll in Wound Healing and Suppurative Disease.," *American Journal of Surgery* 73, no. 1 (1947).
73. Davis, "Understanding Ethnic Women's Experiences with Pharmacopeia.," 425.
74. Libster, *Herbal Diplomats: The Contribution of Early American Nurses (1830-1860) to Nineteenth-Century Health Care Reform and the Botanical Medical Movement*.
75. *Herbal Diplomats: The Contribution of Early American Nurses (1830-1860) to Nineteenth Century Healthcare Reform and the Botanical Medical Movement*.

76. Wall, *Wisdom's Daughters: Conversations with Women Elders of Native America*, 261.
77. William Anderson, *Green Man: The Archetype of Our Oneness with the Earth* (London: HarperCollins, 1990).
78. Larry Dossey, "Being Green: On the Relationships between People and Plants," Alternative Therapies in Health and Medicine 7, no. 3 (2001): 139.
79. Charles A Lewis, *Green Nature/Human Nature the Meaning of Plants in Our Lives* (Urbana, IL: University of Illinois Press, 1996).
80. Carl G. Jung, *Dreams*, Bollingen Series, (Princeton, N.J.: Princeton University Press, 1974).
81. Olayiwola Akerele, Vernon Heywood, and Hugh Synge, eds., *The Conservation of Medicinal Plants* (Cambridge: Cambridge University Press, 1991).
82. Charles Anyinam, "Ecology and Ethnomedicine: Exploring Links between Current Environmental Crisis and Indigenous Medical Practices," *Social Science & Medicine* 40, no. 3 (1995).
83. Ibid., 323.
84. Rosita Arvigo, Nadine Epstein, and Marilyn Yaquinto, *Sastun : My Apprenticeship with a Maya Healer* (San Francisco: HarperSanFrancisco, 1994).
85. *World Health Organization, Guidelines on the Conservation of Medicinal Plants* (Geneva: World Health Organization, 1993); *The Conservation of Medicinal Plants: Proceedings of the International Consultation 1988 Chiang Mai, Thailand*. (Cambridge: Cambridge University Press, 1991).
86. Johann Wolfgang Goethe and Jeremy Naydler, *Goethe on Science* (Edinburgh: Floris Books, 1996).
87. Phoebe Bendit and Laurence Bendit, *Our Psychic Sense: A Clairvoyant and a Psychiatrist Explain How It Works* (London: Quest Books, 1958).
88. Ibid., 109.
89. Ellen Langer, *Mindfulness* (Reading, Massachusetts: Perseus Books, 1989), 138.
90. Ibid., 10.
91. Ibid.
92. Libster and McNeil, *Enlightened Charity: The Holistic Nursing Care, Education and Advices Concerning the Sick of Sister Matilda Coskery, (1799-1870)*.
93. H. C. Alfred Vogel, *The Nature Doctor: A Manual of Traditional and Complementary Medicine* (New Canaan, Connecticut: Keats Publishing, 1991).
94. Libster and McNeil, *Enlightened Charity: The Holistic Nursing Care, Education and Advices Concerning the Sick of Sister Matilda Coskery*, (1799-1870).
95. Shakers, *Receipt Book*, Fruitlands Museum - Shaker Manuscripts - Reel 1.3.
96. Canterbury Shaker Nurses, *Infirmary Recipe Book* (Sabathday Lake, Maine: Sabathday Lake Shaker Village Archives, 1841?-1873), 9.
97. George Wood and Franklin Bache, *The Dispensatory of the United States of America* (Philadelphia: Grigg & Elliot, 1839), 1065.
98. George Vithoullkas, *The Science of Homeopathy* (New York: Grove Press, 1980).
99. Paramahansa Yogananda, *The Bhagavad Gita* (Los Angeles: Self-Realization Fellowship, 1995).
100. J. Duggan and S. Duggan, *Edgar Cayce's Massage, Hydrotherapy, and Healing Oils*. (Virginia Beach, Virginia: Inner Vision Publishing Company, 1989).
101. Martha Libster, *Science of Energy Flow: Foot Reflexology with Herbal Stress Relief* (Wauwatosa, WI: Golden Apple Publications, 2014).

102. Olof Alexandersson, *Living Water: Viktor Schauberger and the Secrets of Natural Energy* (Bath, UK: Gateway Books, 1997).
103. Merriam-Webster, *Merriam-Webster's Collegiate Dictionary*.
104. Norman Farnsworth, Preclinical Assessment of Medicinal Plants. In Baba, Akerele, and Kawaguchi, "Natural Resources and Human Health: Plants of Medicinal and Nutritional Value. Proceedings of the 1st Who Symposium on Plants and Health for All: Scientific Advancement, Kobe, Japan. August 1991.," 87.
105. Balick and Cox, *Plants, People, and Culture the Science of Ethnobotany*.
106. *The name "valerian" is derived from the Latin valere, meaning "to be well." Valerian is a perennial and likes to grow in moist environments and is often found along streams, in damp meadows, and woodlands. Valerian can grow to a height of 2 to 5 feet (0.6 to 1.5 meters).*
107. Harvey Wickes Felter and John Uri Lloyd, *King's American Dispensatory*, 18th ed., 3d rev ed. (Sandy, Oregon: Eclectic Medical Publications, 1983).
108. Igor Zevin, *A Russian Herbal: Traditional Remedies for Health and Healing* (Rochester, Vermont: Healing Arts Press, 1997).
109. Yoga is that "supreme bridge to cosmic attainment." Agni yoga is "a path not of physical disciplines, meditation, or asceticism—but of practice in daily life. It is the yoga of fiery energy, of consciousness, of responsible, directed thought. It teaches that the evolution of the planetary consciousness is a pressing necessity and that, through individual striving, it is an attainable aspiration for mankind."
110. Helena Roerich, *Fiery World 1* (New York: AgniYoga Society, 1933).
111. Levin and Idler, *The Hidden Health Care System*
112. Norman Farnsworth, "Relative Safety of Herbal Medicines.," *Herbalgram* 29 (1993).
113. World Health Organization, "Guidelines for the Appropriate Use of Herbal Medicines," in *WHO Regional Publications* (Geneva1998).
114. Janice Tanne, "Food and Drugs Alter Response to Anesthesia," *BMJ: British Medical Journal* 317, no. 7166 (1998).
115. Uwe Fuhr, "Drug Interactions with Grapefruit Juice. Extent, Probable Mechanism and Clinical Relevance," *Drug Safety : An International Journal of Medical Toxicology and Drug Experience* 18, no. 4 (1998).
116. Jonathan Treasure, "Herbal Pharmacokinetics," *Journal of the American Herbalist Guild* 1, no. 1 (2000).
117. John Kingsbury, "The Problem of Poisonous Plants," in *Toxic Plants*, ed. A. Douglas Kinghorn (New York: Columbia University Press, 1979).
118. James Duke, *Dr. Duke's Essential Herbs* (Emmaus, Pennsylvania: Rodale, Inc., 1999).
119. *Handbook of Phytochemical Constituents of Gras Herbs and Other Economic Plants* (Boca Raton, Florida: CRC Press, 1992).
120. Kingsbury, "The Problem of Poisonous Plants," 5.
121. Farnsworth, "Relative Safety of Herbal Medicines.," 36H.
122. Norman Farnsworth et al., "Medicinal Plants in Therapy.," *Bulletin of the World Health Organization* 63, no. 6 (1985): 965.
123. Loren Israelson and Thomas Aarts, "Industry Needs to Re-Think Dshea," *Herbalgram* 58 (2003).
124. Helena Blavatsky, *The Secret Doctrine: The Synthesis of Science, Religion, and Philosophy* (London: The Theosophical Publishing Co, 1888), 671.
125. Merriam-Webster, *Merriam-Webster's Collegiate Dictionary*.

126. Blavatsky, *The Secret Doctrine: The Synthesis of Science, Religion, and Philosophy*, 672.
127. Hildegard von Bingen and Bruce Hozeski, *Hildegard Von Bingen's Mystical Visions* (Santa Fe: Bear & Company, 1986), xxvii.
128. Gladys Tantaquidgeon, *Folk Medicine of the Delaware and Related Algonkian Indians* (Harrisburg: Pennsylvania Historical and Museum Commission, 1972), 13.
129. Manfred Junius, *Practical Handbook of Plant Alchemy* (New York: Inner Traditions, 1985), 1.
130. Tompkins and Bird, *The Secret Life of Plants*, 278.
131. Goethe and Naydler, *Goethe on Science*, 36, 49.
132. Libster, "The Tao of Integrative Nursing Assessment (TINA): An East-West Model for Precision, Complementarity, and Inclusion in Relationship-Centered Care."
133. John Christopher and Cathy Gileadi, *Every Woman's Herbal* (Springville, Utah: Christopher Publications, 1987), 47.
134. James Duke, *The Green Pharmacy* (Emmaus, Pennsylvania: Rodale Press, 1997), 323.
135. Candice Pert, *Molecules of Emotion* (New York: Scribner, 1997), 81.
136. Edward Bach, Judy Howard, and John Ramsell, *The Original Writings of Edward Bach* (Essex, England: C. W. Daniel Co., 1990), 50-51.
137. Ibid., 62.
138. As cited in Bobette Perrone, H. Henrietta Stockel, and Victoria Krueger, *Medicine Women, Curanderas, and Women Doctors*, 1st ed. (Norman: University of Oklahoma Press, 1989), 75.
139. Paul Wallace, *The White Roots of Peace* (Philadelphia: University of Pennsylvania Press, 1946), 7.
140. Ibid., 31.
141. Ibid., 34.
142. K. Gips, *Flora's Dictionary: The Victorian Language of Herbs and Flowers*. (Chagrin Falls, OH: TM Publications, 1990), 73.
143. Martha Libster, "Transmuting Imperil: Insight on the Healing Art from Mdm. Helena Roerich," *Golden Apple Monographs*, no. January (2010).

References

Akerele, Olayiwola, Vernon Heywood, and Hugh Synge, eds. *The Conservation of Medicinal Plants*. Cambridge: Cambridge University Press, 1991.

Alexandersson, Olof. *Living Water: Viktor Schauberger and the Secrets of Natural Energy*. Bath, UK: Gateway Books, 1997.

Anderson, William. *Green Man: The Archetype of Our Oneness with the Earth*. London: HarperCollins, 1990.

Anyinam, Charles. "Ecology and Ethnomedicine: Exploring Links between Current Environmental Crisis and Indigenous Medical Practices." [In eng]. *Social Science & Medicine* 40, no. 3 (1995): 321-9.

Arvigo, Rosita, Nadine Epstein, and Marilyn Yaquinto. *Sastun: My Apprenticeship with a Maya Healer*. San Francisco: Harper San Francisco, 1994.

Baba, Shigeaki, Olayiwola Akerele, and Yuji Kawaguchi. "Natural Resources and Human Health: Plants of Medicinal and Nutritional Value. Proceedings of the 1st Who Symposium on Plants and Health for All: Scientific Advancement, Kobe, Japan. August 1991." Amsterdam: Elsevier, 1992.

Bach, Edward, Judy Howard, and John Ramsell. *The Original Writings of Edward Bach*. Essex, England: C. W. Daniel Co., 1990.

Balick, Michael, and Paul Alan Cox. *Plants, People, and Culture the Science of Ethnobotany*. New York: Scientific American Library, 1996.

Bendit, Phoebe, and Laurence Bendit. *Our Psychic Sense: A Clairvoyant and a Psychiatrist Explain How It Works*. London: Quest Books, 1958.

Bensky, Dan, and Andrew Gamble. *Chinese Herbal Medicine: Materia Medica*. Seattle, Washington: Eastland Press, 1993.

Bigelow, Jacob. "On Self-Limited Diseases: A Discourse Delivered before the Massachusetts Medical Society at Their Annual Meeting, May 27, 1835." In *Nature in Disease: Illustrated in Various Discourses and Essays*. Boston: Phillips, Sampson, and Company, 1859.

Biodynamic Association. "What Is Biodynamics?" https://www.biodynamics.com/what-is-biodynamics.

Blavatsky, Helena. *The Secret Doctrine: The Synthesis of Science, Religion, and Philosophy*. London: The Theosophical Publishing Co, 1888.

Bowers, W. "Chlorophyll in Wound Healing and Suppurative Disease.". *American Journal of Surgery* 73, no. 1 (1947): 37-50.

Bridges, William, and Susan Bridges. *Managing Transitions; Making the Most of Change.* Philadelphia, PA: DaCapo Press, 2016.

Brown, W. A. "The Placebo Effect." *Scientific American* 278, no. 1 (Jan 1998): 90-5.

Calabria, Michael. *Florence Nightingale in Egypt and Greece.* New York: State University of New York Press, 1997.

Canterbury Shaker Nurses.*Infirmary Recipe Book*. Sabathday Lake, Maine: Sabathday Lake Shaker Village Archives, 1841?-1873.

Capra, Fritjof. *The Tao of Physics*. New York: Bantam Books, 1975.

Christopher, John, and Cathy Gileadi. *Every Woman's Herbal.* Springville, Utah: Christopher Publications, 1987.

Davis, Ruth. "Understanding Ethnic Women's Experiences with Pharmacopeia."*Health Care for Women International* 18 (1997): 425-37.

Dossey, Larry "Being Green: On the Relationships between People and Plants." [In eng]. *Alternative Therapies in Health and Medicine* 7, no. 3 (2001): 12-6, 132-40.

Duggan, J., and S. Duggan. *Edagr Cayce's Massage, Hydrotherapy, and Healing Oils.* Virginia Beach, Virginia: Inner Vision Publishing Company, 1989.

Duke, James. *Dr. Duke's Essential Herbs.* Emmaus, Pennsylvania: Rodale, Inc., 1999.

———. *The Green Pharmacy.* Emmaus, Pennsylvania: Rodale Press, 1997.

———.*Handbook of Phytochemical Constituents of Gras Herbs and Other Economic Plants*. Boca Raton, Florida: CRC Press, 1992.

Eisenberg, David, Roger Davis, Susan Ettner, Scott Appel, Sonja Wilkey, Maria Van Rompay, and Ronald Kessler. "Trends in Alternative Medicine Use in the United States, 1990-1997: Results of a Follow-up National Survey."*JAMA* 280, no. 18 (1998 1998): 1569-75.

Farnsworth, Norman. "Relative Safety of Herbal Medicines." *Herbalgram* 29 (1993 1993): 36A-H.

Farnsworth, Norman, Olayiwola Akerele, Audrey Bingel, Djaja Soejarto, and Zhengang Guo. "Medicinal Plants in Therapy." *Bulletin of the World Health Organization* 63, no. 6 (1985 1985): 965-81.

Felter, Harvey Wickes, and John Uri Lloyd.*King's American Dispensatory*. 18th ed., 3d rev ed. Sandy, Oregon: Eclectic Medical Publications, 1983.

Flaws, Bob. *The Tao of Healthy Eating: Dietary Wisdom According to Traditional Chinese Medicine.* Boulder, CO: Blue Poppy Press, 1998.

Fries, James, and Donald Vickery. *Take Care of Yourself.* Boston, MA: Da Capo Press, 2017.

Fuhr, Uwe. "Drug Interactions with Grapefruit Juice. Extent, Probable Mechanism and Clinical Relevance." [In eng] *Drug Safety: An International Journal of Medical Toxicology and Drug Experience* 18, no. 4 (1998): 251-72.

Fuller, Margaret. "Woman in the Nineteenth Century." https://archive.vcu.edu/english/engweb/transcendentalism/authors/fuller/woman1.html.

Gips, K. *Flora's Dictionary: The Victorian Language of Herbs and Flowers.* Chagrin Falls, OH: TM Publications, 1990.

Goethe, Johann Wolfgang. *The Metamorphosis of Plants.* Cambridge, Massachusetts: MIT Press, 2009.

Goethe, Johann Wolfgang, and Jeremy Naydler. *Goethe on Science.* Edinburgh: Floris Books, 1996.

Griggs, Barbara. *Green Pharmacy*. Rochester, VT: Healing Arts Press, 1991.

Hauck, Dennis. *The Emerald Tablet: Alchemy for Personal Transformation.* New York: Penguin Putnam Inc., 1999.

Israelson, Loren, and Thomas Aarts. "Industry Needs to Re-Think Dshea." *Herbalgram* 58 (2003): 59-61.

Jung, Carl G. *Dreams*. Bollingen Series,. Princeton, N.J.: Princeton University Press, 1974.

Junius, Manfred. *Practical Handbook of Plant Alchemy*. New York: Inner Traditions, 1985.

Kincheloe, Lawrence. "Herbal Medicines Can Reduce the Costs in Hmo.". *Herbalgram* 41 (1997): 49.

Kingsbury, John. "The Problem of Poisonous Plants." In *Toxic Plants,* edited by A. Douglas Kinghorn. New York: Columbia University Press, 1979.

Langer, Ellen. *Mindfulness.* Reading, Massachusetts: Perseus Books, 1989.

Lanius, Ulrich F., Sandra Paulsen, and Frank M. Corrigan. *Neurobiology and Treatment of Traumatic Dissociation: Toward an Embodied Self*. New York: Springer Publishing Company, 2014.

Leung, Albert and Steven Foster. *Encyclopedia of Common Natural Ingredients Used in Food, Drugs, and Cosmetics.* 2nd ed. New York: John Wiley & Sons, 1996.

Levin, Lowell S, and Ellen L Idler. *The Hidden Health Care System* Wauwatosa, WI: Golden Apple Publications, 2010.

Lewis, Charles A. *Green Nature/Human Nature the Meaning of Plants in Our Lives.* Urbana, IL: University of Illinois Press, 1996.

Libster, Martha. "Cultural Diplomacy: Demonstrating Person-Centered Care and Coaching" *Perspectives on Cultural Diplomacy* Vol. 1 (2015).

———. *Demonstrating Care: The Art of Integrative Nursing.* Albany, New York: Delmar Thomson Learning, 2001.

———. "Elements of Care: Nursing Environmental Theory in Historical Context." *Holistic Nursing Practice* 22, no. 3 (2008): 160-70.

———. *Herbal Diplomats: The Contribution of Early American Nurses (1830-1860) to Nineteenth Century Healthcare Reform and the Botanical Medical Movement.* Wauwatosa, WI: Golden Apple Publications, 2004.

———. *Science of Energy Flow: Foot Reflexology with Herbal Stress Relief.* Wauwatosa, WI: Golden Apple Publications, 2014.

———. "The Tao of Integrative Nursing Assessment (Tina): An East-West Model for Precision, Complementarity, and Inclusion in Relationship-Centered Care." *Holistic Nursing Practice*, no. (In press) (2022).

———. "Transmuting Imperil: Insight on the Healing Art from Mdm. Helena Roerich." *Golden Apple Monographs*, no. January (2010).

Libster, Martha, and Betty Ann McNeil. *Enlightened Charity: The Holistic Nursing Care, Education and Advices Concerning the Sick of Sister Matilda Coskery, (1799-1870).* United States: Golden Apple Publications, 2009.

Louv, Richard. *Last Child in the Woods : Saving Our Children from Nature-Deficit Disorder.* Chapel Hill, North Carolina: Algonquin Books of Chapel Hill, 2005.

Mascaro, Juan. *The Upanishads: Translations from the Sanskrit with an Introduction by Juan Mascaro.* New York: Penguin Books, 1965.

Matthews, John. *Drinking from the Sacred Well.* New York: Harper Collins, 1998.

Maveric, Jean. *Hermetic Herbalism: The Art of Extracting Spagyric Essences.* Rochester, Vermont: Inner Traditions, 2020.

Merriam-Webster. *Merriam-Webster's Collegiate Dictionary.* 10th ed. Springfield, Massachusetts: Merriam-Webster, 1999.

Moerman, Daniel E. *Native American Ethnobotany.* Portland, Or: Timber Press, 1998.

Newman, Margaret. *Health as Expanding Consciousness*. New York: National League for Nursing Press, 1994.

Nightingale, Florence. *Notes on Nursing: What It Is and What It Is Not*. Edinburgh, Scotland: Churchill Livingstone, 1980, Originally published 1859.

O'Connor, Bonnie *Healing Traditions: Alternative Medicine and the Health Professions*. Philadelphia: University of Pennsylvania Press, 1995.

Ondrizek, Richard, Philip Chan, William Patton, and Alan King. "An Alternative Medicine Study of Herbal Effects on the Penetration of Zona-Free Hamster Oocytes and the Integrity of Sperm Deoxyribonucleic Acid." *Fertility and Sterility* 71, no. 3 (Mar 1999): 517-22.

Orem, Dorothea. *Nursing Concepts of Practice*. 6 ed. St. Louis, MO: Mosby, 2001.

Perrone, Bobette, H. Henrietta Stockel, and Victoria Krueger. *Medicine Women, Curanderas, and Women Doctors*. 1st ed. Norman: University of Oklahoma Press, 1989.

Pert, Candace. *Molecules of Emotion*. New York: Scribner, 1997.

Ray, Priyadaranjan, and Hirendra Gupta. *Caraka Samhita: A Scientific Synopsis*. New Delhi: Indian National Science Academy, 1965.

Roerich, Helena. *Fiery World 1*. New York: Agni Yoga Society http://www.agniyoga.org/ay_frame.html?app_id=FW1, 1933.

Shakers. *Receipt Book*. Fruitlands Museum - Shaker Manuscripts - Reel 1.3.

Sheldrake, Rupert. *The Presence of the Past: Morphic Resonance and the Habits of Nature*. Rochester, Vermont: Park Street Press, 1995.

Tanne, Janice. "Food and Drugs Alter Response to Anesthesia." *BMJ: British Medical Journal* 317, no. 7166 (1998): 1102.

Tantaquidgeon, Gladys. *Folk Medicine of the Delaware and Related Algonkian Indians*. Harrisburg: Pennsylvania Historical and Museum Commission, 1972.

Thorne, Sally. "Health Belief Systems in Perspective." *Journal of Advanced Nursing* 18, no. 12 (1993): 1931-41.

Tompkins, Peter, and Christopher Bird. *The Secret Life of Plants*. New York: Harper & Row, 1973.

Treasure, Jonathan. "Herbal Pharmacokinetics." *Journal of the American Herbalist Guild* 1, no. 1 (2000): 2-11.

Tyler, Varro, and Steven Foster. *Tyler's Honest Herbal*. 4th ed. New York: Haworth Herbal Press, 1999.

Vithoullkas, George. *The Science of Homeopathy.* New York: Grove Press, 1980.

Vogel, H. C. Alfred. *The Nature Doctor: A Manual of Traditional and Complementary Medicine.* New Canaan, Connecticut: Keats Publishing, 1991.

von Bingen, Hildegard, and Bruce Hozeski. *Hildegard Von Bingen's Mystical Visions.* Santa Fe: Bear & Company, 1986.

Wall, Steve. *Wisdom's Daughters: Conversations with Women Elders of Native America.* New York: Harper Perennial, 1993.

Wallace, Paul. *The White Roots of Peace.* Philadelphia: University of Pennsylvania Press, 1946.

Wood, George, and Franklin Bache. *The Dispensatory of the United States of America.* Philadelphia: Grigg & Elliot, 1839.

World Health Organization. *The Conservation of Medicinal Plants: Proceedings of the International Consultation 1988 Chiang Mai, Thailand.* Cambridge: Cambridge University Press, 1991.

———. "Fact Sheet No. 134 Traditional Medicine." Geneva, Switzerland: W.H.O., 2003.

———. "Guidelines for the Appropriate Use of Herbal Medicines." In *WHO Regional Publications.* Geneva, 1998.

———. *Guidelines on the Conservation of Medicinal Plants.* Geneva: World Health Organization, 1993.

Yogananda, Paramahansa. *The Bhagavad Gita.* Los Angeles: Self-Realization Fellowship, 1995.

Zevin, Igor. *A Russian Herbal: Traditional Remedies for Health and Healing.* Rochester, Vermont: Healing Arts Press, 1997.

Index

A

ablution, 88
adaptation, 32, 119, 186, 188–89, 197
adaptogen action, 186–87
Adaptogen Action and Thinking Plants, 186
adverse effects, 78, 80, 159, 161–62, 182
african violets, 191
agni, 155, 173
air element, 34, 41, 82, 103, 105, 177
alchemy, 176–77, 179–80, 183, 195
American Botanical Council, 112, 160
anatomy, 64, 82, 85–87, 94, 144, 182
ancient Greeks, 34, 52–53, 94, 152
anxiety, 32, 54
apothecaries, 35, 77, 101
applications, right, 154, 160, 162–64
archetype, 53, 98
aromatherapy, 140–41
awareness, 15, 56, 66, 98, 102, 104, 106, 151, 155, 175
axis mundi, 99
Ayurveda, 52, 75, 121, 126

B

babies, 20, 22, 184–85
Bach, Edward, 186–87,
Bach flowers, 187–88, 196
barometers, 15, 17, 190–91
baths, 8–9, 17, 119, 123, 132, 141–43, 145
    five elements herbal foot, 87
beauty, 5, 13, 19, 26, 118, 147, 172, 188–89
beliefs, 3, 6, 12, 37, 52–53, 56, 59, 64, 70, 74, 78, 172, 176
Bendit, Laurence and Phoebe, 104-5
benefits and risks of self-care, 156–57
benzodiazepines, 152
Best Precision Self-care Plans, 152
Best precision Self-care practice, 148
beverage teas, 116, 123, 152, 161, 165, 182
Biodynamic gardening, 58
biomedical care, 10–11, 164
biomedical culture, 12, 37, 75, 77, 107
biomedical paradigm, 65–67, 70, 72, 76–78, 112, 169
biomedical science, 67, 73, 91, 147
biomedical world, 67, 77, 107, 146–47, 150, 152, 164

biomedicine, 37, 68, 73, 115, 156, 158
bitter, 48, 57, 121, 161
bitter tastes, 86, 121
black currants, 103
blood, 58, 102, 138, 156, 197
body circuitry, 105
botanical gardens, 101, 144, 182
botanical names, 40, 55, 70
botany, 40, 112, 182
breath, 19, 33, 62, 89, 91, 102, 161, 196–97
Breath and Body Scan, 102
breathe, 55, 89, 91, 102–3, 132, 141
breathing
    4-Part, 102–3
broths, 124–25
Burbank, Luther, 190
burner
    lower and upper, 15, 63

C

Cannabis sativa, 8, 93–94
caregiver's crisis, 110
castor oil, 134–35, 160
castor oil pack, 135
Cayce, Edgar, 134
cayenne peppers, 18, 162
CBD, 94
Celtic tradition, 50, 97–98
centering, 86
chalice, 173, 181
chamomile, 36, 140–41, 151–52
chamomile inhalations, 140
change, forces of, 30
change and transition, 28, 106, 109, 184, 197
checkerberries, 4, 57
chemistry, 167, 176, 180, 182
chemotherapy, 146, 165
chest, 55, 102, 136
Chinese Herbal Medicine, 73, 161
Chinese Materia Medica, 126, 160, 165
chlorophyll, 66, 88–90, 93, 147
chlorophyll connection, 81, 86, 89
Christopher, John, 185
cinnamon, 15–16, 139
climate change, environmental, 31

clinical trials, 35, 37–38, 65–66, 68, 111–13, 166
Coffea arabica, 163
comfort, 1, 3–5, 9, 13, 17, 23–24, 26, 52–53, 104–5, 111, 113
comfrey, 46, 157
complexity, 59, 67, 151–52, 158, 162, 166, 168
compresses
  cold, 33, 133
  hot, 132–33
  lemon, 38
connection, human-plant, 174–75
consciousness, 13, 21, 23, 25, 29, 32–33, 50, 53, 96–98, 151–52, 154–55, 172, 174–77
constituents, single, 71, 75, 140, 164
corticosteroids, 185
cosmic consciousness, 131
cost savings, 67, 154
cough, 58, 152
cough syrup, 134
  homemade, 152
coumarins, 48
creation stories, 96, 194
creativity, 82, 110, 174
Culpeper's classification, 150
cyanide, 47, 168
cycles, 29, 31, 107, 144, 181
Cytochrome P-450, 165

D

dandelion, 47, 121
decoction, cinnamon, 16
decoding, 111, 114
design, 3, 9, 13, 44, 51, 53–55, 80, 83, 114, 189
diet, 33, 64, 76, 90, 164
diet therapies, 65
dill, 4, 41, 121
diplomacy, 195
  health culture, 64
discern, 8, 36, 57, 78–79, 162, 191
discernment, 85, 105, 160
disease focus, 59
Doctrine of Signatures, 58
dose, right, 153, 162, 167, 169
dreams, 51–52, 82, 98, 108, 147
drug absorption, 163
drug development, 9, 147
drug-herb interaction information, 166

Drug Interactions, (see interactions)
drug metabolism, 164
drugs, plant-derived, 150
DSHEA (Dietary Supplement Health and Education Act), 170–71

E

ear infections, 89
ecosystem, 7, 171
effectiveness, 10, 76, 79, 93, 155, 163
efficacious, 65, 67, 113
efficacy, 38, 57, 65, 68, 72, 163, 170
effort, 14–15, 25–26, 66, 86, 104, 172
elderberries, 103, 127
elders, 32, 75, 82, 127, 192–93
elements, five, 31–33, 50, 52–54, 59, 80–81, 83–85, 102, 142, 190, 192, 194
Elements of Care, 2, 11, 13, 34, 59, 81, 84, 190
elements of self, 51, 74, 81, 103, 118, 131, 172
Eleutherococcus senticosus, 185
Emerald Tablet, 50, 176
emotion, 11–12, 14, 16, 19, 24, 59, 106, 110, 118, 175–76, 183, 187, 196
energetic patterns, 17, 33, 56–57, 60, 86, 97, 151, 155
energetics, 16–17, 39, 57–58, 60, 91, 111, 155, 182
energy, 26, 28, 42–43, 56, 58–59, 86–87, 92–93, 109–10, 118–19, 142, 146, 181, 183–84, 190–91, 196
energy balance, 95
energy fields, 17–18, 143, 184, 196
energy flow, 29, 59, 86–87, 105, 110, 118–19, 142, 181
Enlightened Charity, 208
EOC (Elements of Care®), 2–3, 11, 13, 34, 59, 81–82, 84, 102, 155, 190, 198
EOC precision Self-care program, 26, 34, 60, 149
EOC program, 5, 10–13, 17, 24, 33–35, 38, 52, 54, 59, 64, 110–11, 156–57
Ephedra sinensis, 115, 160-161
epilepsy, 93–94
Equisetum arvense, 43, 180
essential oils, single, 171
estrogens, 165, 185
ether, 32–33, 48, 51–52, 59, 80–81, 118, 142, 174–75, 179
ether element, 81, 174–76
ethic, 96–98, 108, 159, 194

ethnobotanists, 111, 149–50
ethnobotany, 112, 149
eucalyptus, 139, 142
European folklore, 152
evidence, 22, 37, 68–69, 111–12, 114, 149, 153, 155, 158, 171
  biomedical, 72
  clinical, 151
  clinical trial, 112
evidence-based practice, 68
excess, 60–63, 126, 133
experiment, 69, 193
expertise, 13, 52, 101
extraction, 119, 122, 129, 179
extracts, 9, 71, 120, 128–29, 163, 168, 172
  standardized, 69–70, 72, 131, 140, 161

F
faith, 78
FDA (Food and Drug Administration), 37, 66, 169–71
FDA and pre-market approval of evidence, 171
fever, 38, 62
Fibonacci sequence, 189
Fiery World, 154
first aid treatment, 156
First Nation, 50, 74
Five Element Foot Bath, 142, 196
five elements of care, 52, 81
five elements structure, 34
Five Nations, 194
Five Rights of Precision Plant Partnership Self-care, 153
flavor, 21, 57
floral waters, 17, 192
flow, 81–82, 102, 118–19, 134, 145, 181, 197
folklore, 35, 73, 112
Food and Drug Administration. See FDA
footbaths, 17, 142–44, 160
  five-element, 143–44
foot reflexology, 87
forces, 30, 107–8, 175, 192–93
forests, 1, 21, 76, 94, 100–101, 188, 193
formic acid, 46
formulations, 39, 98, 115, 161, 163, 165, 167, 171, 179, 181–83

fragrance, 1, 13, 18, 21, 48, 139, 172, 177
framework, 31, 34, 59, 82
fun, 5, 79, 99, 116, 147

G
garlic, 69
garlic oil study, 114
Gaultheria procumbens, 57
generalization, 124
genetic factors, 169
gentle medicines, 1–2, 10, 12, 85, 90–92, 109, 111, 144, 146, 154, 156, 160, 164, 166, 172–73
Gentle medicine Self-care, 92, 153, 160
Gentle Medicine Self-study, 3, 6, 11, 14, 16, 27–29, 38, 53, 55, 102, 133–34, 191, 193
ginger, 124, 139, 163
Ginkgo biloba, 41
ginseng, 58, 95, 185
glycerites, 130
glycosides, anthraquinone, 47
goals
  long-term, 108–9, 111
  personal, 59
Goethe, 26, 103, 180

golden ratio spiral, 189
good manufacturing practices, 171
grace, 25, 86
grasses, 41–42, 174, 195, 197
gratitude, 15, 94
Green Nature, 97
green pharmacy, 81, 98
Green Woman, 97
growth, 15, 18, 43, 91, 99, 150–51, 189, 193, 197
growth cycle, 144
growth patterns, 18–19, 35, 40, 49, 182

H

habits, 110
Hahnemann, Samuel, 130, 187
hallucinate, 91
Hamamelis virginiana, 121, 132–33
harmonious, 96, 164, 189
harmony, 29, 34, 50, 63, 74, 81, 122, 174, 188
harvesting, 13, 74, 95, 120, 145, 150, 192
headaches, 84, 138, 142
healers, 9, 30, 50, 75, 78, 116, '120, 175, 177, 185, 187
 indigenous, 18, 74, 77
 inner, 154, 173
healing relationship, 77, 147
healing traditions, 1, 3, 24, 56, 59, 75, 92, 110, 112, 118
health beliefs, 6, 12, 50, 64, 96, 147, 177
health benefits, 1, 69, 72, 89–90
healthcare reform, 96, 145
health care systems, 9, 52, 169
health culture diplomacy approach, 78
health cultures, 64
health decisions, 10, 106–7, 111, 117, 155, 157, 166
health outcomes, 144
health pattern recognition, 182
health patterns, 55, 59, 84–85, 98, 100, 103, 106, 108, 111, 155–56, 160, 163, 183
 energetic, 85, 95, 149, 156, 163, 170
 primary energetic, 33
 symptom-sign, 59
 unique, 13, 36
health promotion, 34, 37, 57, 59, 77, 157
hemoglobin, 88, 90
hepatoprotective, 72
hepatotoxicity, 157
herbal application, 36, 142, 158, 163

herbal baths, 139, 141
herbal community, 151
Herbal Diplomats, 13
herbal extracts, 130
herbal foot baths, 142
herbal formulas, 67, 121, 126
herbal formulation, 81, 183
herbalism, 29, 36, 70, 112, 115, 118, 130–31, 140, 175–76
herbalists, 39, 43, 72, 74, 98, 116, 119–20, 149, 151, 175, 177, 180
herbal laxatives, 84
herbal medicines, regulation of, 159, 170
herbal oil, 132, 134, 136–39, 145, 192
herbal pharmacy, 168
herbal poultices, 135
herbal practices, 68, 77
herbal practitioner, 116
herbal products, standardized, 72
herbal recipes, 76, 175
herbal remedies, 66–67, 69, 114–16, 121, 124, 126, 142, 146–47, 149, 151–52, 163–64, 166, 181–82, 185
herbal salves, 138
herbal Self-care, 162, 166
herbal steam inhalation, 140
herbal supplements, 11, 36, 170
herbal teas, 17, 36, 79, 119, 183
herbal therapies, individualizing, 116
herbal tincture, 127
herbal topical applications, 131
herb-drug interactions, 164
herb-herb interactions, 165
herb-herb synergy, 165
herb industry, 92, 160, 170
herb production, high-volume, 150
herb products, 72, 171
herb research, 112
herbs, 14–16, 18, 35–39, 46, 60, 63–65, 67–69, 73–77, 79, 92–94, 97–100, 105, 111–16, 121–26, 132–34, 136–38, 140–42, 146–52, 154–72, 182–86
 culinary, 121, 152
herb safety, 158
Hermes Trismegistus, 50, 176
Hermeticism, 49–51
Hermetic philosophy, 176
Hermetic texts, 50

heroics, 146
Hiawatha, 194
high altitudes, 100
history, 1–3, 9–10, 17, 35, 49, 51, 53, 71, 73, 75, 119, 121, 146–47, 182, 184
holistic, 19, 78
holographic, 192
homeopathic medicine, 130
homeopathic remedies, 130
homeopathy, 130, 140, 187
home remedies, 76
honey, 127, 134
hops, 136, 152
horsetail, 43, 180
horticultural therapy, 144
human consciousness, 131, 154
humors, 51, 58
Humulus lupulus, 152
Hydrastis canadensis, 121
hydrotherapy, 132
Hypericum perforatum, 7, 21, 137, 166

I
ignorance, 156
illness
  chronic, 62, 157
  common, 52
imagination, 55, 110
inclusion, 111, 119, 148
Indigenous knowledge systems (IKS), 74
indigestion, 79, 86
individuality, 166, 194
industry, 2, 160, 170
  pharmaceutical, 92
infant, 20, 32, 116
infant communication, 20–21
informed consumers, 36
infusions, 122–24, 126, 132–33, 135, 141–42, 172
ingredients, active, 65, 113, 131, 150
injuries, 22, 26, 79, 169, 171, 175
insomnia, 108, 142
instruments, 18, 52, 83, 86, 176
integration, 13, 25–26, 68, 81, 192–93
integrative insight, 13–14, 19, 21, 26
Integrative Nursing Assessment, 60
intentions, 5, 8–9, 11, 52, 82, 157, 190–91
interactions, 30, 65, 108, 164–65, 175, 188
  drug-food, 164

drug-herb, 164–65
intuition, 18, 49, 103–5, 109, 162
Iroquois Confederacy, 75, 194
Iroquois Nation, 194
Iroquois people, 194
isoquinolines, 46
itching, 108, 130

J
Japanese Kampo, 50
judgment, 59, 103, 107
Jung, Carl, 98

K
Kampo medicine in Japan, 74
Kannonsionni, 194
kindness, 85, 155
Kirlian photography, 184
kitchen, 14, 41, 92, 100, 128, 134, 178
kudzu, 125

L
labor, 22–23
laboratory, 68, 91, 99, 114, 158
Laminaria spp, 156, 180
language, 12, 23, 60, 76, 84, 104, 111, 195
lavender, 141
LD50, 168
lemon balm, 140, 152, 195–96
lemon balm lawn, 195–96
Lemon Bread, 176, 178–79
  secret recipe, 179
life force, 18, 21, 92, 131, 146, 177, 184, 193
life forms, 41, 96, 177, 189
life purpose, 106, 109, 196
lifestyle, 10, 60, 63, 78, 108, 164, 182–83
lifestyle patterns, 33
ligands, 186
liniments, 131, 136, 138–39
  witch hazel, 132
Linnaeus, Carl, 40
liquid extraction, 129
liquid extracts, 119, 127–31, 160
Living Water, 143
Lobelia inflata, 138, 185
long-term storage, 100
long-term use, 157
lotions, 131

M

maceration, 128–30
marijuana, 8, 93–94
massage, 102, 139
mastery of fear and anxiety, 31
materialization, 174
Materia Medica, 149
Matricaria chamomilla, 36, 140
measurable goals, 109
mechanism of action, 94
media reports, 111, 161
medicine
　botanical, 72
　making, 92, 119, 172, 174, 179
　traditional, 50, 73, 95, 159
medicine wheel, 50
meditation, 15, 86, 176
Melissa officinalis, 140, 152, 195
memories, 2–4, 7, 9, 14, 17, 26, 55–56, 73, 108, 195
memory loss, 192
menstruum, 120, 127–29
　excellent, 127
Mentha piperita, 14, 60
metabolism, 159, 161, 163, 165
migraine, 8, 109, 138
migraine headaches, 96
milk thistle, 72
mind, turtle, 192
mindfulness, 110
mindfulness meditation, 110
Mindful Tea Tasting, 16
mindlessness, 110
miscarriage, threatened, 185
Mitchell, Cecilia, 75, 94
Mohawk, 194
Mohawk tradition, 181
morphic resonance, 56
mother tincture, 130, 187–88
movements, 19–20, 27, 30, 34, 61–62, 72, 96, 102, 118, 143, 161
muscle testing, 105
mustard plaster, 67
mystical experience, 49, 51

N

NAPRALERT, 112
Native American, 74, 177
nature care, 119
nature cure, 24
negative psychism, 104–5
nervous system
　central, 46, 140
　peripheral, 131
nettles, stinging, 46, 90, 147, 153, 158
neural pathways, 97
neurotransmitters, 186
Nicotiana tabacum, 93, 158, 177
Nightingale, Florence, 10
noxious weed, 7
nurse-herbalism, 22, 150, 175
nurse-herbalists, 13, 116
nursing, 10, 13, 84, 91, 104, 148, 182
nursing care, 156
nursing practice, 22, 59–60, 186
nursing process, 106–7
　five-step, 85
nursing science, 36, 107, 142

O

objects, personal power, 193
oil, 22, 105, 120, 123, 133–39, 143, 172
　carrier, 139
　infused, 17, 22, 132, 136, 138
oil compress, 134, 160
oil infusions, 136–37
ointments, 17, 131, 136, 138–39
Oma, 87, 104
Oneida, 194
oneness, 25
onion poultices, 36
onions, 36, 121, 125, 127, 134, 136, 172
onion soup, 125
onion syrup, 127, 134
opioid crisis, 169
opium poppy, 8, 46
opposites, union of, 25–26, 49
oral applications, 17, 160
oral remedies, 119–20, 160–61
oral use, 105
orchids, 41, 97

P

P-450 system, 165–66
paganism, 50

pain level, 63, 109
Panax ginseng, 95, 185
Panax quinquefolium, 95
Papaver somniferum, 8, 46, 150
Paracelsus, 50, 58, 167, 176, 179
paradigms, 12, 56, 64, 72, 77–78
  clinical, 153
  ecocentric, 101
pathology, 59, 187
pathways, multiple, 67
pattern recognition, 56–57, 59–60, 76, 85, 107, 109–10
patterns, 17, 19–20, 33–35, 56–61, 64, 81–82, 85, 87, 95, 98, 108–9, 111, 183, 188, 191
Peacemaker, 194
peacemaking, 81, 193, 195
peppermint, 14–16, 60, 139, 155
perceptions, 12, 29–31, 33, 56–57, 59, 61, 103, 177, 180
  intuitive, 26
person, right, 153, 170
perspective, 12, 20, 109, 114, 149, 156, 167–68, 178, 180
Pert, Candace, 186
pesticides, 99–100, 119, 171
pharmaceutical drugs, 10, 12, 52, 55, 66–68, 70–71, 76, 79, 146, 149, 157, 160, 166, 169, 184
pharmaceuticals, 9, 11–12, 67, 72
pharmacists, 65, 76, 78, 165
pharmacognosists, 149, 169
pharmacognosy, 94, 149
phlegm, 51, 58, 125
phosphorus, 179
photosynthesis, 42–44, 90–91
  process of, 45, 90–91
physics, 17, 25, 56–57
physiology, 81, 84–85, 93, 143, 157, 183
phytochemicals, 185–86
phytoestrogens, 185–86
pills, 72, 80, 125–26, 160
placebo, 68, 79
plant alchemy, 81, 179
plant applications, 113, 157–58
plant constituents, individual, 46, 71, 120
plant designs, 40, 44
plant drugs, 66, 113
plant growth, 26, 43, 64, 146
plant partnerships, precision, 81

plant patterns, 20, 58
plant personalities, 40
plant perspective, 70, 93, 112
plants
  right, 53, 153, 155
  sacred, 94, 177
plant science, 71
plant's consciousness, 177
plants in self-care and comfort, 4, 9, 23
plant therapies, 68, 158
plasters, 9, 131, 135–36
poison, 57, 167–68
pollen, 45, 119
pollination, 44–45
potency, 71, 120, 129–31, 145
potentizing, 187
potherb, 90
poultices, 8–9, 17, 131, 135–36, 146
  onion slurry, 136
powders, 125, 127, 137
power, 29–30, 50–52, 56, 92, 98, 146–47, 151, 172, 174, 181–82, 184, 193, 197
Power Object, 7, 193
practice plan, 82
prayer, 86, 92, 142, 146, 176, 194
precision, 111, 126, 153–55, 160, 170
precision Self-care, 2, 5, 12, 21, 24, 31, 34, 36, 84–85, 105–7, 148, 170–71, 180–82, 184, 195–96
precision Self-care Model, 35–36
prescription, 66, 79, 89, 182
preservation, 150
prevention, 22, 26, 99
  tertiary, 36
primary prevention, 34–36, 109, 156, 197
Principle Patterns, 59–60, 63–64, 84, 109
problem-solving process, 84, 107
properties, 8, 40, 139, 195
  calming, 151
protection, 19, 98, 147, 172, 188, 190
public safety, 37, 170
pungent, 49, 121, 161
purgatives, common, 86
purification, 154, 179
purity, 87, 120

Q

qi, 58, 92, 102, 149
qi tonic, 95
quantum physics, 25, 56
quercetin, 8
quinine, 46, 150
quintessence, 175–76

R

radiation treatments, 146
ratio, golden, 81, 188–89
RCTs (randomized clinical trials), 67–69
Receipt Book, 35, 127
Recipes for Making Herbal Simples, 119
regulation, legal, 158
regulatory agency, 126, 162
reimbursing, 113
relationship-centered care, 1
relaxation response, 143
relief, 52, 66, 118
religion, 24, 50, 149, 167
religious rituals, 140
relinquish, 28, 190
Rescue Remedy, 187–88, 196
responsibility, 11, 32, 93, 109, 148, 158, 164, 170
rhythm, 55, 102, 134, 196
Right action, 194
rights, five, 153–55, 157, 171, 182
rituals, 20, 70, 73, 75, 112, 178
Roerich, Helena, 154
room temperature, 16, 38
roses, 40–41, 127, 147, 188, 190

S

safe place, 52, 54–55, 107, 131, 143, 193
safe practice, best, 171
safety and efficacy, 38, 68, 163
safe use, 71, 162, 169
safe use system, 121
salicylates, 57
salves, 8, 17, 131, 136, 138–39, 163
  topical, 160
scale, 1-to-10-point, 109
scaling, 109
school nurse, 77, 118
scientific inquiry, 73
scientific process, 14, 37, 85, 115
scientific study, 29, 158

seasons, 29, 31, 43, 144, 152
seaweeds, 121, 156, 180
Secret Life of Plants, 18
self
  enduring, 24
  five elements of, 32, 50, 82
Self-awareness, 177
Self-care coaching, 63
Self-care decision, 78
Self-care Model, 35, 39
Self-care process, 107, 146, 148
Self-care solutions, 110, 118
Self-concept, 108
Self-study, 14–15, 27, 29–30, 38, 54, 57, 63, 82, 190–91
Senna, 47, 71
sensations, 15, 55, 62, 131
senses
  five, 18, 104, 162
  psychic, 104
sensitivity, 13, 58, 70
sensory experiences, 1–2, 18, 20, 56, 58, 126, 140, 162, 188
sentient, 18, 23
sentient life, 20–21, 73
Shakers, 92, 96
Sheldrake, Rupert, 56
shelf life, 100, 120, 127
Shen Nung, 150
sick room management books, 21
simples, 38–39, 76, 119, 139, 149, 171, 179, 181–82, 196–97
  making, 119
  single plant, 76
  whole-plant, 153
single herb remedy, 38
skin, 62, 67, 71, 90–91, 119, 123, 131–39, 141, 145, 153, 156, 161
sleep, 33, 59, 108, 151
soups, 9, 17, 92, 119, 124–25, 146
  boiling, 125
Spagyric preparations, 179
Spagyrics, 179
spiral, 181
  downward, 107
  positive, 196
spiritual experiences, 174–75
spiritual inspiration, 9

spirituality, 181
spiritual practices, 94, 151
spiritual Self, 81, 187
spiritual transformation, 33
stagnation, 110
  blood and dampness, 63
standardization, 67, 70–72
state, negative psychic, 104
steams, 8–9, 16–17, 36, 51, 119, 139–40
St. John's Wort, 7, 21, 23, 47, 49, 67, 93, 147, 166, 174–75
stories of healing, 2, 26, 36
stress, 95, 142, 196
  excessive, 110, 188
stress levels, 144
sun, 26, 53, 58, 96, 98, 146, 172, 187, 191, 197
sunflower, 137
supplement industry, 161, 169
supplements, 36, 126, 149, 151, 161, 170–71
  dietary, 126, 161, 170
support, 10, 23, 37, 39, 43–44, 52, 66–68, 95, 142, 146, 183
survival, 31, 42, 91, 97, 192–93
sustainability, 9
sweet potato, 63
Symmetria, 93, 118, 147
symptom-sign patterns, 58, 60, 62, 81–82
  energetic, 86
  unique energetic, 84
syrups, 9, 17, 127, 134, 172
system
  endocannabinoid, 93
  tiered, 9, 78

T

tannins, 46, 129
Tao, 60
Taoism, 50
Taoist philosophy, 60, 63
Tao of Integrative Nursing Assessment (TINA), 60
TCM, 14, 50, 59–60, 63, 74, 77, 95, 116, 121, 126, 165
TCM diet therapy, 60
TCM energetics, 60
TCM system, 60
tea ceremonies, 119
teapot, 122–23
teas, 9, 14–16, 79–80, 87, 118–23, 126–27, 130, 134, 145–46, 152, 155, 161–63
tea tastings, 1, 14–17, 39, 86, 182
  learned, 14
technology, 9, 11–12, 52, 65, 150, 161, 193
THC, 94
theory, 22, 92, 185
  germ, 136
  humoral, 51, 58
therapies, 22, 33, 65, 79, 156–58
  heroic, 10
thermal nature, 15
thinking herb, 185
thinking plants, 81, 184–85
thorns, 147, 162, 190–91
thoughtforms, 17
  negative, 31
thyme, 40, 123, 127
Thymus vulgaris, 123, 127
Tiered Healthcare System, 9
tinctures, 22, 127–35
Tinctures and liquid extracts, 127, 129
tisanes, 122
tobacco, 93–94, 158, 177
tongue coating, 62–63, 108
  normal, 62
topical applications, 8, 17, 38, 100, 119, 122, 131, 134, 139
Topical remedies, 131
topicals, 152, 162
toxic compounds, 169
toxicity, 35, 51, 67, 163, 167–69
toxicity data, 168, 170
toxic reactions, 158
Traditional Chinese Medicine, 59, 189traditional healers, 72–74, 98, 101, 149–50, 157, 159
transmutation, 87, 179
traumas, 110, 175, 187
Tree of Peace, 194
triage, 11, 157
trickster mind, 104
truth, 22, 32, 104, 175

U

union, 25, 51, 53, 194, 197
unity, 24–26, 49, 51, 53, 181, 194
unity of opposites, 49, 51
universe, five-element, 145

V

valerian, 46, 150–53
Valeriana officinalis, 46, 150
vegetables, 41, 47, 76, 124, 129
vibration, 21, 187, 196
  beautiful, 187
  rhythmic, 56
Vickery, Donald 11, 157
violets, 58, 191
viriditas, 177
vision, 28, 66, 83, 94, 108, 139, 162, 187
  dedicated, 154
visualizations, 87, 92
vitamin, high-dose, 76
Vogel, Alfred, 125
volatile oils, 39, 48, 100, 120, 123–24
  oxidized, 48
vulnerary, 29, 131

W

watchful waiting, 10
watercress, 125
water element, 33, 81, 111, 117–18, 131, 160
weighing benefits and risks, 155, 157
welcome, 1–2, 5, 21, 78, 98, 118, 154, 197–98
wellness, 31, 59
White Roots, 75
WHO (World Health Organization), 5, 73–74, 99, 101, 112, 159, 170
wholeness, 181
whole-plant applications, 152
wildcrafting, 81, 99
wisdom, ancient, 2, 51
wisdom keepers, 74
Wisdom of Elders, 192
wisdom tradition, 75, 182, 192
witch hazel, 121
women
  pregnant, 139
  premenopausal, 185
women's estrogen production, 185
world tree, 98
worldview, 21, 25, 64
wound healing, 137
wounds
  infected, 136
  localized, 131
  open, 139

Y

yin deficiency, 60
yoga, 25, 131
Yogananda, 131

Z

Zuni, 75

Gentle Medicine for Balance in Body and Peace of Mind

EXPERIENTIAL GUIDE

Martha M. Libster PhD, APRN

The Elements of Care® Program

CHAPTER 1

Welcome Back to the Plant World

Plants provide a vessel for carrying out our hearts' intentions for healing, energy, and comfort in the care of Self and others.

As you think about plants in nature, reflect and describe any fragrances, shapes, tastes, or textures associated with your experiences.

What is the foundation for safe and effective plant partnerships?

How do we gain an understanding of plant medicine?

What are some of your own stories about plants?

—*Gentle Medicine Self-Study #1*—
Plant Memories

What are your earliest memories of plants? How old were you?

What happened with the plant(s)?

What did you learn about the plant?

Use a journal to record your memories and reflections.

MEMORIES AND PLANT PARTNERSHIP

How will you use this book to either ignite or deepen your relationship with healing plants in the care of Self and family?

PLANT TEACHERS

How have you learned to care for yourself and others over the years? What do you believe and think about healing plants?

—Gentle Medicine Self-Study #2—
When Does Food Become Medicine?

Pick or purchase a fresh orange (Citrus sinensis). Wash it thoroughly. Cut the orange into quarters. Set a timer for 5 minutes. Quiet yourself in a comfortable chair. Use all of your senses to focus mindfully on the orange. Smell, feel, look at, listen to, and taste the outer peel, the inner peel, and the fruit.

1. What are the qualities of the orange?
2. Is it "medicine"?
3. When is a plant food and when is it medicine?
4. Who decides? How is this decided?

List the 5 types of plant-human partnerships. Give an example of a plant that can be categorized within all 5 types.

1.

2.

3.

4.

5.

What is the difference between a plant as food and a plant as medicine?

It is time to restore the knowledge of healing traditions with plants.

SELF-CARE AS FIRST STEP IN A TIERED HEALTHCARE SYSTEM

How can people partner with plants in Self-care and comfort of others?

How can a person practicing Self-care restore or promote their own health?

Outline each step in the four-tiered system healthcare system that exists in most communities:

1. First Tier

2. Second Tier

3. Third Tier

4. Fourth Tier

Each person is responsible for the health choices that they make.

What is it important about having gentle medicine with conservative, watchful, and active Self-care as a foundational part of any healthcare system?

How do we consider all health care paradigms?

—*Gentle Medicine Self-Study #3*—
Self-care Survey Question

Would you rather be asked what you would like to do about your health or told what to do about your health?

Ask this question of yourself or a friend or family member you are helping. The answer serves as an indicator for the tier of care that may be required.

CHAPTER 2
The Elements of Care® Program: A Guide for Self-Care

Describe integration, insight, and integrative insight as defined in the book.

When tasting tea, traditionally one begins with _____ and ends with _____ .

What two primary questions do you need to ask when tasting herb tea?

1.

2.

What are the 3 burners in Traditional Chinese medicine (TCM)?

1.

2.

3.

What is the energetic scale used for tea tasting when asking about the thermal nature of an herb?

How do we use the body as barometer in partnering with plants for Self-care?

Gentle Medicine Self-Study #4—
Managing Expectations with Mindful Tea Tasting

Cinnamon Decoction

Purchase 5 small or 2 large cinnamon sticks (the bark of Cinnamomum spp.). Wash them thoroughly and place in small pot. Cover with spring or distilled water. Raise water to the boil and take off stove. Cover with lid and allow to sit for 4 hours as the herb expands. After expansion period, check water level and add enough water so that the level is about 2 cm above the herbs. Decoct (gentle boil) the herb for 45 minutes at a temperature where the steam just rises from the water – not a rolling boil. The water level should be about ½ of the original level after the cooking. Strain the decoction and discard or compost the herb. Sip the tea at room temperature. Cinnamon is classified as opening and warming the energy channels in the body. Record your reflection of cinnamon decoction – body, mind, emotion, spirit.

Mint Infusion

Harvest or purchase fresh or dried mint leaf (Mentha piperita). Chop the fresh leaf or gently crush the dried leaf prior to infusing in boiled water. Put 1-2 teaspoons of fresh or 1 teaspoon of dried herb in a tea pot or tea ball. Pour one cup of boiled water over the herb. (Put the herb in the cup first and splash with the water rather than put the water in the cup first and try to submerge the leaf.) Strain and sip. Peppermint is energetically cold and opens and cools the channels of the head. Record your reflection of the mint infusion.

SENTIENCE AND COMMON SENSE

Plants are energy fields and sentient life forms.

How can we use all of our senses to learn about healing plants?

Discuss the concept that the "whole is greater than the sum of the parts" when talking about plants.

We can use all of our senses to learn about healing plants.

What are some examples of how plants become part of our celebrations and rituals?

What is one way that we can understand a plant's healing ways?

What is the backdoor theory of plant-human interaction?

SELF-CARE WITH A CAPITAL S

Self-care is a healing tradition as well as a _____.

Distinguish between the Self (capital "S") and the self ("s").

The path of Self-care is one of _____ and _____.

What is the outcome of an integrative Self-care process?

A SEASON FOR CLIMATE CHANGE

List the 3 approaches to reframing as it relates to change in health.
1.

2.

3.

List and define the 3 stages in the process of transition.
1.

2.

3.

How do plants remind us that everything in life changes over time?

What must be present for any kind of change to occur? Provide an example from your reading.

This sentient plant world is a ready source of inspiration and natural instruments for creating Self-care.

—Gentle Medicine Self-study #5—
Comfort Level with Change

Try this change Self-study with some friends and family. First have each person select a partner to work with. Have each one face their partner and study the appearance of the partner for 30 seconds. Then have the partners turn back to back and give them the following simple instruction: "Change Your Appearance in 3 Ways." After one minute, have the pairs turn around to face each other and give them a few minutes to discover what changes were made. After everyone finishes the Self-study, have them sit down and record on a board the number of changes in which the person either added to, gave up, or moved around something in their appearance.

What is the reason that we perceive "climate change" in the negative?

—Gentle Medicine Self-Study #6—
Change and Transition

Reflect on your Self-care practices as they are today. What would you change—that is add, give up, or move around? Write down your vision for change.

1. Change – Relinquish:

2. Change – Add:

3. Change – Move around

Where are you in the process of transition?

4. Letting Go:

5. Neutral Zone:

6. Renewal:

FIVE ELEMENTS OF CLIMATE CREATION

What are the 5 elements that form the foundation of science and medicine in many cultures?

1.

2.

3.

4.

5.

Reflective Moment

Consider what compels you to make changes in your life and health that you perceive as leading toward greater balance in body and peace of mind. What forces keep you from making those changes?

—Gentle Medicine Self-study #7—
The Power of Perception
Count the F's you see.

> FINISHED FILES ARE THE RESULT OF YEARS OF SCIENTIFIC STUDY COMBINED WITH THE EXPERIENCE OF MANY YEARS.

How many F's do you see? I have shown this Self-study as a slide at conferences and asked people to count the F's that they see. On the count of three, I ask them to call out the number of F's that they see. People call out numbers from two to six. They then look around wondering how people in the room can see different numbers of F's on the same slide!

There are in fact six F's in the sentence and yet few people actually see the six F's. Moving slowly from word to word I point out the F's using a laser pointer. I point out that studies on perception suggest that on any given day we may or may not see all of the F's. However, once we have been shown the F's, our brains do not "un-see" the correct number of F's.

This Self-study really causes people to think about perception and the mind. People begin to realize that we may not always see what is right in front of us. The lesson of this Self-study can be applied to plant partnership and Self-care as well.

Mental transformation includes:
1.
2.
3.

Complete the following table with the corresponding element and key characteristics of Transformation

CHANGE	CORRESPONDING ELEMENT	CHARACTERISTICS
Physical Transformation		
Mental Transformation		
Emotional Transformation		
Spiritual Transformation		

Describe ether, the fifth element:

Balance of the elements as they manifest in a person is created by

___

*Changes in perception often signal
a spiritual change in consciousness.*

___

CHAPTER 3
The 5 P's of the Self-care Model

List the 5 P's of the Self-Care Model.
1.
2.
3.
4.
5.

THE SELF-CARE MODEL FOR PRIMARY PREVENTION

How do we develop plant partnerships in Self-care?

What differentiates an herb from and herbal product? Provide examples of each from your reading.

What factors make it important for us to use alternative language to the word "prove" when referring to the scientific process?

THE SOLUTION IS SIMPLES

Define the term "simple" as it relates to herbal Self-care.

— *Gentle Medicine Self-study #8*—
A Simple Lemon Compress for Fever Reduction

Try this Self-study in cooling the body. Lemon Compress is a topical application of an herbal infusion (water extraction) of lemon using a cotton, silk, or wool material. The temperature of the room should be regulated so that the person is not chilled by drafts or by the room temperature itself. The person is covered for warmth. A woolen cloth with safety pins attached is placed on the bed in preparation for being placed around the lower legs. Place another piece of soft material on top of the wool that will fit around the legs. Then the dipping cloth is prepared.

A bandage-type material that will go around the lower legs is folded to fit the legs and then rolled on both sides up to the middle. Place the bandage on another cloth that can be used to wring out the bandage. This cloth should have both ends rolled, too. Place tepid water, temp 37.6 °C / 99°F, in a bowl and, using a fork to hold a lemon submerged in the water, use a paring knife to cut the lemon in half into a star shape.

Use the base of a glass or small bowl to press the lemon halves. The lemon is cut under water so that the volatile oil does not escape. Then put the cloth with the bandage on it in the lemon water, holding onto the rolled ends so that they do not get wet. Wring out until cloth is not dripping. Use the cloth to sponge the person who is fevering. Begin sponging by wrapping the ankles in the cloth. Flip the compress as soon as the cloth draws heat from the body. The compresses are wrapped around the lower leg from the top of the metatarsals to below the kneecap and left in place for 60 – 120 minutes while the person is reclining. Monitor temperature, blood pressure, and perspiration to be sure that the person's temperature is lowered gently.

What is the best Self-care approach when considering an herbal formulation?

PLANTS, PERSONALITIES, AND BOTANY

What is gained when we learn botany to partner with plants?

PLANT DESIGNS AND GROWTH PATTERNS

What is the purpose of using the Latin name for plants in botanical science?

Naming Your Favorite Plants: Search the internet or plant books that you have. Find and record the Latin binomial nomenclature for 5 of your favorite healing plants.

1.

2.

3.

4.

5.

PLANT PARTS

What are the four parts of each plant?

1.

2.

3.

4.

Define the terms cotyledons, angiosperms, and gymnosperms. Provide examples of each.

What purpose do roots serve for plant survival?

What are the 3 basic leaf patterns or arrangements on the stems of plants?

Three parts of the leaf are:
1.

2.

3.

The plant can use the _____ of the flower to attract insects or animals that assist in pollination or to deter predators.

PLANT CONSTITUENTS

What effects do plant tannins have on body tissues?

What effects do plant alkaloids have on the body?

Plant carbohydrates are classified into 2 groups: _____ and _____.
Explain the differences between these 2 groups.

Explain how the anthraquinone glycosides create a laxative effect on the body.

What is the cause of the fragrance associated with a plant?

What causes the release of resins from a plant?

PEACE AND PLANT-LIKE GENTLENESS

What is the relationship between peace and Hermeticism?

Describe some of the differences between Self-care and the One Cause-One Cure philosophy of health?

What makes an environment healing?

Hermeticism is a philosophy of the five elements of all creation that suits every creed, philosophy, and health belief and clashes with none.

— *Gentle Medicine Self-study #9—*
Designing a Peaceful Safe Place

Design a peaceful "safe place" for doing the next phase of your Self-care Self-study work – within and without. Find a physical space in your home or elsewhere where you can close your eyes and know that you will be completely safe and not be interrupted or disturbed. Take a comfortable position and close your eyes. Place your fingers on your radial pulse and notice the rhythm and rate of your pulse. Then move your awareness to the center of your chest and your heart – the heart that beats as pulse. Using your memory and imagination, find or create a place in your mind in which you are completely safe ... and by yourself. Carefully note all sounds, shapes, colors, smells, sensations, and tastes associated with your safe place. Take your time. Notice any plants in your safe place. As with the tea tasting Self-study, do not attempt to name the plants. Remember their color, shapes, smells, taste, and sensations that you experience with them in your safe place. After your creative reflection, try to synthesize this reflection of creating a safe place into one word that represents the essence of the safe place. Breathe in and out and move your awareness back to your radial pulse. Notice the rhythm and rate of your pulse now. Note the name of your safe place in a journal dedicated to your plant experiences and Self Studies. Be sure to research any plants that you found in your safe place. What is its botanical name and personality? Where does it grow? Does the plant or any of the botanical patterns have meaning for you? Record what you learn about the plant in your journal. You can re-create this safe place at any time of the day and anywhere you go. Lock it in to your memory now for future reflection.

Patterns in Health, Physics, and Paradigms

Describe physis, physics, and morphic resonance.

Do you have memory of a Self-care partnership with plants?
If so, reflect on that memory now.

PUTTING PATTERNS FIRST

Health is described in terms of patterns.

What are patterns and why is pattern important?

What is the Doctrine of Signatures and how does it relate to knowing plants? Provide examples from your reading.

What is a symptom-sign pattern? How does this expand our ability to partner with plants?

Energy flow manifests in patterns known as the 5 elements. List the 5 elements and describe them energetically.

1.

2.

3.

4.

5.

Each person-plant partnership for healing is distinct.

EIGHT PRINCIPLE PATTERNS

What are the eight principle patterns?

1.
2.
3.
4.
5.
7.
8.

What is the importance of using all 4 groups to describe general energetic qualities when viewing a health pattern?

The goal of interventions in TCM is to move the health pattern toward greater _____.

What is the best way to evaluate heat/cold patterns?

List characteristics of a cold pattern.

List the possible symptoms found in a heat pattern.

One of the most important symptoms differentiating between excess and deficiency is the _____.

What differentiates an exterior from interior symptom-sign pattern?

In terms of physical health, _____ is the ability of the body to calm and cool itself and _____ is the ability of the body to heat and energize itself.

PARADIGMS ABOUT PLANT PARTNERSHIP

Define cultural diplomacy. What is the goal and purpose of cultural diplomacy?

The 3 paradigms that impact Self-care with plants include:
1.
2.
3.

Applied in whole plant form,
the action of plant remedies is very complex.

BIOMEDICAL PARADIGM

How should we ask questions beyond those asked from a biomedical worldview when determining the benefit of plant remedies?

PLANTS AS POTENTIAL DRUGS

What are some of the prescription and over-the-counter drugs for which plants or their derivatives are used to make?

RESEARCHING SAFETY AND TOXICITY

What will provide the best evidence for each person as to how all foods, herbs and drugs that they ingest and apply influence and interact in the whole body?

What might provide the most reasonable approach to informing Self-care?

SHARING THE EVIDENCE

Can the consumer feel confident that findings from a research study regarding a "constituent" of a plant be generalized to the whole plant? Why or why not? Explain your response.

From a plant science perspective, research reports about herbal remedies should include what information?

1. A Plant Perspective

a.

b.

c.

d.

2. Control bias

a.

b.

c.

STANDARDIZATION

What is a standardized extract?

Does your body get the identical energy boost from an apple as it does from a spoonful of fructose? Explain what the difference between the two might be.

What is a potential risk of using standardized plant extracts?

THE TRADITIONAL PARADIGM

Plant knowledge in the traditional paradigm is most often embedded in a story.

The World Health Organization defines traditional medicine as:

Define indigenous knowledge and ways of knowing.

What is the difference between the question of those in the biomedical culture "What makes this plant work?" and the question of those of a traditional paradigm "What is the healing spirit of this plant?" Explain how each paradigm might provide a different answer for those engaging in Self-care.

Traditional and indigenous practitioners use _____ and _____ when describing illness.

What are some of the reasons that people choose to use traditional healing methods?

SELF-CARE PARADIGM

Self-care focuses on _____ and _____, and _____ that promote well-being and prevent illness through that which is perceived and experienced as creating balance in body and peace of mind.

There are many reasons for considering partnership with plants in Self-care.

What are some reasons to consider a partnership with plants for Self-care?

STARTING A SELF-CARE PLAN

The process of designing a Self-care plan is just like designing a garden.

What is the ONE rule for creating your Self-care plan?

What is your vision for your Self-care plan?

Consider what compels you to make changes in your life and health that you perceive as leading toward greater balance in body and peace of mind. What forces keep you from making those changes?

Herbs are gentle in how they convey their medicine to humans.

CHAPTER 4
Start Your 5 Elements of Care® Self-care Plan

The earth element is associated with the _____ body.

The air element is associated with the _____ body.

The water element is associated with the _____ body.

The fire element is associated with the _____ body.

The ether element is _____.

STARTING A SELF-CARE PLAN

What are your intentions and plans for your Self-care plan?

In addition to this experiential guide, what medium do you intend to use for your Self-care plan? Briefly describe how you will design your plan with the medium that you have chosen.

Coloring is a very effective technique for locking into your memory what you learn about each organ and system.

CHAPTER 5
Entering the Earth Element

KNOW YOUR SELF – ANATOMY, PHYSIOLOGY, AND PATTERNS

Do you know anatomy and physiology of the human body? Anatomy is what the body structures are, and physiology is how they work. Some basic anatomy charts are provided here, but if you wish to have a more in-depth study of the body systems, purchase an **anatomy coloring book.**

Reflective Moment
What would you say is the current state of balance and peace in your physical body?

ANATOMY SELF-STUDIES

As you learn about and color each anatomical system, please use the following scale to rate your perception of the state of your "balance in body" for each system.

Balance in Body:

Physical Health (Earth Element)

Mental Health and Knowledge (Air Element)

Emotional Health and Feelings (Water Element)

Spiritual Health and Well-being (Fire Element)

All Senses and Intuition (Ether Element)

Endocrine and Reproductive Systems	Balance in Body Now 1 Low – 5 High	Balance in Body 3 Months from Now 1 Low – 5 High
Record Here		

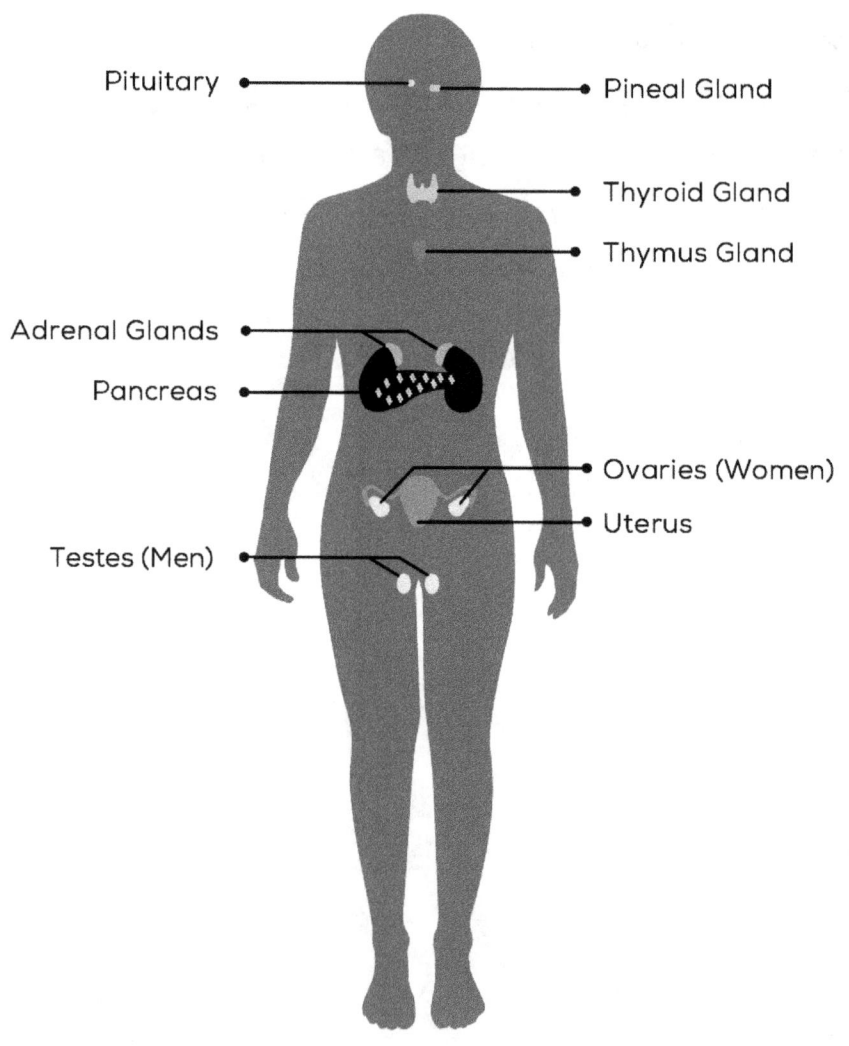

Cardiovascular System	Balance in Body 3 Months from Now 1 Low – 5 High	Balance in Body 3 Months from Now 1 Low – 5 High
Record Here		

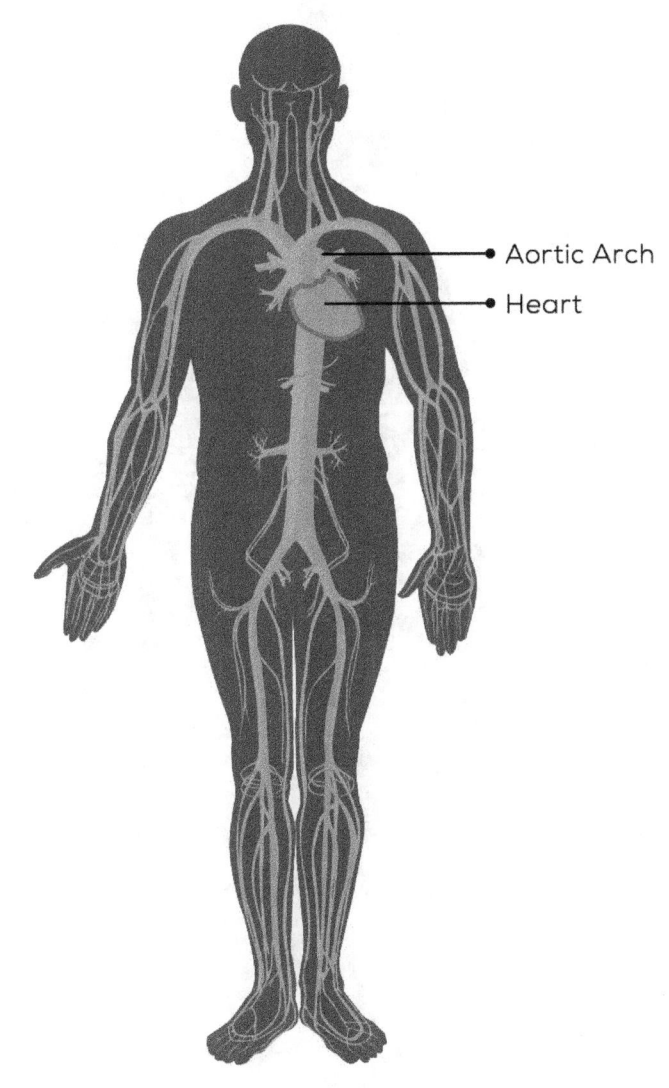

Lymphatic System	Balance in Body Now 1 Low – 5 High	Balance in Body 3 Months from Now 1 Low – 5 High
Record Here		

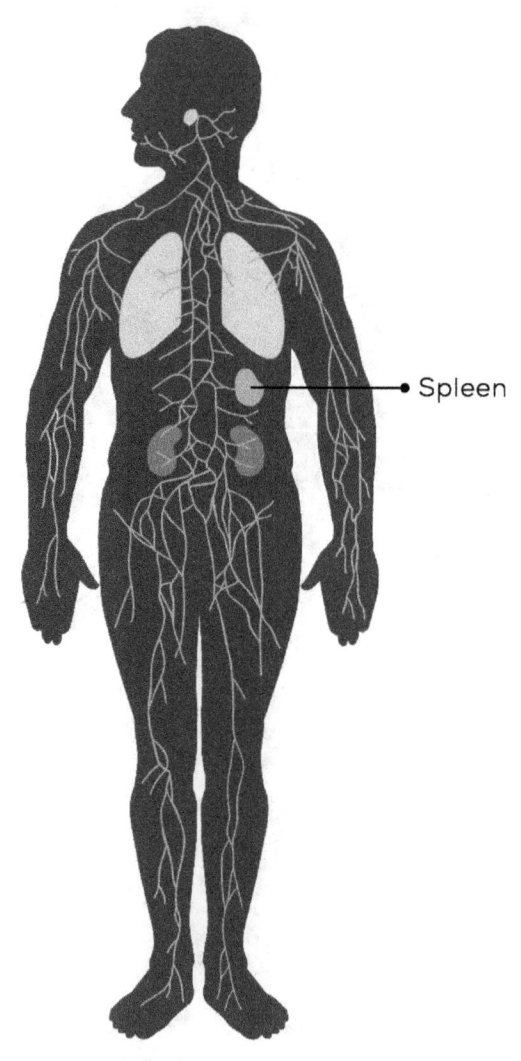

Musculoskeletal and Nervous Systems	Balance in Body Now 1 Low – 5 High	Balance in Body 3 Months from Now 1 Low – 5 High
Record Here		

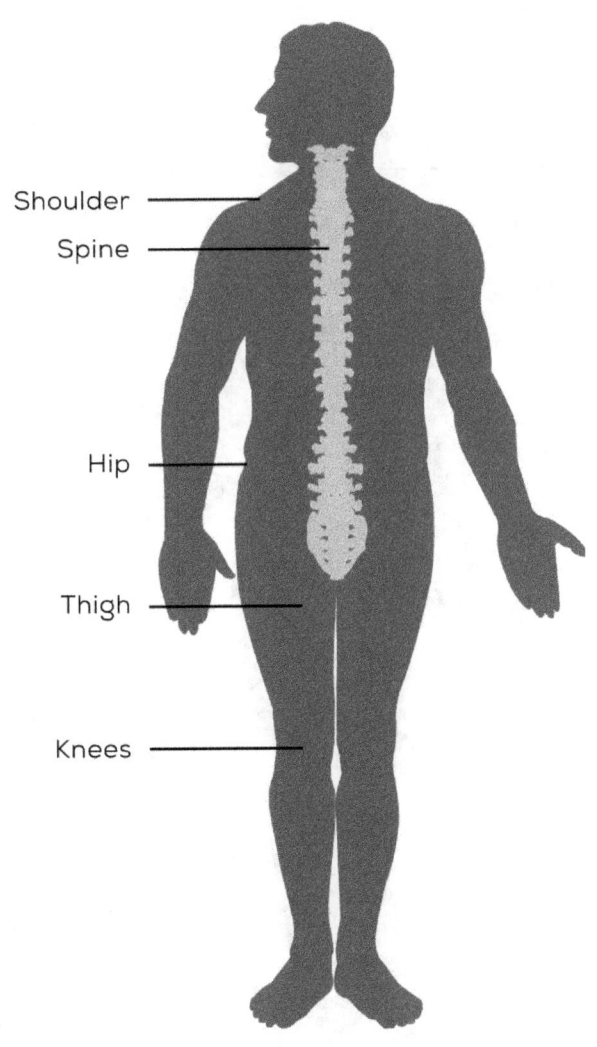

Respiratory System	Balance in Body Now 1 Low – 5 High	Balance in Body 3 Months from Now 1 Low – 5 High
Record Here		

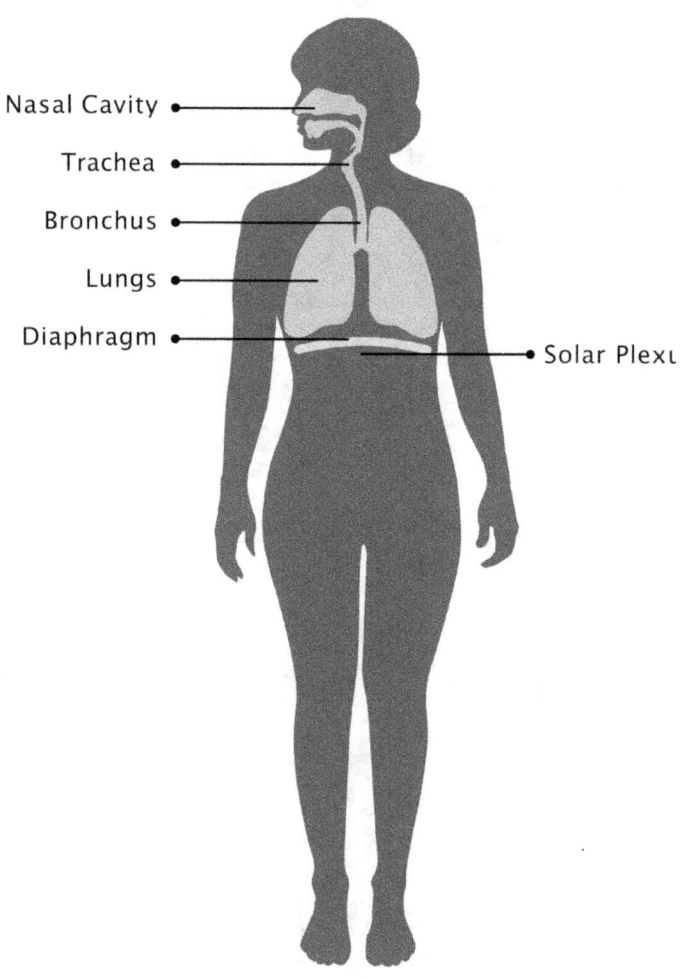

Gastrointestinal System	Balance in Body Now 1 Low – 5 High	Balance in Body 3 Months from Now 1 Low – 5 High
Record Here		

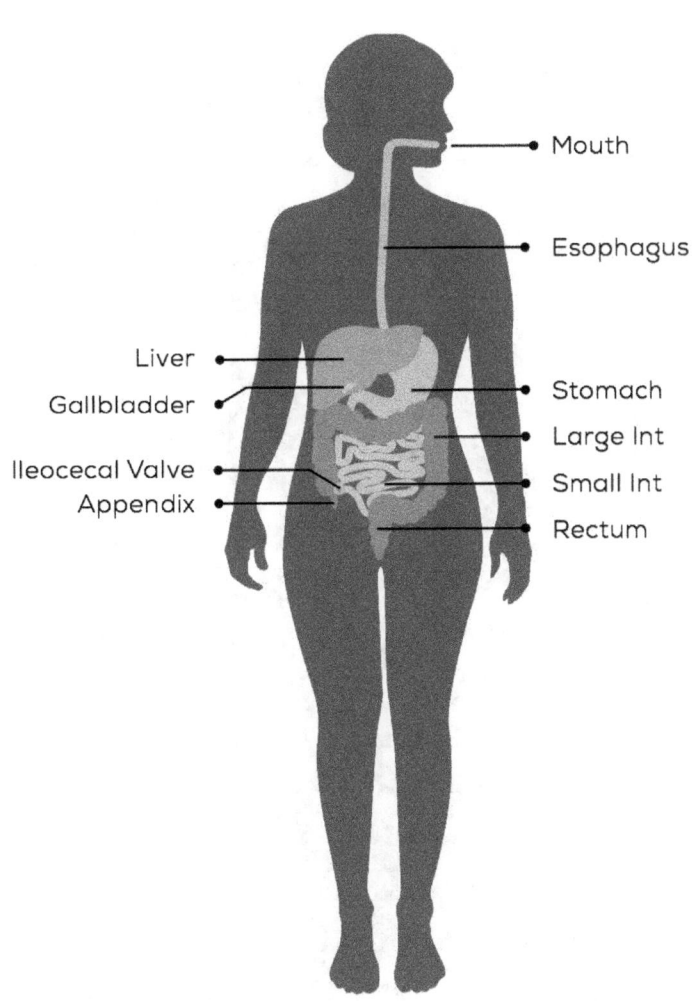

Urinary System	Balance in Body Now 1 Low – 5 High	Balance in Body 3 Months from Now 1 Low – 5 High
Record Here		

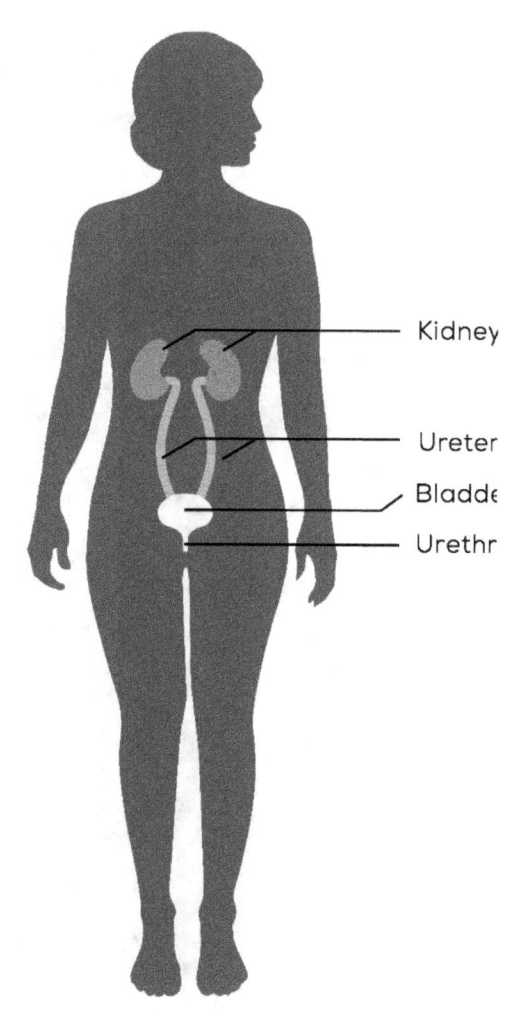

Integumentary System	Balance in Body Now 1 Low – 5 High	Balance in Body 3 Months from Now 1 Low – 5 High
Record Here		

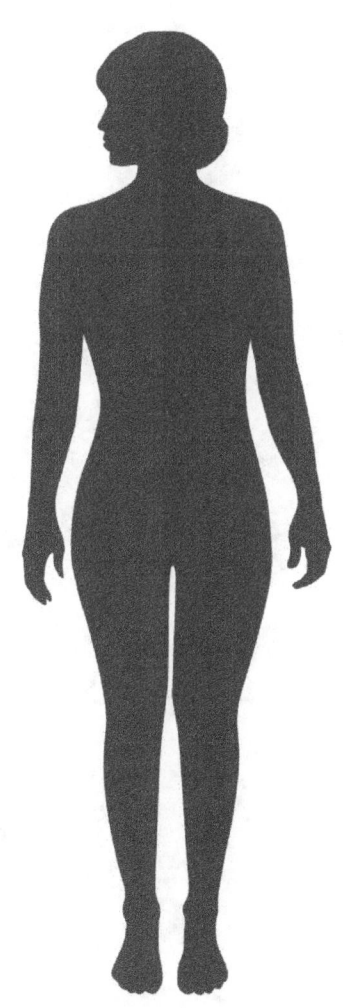

Outline the 5-step problem solving process discussed in your reading.

1.

2.

3.

4.

5.

What is the purpose in following a systematic approach to problem solving?

THE CHLOROPHYLL CONNECTION

What is centering? How does centering effect balance in body and peace of mind?

Draw and color the symbol of the self-care creative process.

What is one way to leave the world outside and center in the present moment?

—Gentle Medicine Self-study #10—
Entering the Green World

Make a list of the 5 elements. Then go outside and find a representative in nature for each of the 5 elements that you can legally and ethically take into your home.

Create a healing environment in your home and position your 5 element representatives in that space. You can integrate the representatives into an existing space or create a new space

Record your reflections. What drew you to the objects you chose? Did you choose any plants? What do the elements mean to you?

Plants are all around us in the physical space we call earth.

Discuss the health benefits and any risks of taking chlorophyll internally or applying externally.

The release of oxygen from plant photosynthesis and the absorption of carbon dioxide from the environment by plants is critical to human survival.

GENTLE MEDICINE BEGINS AT HOME

What are your beliefs about making your own medicine?

"The way in which those remedies are made and how they are applied are as important to the healing outcome as the remedy itself." Discuss your personal experiences of making your own medicine.

COMMUNITY ETHICS AND CANNABIS, TOBACCO, AND AMERICAN GINSENG

Consider the three plants, tobacco (*Nicotiana tabacum*), marijuana (*Cannabis sativa*), and American ginseng (*Panax quinquefolium*). What do you know about these plants? Discuss how you and your family talk about the ethics related to partnership with these plants?

BECOMING ECOCENTRIC AND GREEN

What is an ecocentric philosophy?

How does Self-care with plants as partners contribute to your connection with nature?

What is the *axis mundi* or world tree? Explain the three realms of being as represented here.

The world tree is a place where the strengths of the spirit and dream worlds are drawn toward earthly manifestation and the energy of the earth dimension is drawn toward the spiritual.

PROTECTING YOUR SELF-CARE GREEN PHARMACY

What are some examples of regulations on gathering plants?

What are some of the reasons for purchasing organically grown herbs and plants?

Discuss how you will store herbs in your own apothecary.

CHAPTER 6

Awakening the Air Element
ALL LIFE BEGINS WITH BREATH

MINDFUL DECISION-MAKING AND PROBLEM-SOLVING

What are the differences between Thought, Intuition, and Perception:

Interacting with the plants that provide medicine or the inspiration for medicine is one way that people move into a more Ecocentric paradigm.

Reflective Moment

What do you think and how do you think about Self-care?
What do you know and how do you know about plants as partners?
What would you say is the current state of balance and peace in your mental body?

— Gentle Medicine Self-study #11 —
Breath and Body Scan

One of the largest muscles in the body is the diaphragm. This muscle sits under the ribs and moves in rhythm with other chest muscles and the lungs to support breathing. Begin by letting go of or releasing any muscle tension you may feel around your diaphragm or chest. Do not tell your body to "relax!" This typically makes the body tense the muscles more. You may wish to massage your abdomen to help the muscles release any tightness.

4-Part Breathing

Breathe in slowly for a count of eight. Lift your ribs and sustain the breath for eight counts; then release fully over the count of eight as you drop your jaw and allow the breath to release with a pop of the lips (like a balloon). Continue to gently push the breath out of the lungs for the final count of eight. Repeat the four-part breathing of eight counts each two to three times. Finish by breathing in and out and then normally. The four-part breathing can also be done with four counts instead of eight.

Body Scan

Close your eyes to avoid distraction. Turn your attention inward to the top of your head. Move your awareness from the top of your head to the tips of your toes as you assess where your tensions are held. When you observe tension, breathe in as if you can breathe into that part of your body, tense all muscles and release the tension into the ground. Perform a body scan before and after the 4-part breathing. Notice any effects the 4-Part breathing had on the tension in your body. Journal your results.

Reflective Moment

To start the solution-focused process, ask this goal-oriented question,

"How will I know that I have achieved what I want?"

Set a three-month timeline and ask yourself,

"What will I be doing differently or how will I be feeling differently in 3 months if I am successful in my Self-care plan?"

What is the coeliac plexus?

What is meant by a "negative" psychic or intuitive state?

What is one way to shift to a positive psychic or intuitive state?

When might muscle testing be used to determine which herbs could be applied in Self-care? Note your thoughts, beliefs, or experiences with muscle testing.

What are the benefits of Self-care educational preparation for partnership with plants?

SELF-CARE PROCESS FOR PROBLEM SOLVING

Discuss the phrase "man know thyself."

OBSERVATIONS AND ASSESSMENT

Return to your safe place (Gentle Medicine Self-study) and ask yourself these questions and take some notes for your journal:

"Why is this health behavior, experience, or concern happening now?"

"What plants are in my life?"

"What are my dreams about?"

Next, write down or draw pictures of your observations of the following health patterns:

1. Respiratory Pattern and Breathing
2. Lifestyle (Work, Play, Habits)
3. Intake (Thirst and Appetite)
4. Outflow (Urine and Feces – color, quality, smell, and consistency)
5. Thermal (Hot and Cold in the Body)
6. Pain (Location, Quality, and What makes it better or worse)
7. Skin (Dryness, Itching, Color)
8. Senses
9. Sleep/ Rest (Patterns, Insomnia, Dreams)
10. Motion (Gait, Speed)
11. Speech (Speed, Pitch, Loudness, Force)
12. Tongue Coating (Color, Presence, Moisture, Thickness, Pattern)
13. Tongue Tissue (Color, Shape, Fissures)
14. Behavior and Thoughts (Moods, Interactions, Self-concept, Body Image, Ideals, Ethics)
15. Roles and Relationships (Home, Work, Environment, Global)

PATTERN RECOGNITION

Pattern recognition is the phase that follows observations. Refer to the section in your workbook for the Principle Patterns (Chapter 3).

PLANNING

Primary prevention begins with _____.

What is scaling? Provide an example.

REFRAMING SELF-CARE INTERVENTIONS

What is the purpose of reframing?

Langer describes mindfulness as :

EVALUATION

If necessary, revise your Self-care plan for change and do some further observation of behaviors.

HOW TO DECODE HERBAL SCIENTIFIC DATA

Develop a list of what should be included with responsible reporting and writing about research into medicinal plants.

Questions that are plant focused are critical when designing a Self-care plan. List 5 questions that are plant focused.

Provide some examples of questions that will help you decode the scientific data about specific plant partners.

What is the purpose of the scientific process in herbalism?

List the 4 questions that you might ask yourself as you use information and resources in decision making about plants as partners.

REFERRAL BEYOND SELF-CARE

When would it be considered prudent to self-refer to an herbal practitioner?

CHAPTER 7

Welcoming the Water Element

What does the word Symmetria mean?

Emotion is _____.

Medicine making is a cultural experience that starts with foods and beverages. Do you have a tea ceremony in your culture? Perhaps a ceremony with a different plant beverage (ex. coffee, dandelion wine, beer etc.)

RECIPES FOR MAKING HERBAL SIMPLES

How does timing of planting, harvesting, and preparing remedies affect the hardiness of medicinal plants?

How to Make an Infusion

- A china or glass teapot (for 2+ cups [500 ml]), a tea ball or net for 1 cup (Note: Do not use aluminum when making herbal teas. Tea nets made of cotton do not compact the herb as tightly as the stainless steel tea balls and allow for greater circulation of the water around the plant material during extraction)

- Tea strainer to place in cup when infusing loose herb (not teabags) in a teapot

- Herb of choice, usually leaf or flower, cut or ground in small but not minute pieces

- Boiling water

METHOD

Boil the water and choose your herb. When using large dried flowers or leaves, break up the amount of herb needed in the pot or tea net. If using fresh herbs, cut them into pieces and bruise them with a knife so that volatile oils will not be absorbed into the skin of the hands. Measure the herbs for the tea. The rule of thumb for quantities is 1 to 2 rounded teaspoons (about 5 g) per cup of water. Pour the boiling water over the plant material and cover the cup or teapot to prevent the volatile oils from escaping. These oils will accumulate with water on the underside of the lid. Be sure to shake the condensation on the lid back into the tea. For very thin and tender parts of plants, steep for approximately three to five minutes. For other plant materials, steep for approximately ten minutes. Strain and drink tea hot.

How to Make a Decoction

- The same supplies as for making an infusion are needed, but the plant material is usually the harder part of a plant such as the root or bark. With roots, the pieces are often much larger than with leaves or flowers.

METHOD

Use approximately 30 g (1 ounce) of herb per 750 ml (1 1/2 cups) of water. Place dried, hard herbs in a pot and cover completely with cold water. Bring water almost to the boil, cover, and remove from heat. Allow to stand four hours to allow dried herbs to expand. (This step can be skipped when using fresh herbs.) After standing, the herbs are simmered in a pot (not aluminum) for approximately fifteen minutes. Volatile oils will escape during simmering. These instructions are a generalization and specific instructions (as with TCM formulas where the herbs are cooked for 2 hours) should be followed whenever possible. The decoction is strained after cooling slightly and then taken warm. Decoctions are considered more potent than infusions. Larger quantities of decoction often are made. The rule of thumb is that decoctions can be kept refrigerated for up to 72 hours and portions reheated, without boiling, for use during the day.

Broths and soups are still an easy and effective herbal remedy to employ in self-care.

Winter Watercress and Onion Soup

- Slice two large onions and place in a 3-quart saucepan or soup pot.
- Cover with 3-4 cans organic chicken or vegetable broth ro make your own!)
- Add 1-2 cups water.
- Add Braggs Liquid Aminos to taste.

METHOD

This soup should be a little on the salty side to cut the phlegm in the throat. It will also be balanced out by the sweet taste of onions after they cook. Add freshly ground pepper to taste. Bring to a boil and then cover and simmer until onions are soft. Take 1 tablespoon of Kudzu (Pueraria lobata) powder (from macrobiotic section of health food store) and cover with a little water. Stir to paste. Add 1/4 cup of the broth to kudzu and stir until thoroughly mixed and then add to the pot. This mixture will thicken the soup slightly.

Kudzu is a cooling herb that heals the gastrointestinal lining where the viruses that cause the common cold take hold. When the onions are soft and you are ready to eat, cut the watercress leaves gently and place 1/4 to 1/2 cup of leaves in a soup bowl. Cover with very hot soup and by the time you get to the table, the greens will be ready to eat. They are slightly spicy. Substitute chard, kale, or other chopped green leafy vegetable if you do not have cress available.

HEALING FOODS AND ORAL REMEDIES

Explain how taste assists one with Self-care in partnering with plants.

Provide examples of "tastes" found with herbs:

Sour

Bitter

Pungent

Astringent

Sweet

Salty

TCM herbal formulas are designed for the patient with the goal of greater _____ in mind and body.

TEAS—INFUSIONS AND DECOCTIONS

Describe how infusions are made.

Describe the difference between and infusion and a decoction.

What plants do you like in healing soup or broth? Think about vegetables, fruits, and herbs.

The body is said to crave that which assists its natural tendency to seek greater balance and harmony.

PILLS AND CAPSULES

What are some of the risks and benefits of ingesting herbs in in pill or capsule form as part of your Self-care plan?

TINCTURES AND LIQUID EXTRACTS

Explain the difference between a liquid extract and a tincture. How and when do we consider liquid extracts and tinctures?

How to Make an Alcohol Tincture or Extract

- Fresh or dried herb (see information following method for selecting)
- Wide-mouthed jar with lid
- Food grade ethyl alcohol (Pure grain spirits up to 190 proof [e.g., Everclear] are used for maceration.) Amount of alcohol used is discussed after method.

METHOD

Maceration begins with cutting up fresh herb or powdering (coarse not fine) dried herb and putting the plant material in a wide-mouthed jar. The appropriate amount and type of menstruum is then poured over the plant material and the lid to the jar is placed on tightly. The jar is then put in an accessible but dark corner of the kitchen. Shake the jar at least twice daily so that the menstruum can thoroughly penetrate the plant material. Shake and store the jar for two weeks. Heat is not necessary because of the longer maceration period.

At the end of the two weeks, the plant material is strained into a bowl. Use cheesecloth to press out the remaining menstruum from the plant material. Take the alcohol extract, pass it through a coffee filter, and transfer the strained liquid to dark-colored dropper bottles.

A NOTE ABOUT HOMEOPATHY

Describe the process of "potentization."

What menstruum is a good option for children and those avoiding alcohol?

TOPICAL APPLICATIONS

COMPRESSES OR STUPES

What is a compress and how is it used in Self-care?

Applications to the skin and nervous systems provide a comforting way to stay aware of your body and fully engage in the healing process.

How to Make a Compress

- Natural fiber cloths cut to size and shape of body part to be covered
- Cold, warm, or hot herbal infusion, decoction, or tincture to be used
- Bowl to soak compress
- Bath and hand towels for warm/hot compress

METHOD:

Cool compresses are made by dipping the cloth into the infusion, decoction, or tincture, wringing out the cloth and applying it to the body part. The compress is not necessarily covered because the compress is changed as soon as the heat from the body warms the compress, as in the case of fever. With warm and hot compresses, your goal is to keep the compress as warm as possible. The cloth is dipped in the hot or warm infusion or decoction and is placed in a wringing towel so that you do not have to touch the steaming compress directly and it can be wrung out thoroughly. Hot compresses are not applied wet and drippy because they cool too quickly. After wringing, the compress temperature is tested against your arm and if tolerable to the skin is applied as hot as possible to your skin. After the compress is applied, it is completely covered with another cloth and then a wool cloth or towel to keep the heat in. Each successive cloth covers the previous one by a few centimeters to be sure to seal in the heat. The compress is left in place for about 20 minutes. Some people use a piece of plastic, like a plastic bag, to seal in the heat of a compress. If the compress turns cold, you will become uncomfortable and it should be removed and replaced with a warm one.

You may find that you relax deeply and fall asleep. Set an alarm so that if this happens you will awaken to remove the compress after 20 minutes. Compresses that are secured and worn for longer periods of time are kept moist by adding a small amount of the infusion, decoction, tincture, or oil at intervals throughout the day. For certain conditions, hot and cold compresses using different herbs may be alternated.

Gentle Medicine Self-study #12
Comforting Ginger Compress

Grate 4 to 5 ounces (150 g) of fresh ginger root. Put the ginger into a small cloth bag and add it to 1-gallon (3.8 liters) of simmering (not boiling) water. Allow the decoction to steep gently for five minutes. Holding both ends of a hand towel, dip the middle into the ginger water. Wring it out and fold it to the size of the client's mid-back where the kidneys are. Take care in applying the hot compress, making sure that the skin does not burn because of the heat. The compress should be applied as hot as is tolerated. Place a dry towel over the compress and a blanket over the towel, tucking each layer around the client so that air does not enter the compress and cool it. Prepare a second compress as the first. Replace the first compress after three to four minutes. Remove the blanket and dry towel. Place the second hot compress on top of the first and flip the compress over, making sure that the temperature is tolerated. This technique ensures that the connection with the ginger and moist heat is maintained.

The compresses should be flipped every three to four minutes for twenty minutes. The ginger compress will create increased circulation of blood and body fluids and move qi and blood stagnation that usually manifests as pain, inflammation, swelling, or stiffness. Many people with chronic pain benefit from ginger compresses to the kidneys as a systemic remedy rather than applying the compress to individual joints. Ginger compresses should not be used when high fever is present (too warming), on the head area, on the abdomen in pregnancy, for infants or the very old (too stimulating), or on an area of the body experiencing infection (heat) such as chest/lung area during pneumonia.

I taught this compress to teenage women who were preparing to go to nursing school. They were taking NSAIDS every day for "pain." They were so surprised and happy to experience such pain relief with the ginger compress to the kidneys. They asked me if the effect was due to "the ginger, the hot water compress, or the loving kindness with which they had applied the compress?" I asked them what they thought was the answer. They said, "All three!" Yes, the ginger is warming and stimulating as is the hot water. But the feelings of love with which the ginger compress is applied is just as important to the connection through comfort that can be made between you and the plant.

How to Make and Use an Oil Compress

- Cotton flannel cloth (two swatches a size that when doubled will completely cover the body part)
- Castor oil—warmed
- One large thin hand towel and one large bath towel for each body part treated
- Hot water bottle filled and burped

METHOD FOR CASTOR OIL PACK TO YOUR FEET:

Try applying a castor oil pack to your own feet! There are two ways of doing a castor oil pack to your feet or any part of your body. The Cayce method is to completely soak the flannel with the warmed castor oil and apply it to the feet or body part. These packs are reusable if refrigerated. In clinical practice, I use another method that is not reusable. I use significantly less oil by applying the oil directly to the feet or body part and then applying the flannel soak in very hot water. Either way, the pack is applied warm and moist to facilitate the update of the oil. A piece of thin plastic can be used to protect the heat of the pack. For the feet, large plastic baggies are put easily over the foot after the compress is applied and squeezed next to the foot so that all air escapes. After the plastic is applied, the small hand towel is wrapped around the foot in a way to keep air from entering the pack. After both feet are wrapped and tucked in, place them at the center edge of a larger towel, and the hot water bottle at the bottom of the feet outside the small towels. The edge of the large towel away from the patient is folded up over the bottle and pack. Then the towel ends are wrapped up and around the feet, securing the bottle in place and keeping the warmth in. Cover yourself with warm blankets and keep the castor pack in place for up to an hour. After the castor oil pack is removed be sure to keep the body part treated with the pack, warm.

POULTICES AND PLASTERS

How to Make a Poultice

- Linen, cheesecloth, or a light natural fiber fabric cut to size

- Cut or chopped herb chosen for poultice. May be raw and cut or mashed, or may be lightly sautéed

METHOD:

Prepare the herb of choice. Place the slurry of the raw or cooked herb in the center of the cheesecloth or fabric and fold the fabric to enclose the herb. The poultice should be a size that fits the body part to be treated. The poultice is left in place for a certain amount of time determined by the energetic quality of the herb and the amount of moisture in the poultice. Drier poultices can be secured with a bandage and left in place for hours if comfortable whereas a moister poultice such as an onion slurry poultice applied to the chest might be removed after 15 – 30 minutes.

INFUSED OILS, LINIMENTS, SALVES, AND OINTMENTS

How to Make an Herbal Oil

- Use fresh or dried plant material, depending on which plants are best used as oils and whether they must be prepared from fresh or dried herb. You may need to do some research to answer these questions. Some plants such as St. John's wort must be used fresh.

- Wide mouth glass jar

- Cheesecloth

- Oil (Olive, Sunflower, Canola)

METHOD:

An oil of the flowers and tiny leaves of the St. John's wort (*Hypericum perforatum*) plant are used as an example here. St. John's wort oil is applied to first- and second-degree burns and is used in wound healing and for muscle and trigger point pain. I prefer the solar method for making herbal oils. The aerial parts of the *fresh* plant (flowers and small leaves) are collected, and left out to wilt slightly. Then the plant is chopped, and placed in a wide-mouthed jar. Do not use dried St. John's wort. A little oil (preferably olive) is added to the plant material, and then the flowers are crushed again with the back of a spoon. Then more oil is added to cover the plant material completely. The jar is shaken and placed in a warm location for two weeks. The oil must be approximately 37.7°C or 100°F during the infusion time. The plant material is strained out of the oil.

How to Make an Herbal Salve

- Herbal infused oil already prepared or plain oil can be used (Plain vegetable oil is used when drops of essential oils are to be used.)

- Beeswax (approximately 28 g per 250 ml oil or 1-ounce wax per 1 cup oil)

- Tincture of benzoin (1 drop per 30 ml or 1 ounce of oil) as a preservative

METHOD:

This is a basic process for making a salve. The ingredients must be adjusted, based on the herbs used and the consistency desired. The oil and shaved beeswax are placed in the top of a double boiler and the wax is melted. Test the consistency by pouring a small amount of the salve into a jar. It should harden quickly and be the consistency that you want. Add more oil if you want the salve to be softer and more wax if you want it harder, depending on the nature of the application. For example, in the care of an open wound, a hard salve would not be used because applying it takes a little more rubbing, which is not helpful when the wound is healing. A softer salve would be needed that can be applied on the wound easily. When the consistency of the salve is right, add the tincture of benzoin as a preservative.

Discuss examples of liniments and their uses.

SIMPLES FOR A HEALING ENVIRONMENT

Using words, pictures, drawings, or any other form of creative expression, visualize your healing environment. What will be key components and a major area that you will need to focus?

AROMATHERAPY, INHALATIONS, AND STEAMS

Explain how aromatherapy is more like a pharmaceutical drug or standardized extract than a whole herb.

Explain proper dilution of essential oils for use in Self-care.

What part of the human body connects the central nervous system directly with the external environment?

How to Make an Herbal Steam Inhalation

- Plant to be infused—usually an aromatic herb such as chamomile (Matricaria chamomilla) or lemon balm (Melissa officinalis)
- Large bowl
- 1 large and 1 small towel
- Hot water bottle

METHOD:

Prepare a warm room and sit next to a table. Dress warmly, with socks on and rest your feet on a hot water bottle. The herb is placed in the bowl and boiling water is poured over the plant material. Cover your head and shoulders with the large towel and place the towel over the bowl so that the vapors (essential oils) do not escape. Breathe in the vapors for about fifteen minutes. Dry your head and cover yourself with a dry towel to prevent chilling.

HEALING GARDENS

Experiences in nature can promote balance in body and peace of mind.

Use the area below to write about or sketch out an image of a garden space that you currently have or design a space that you would like to have for growing and harvesting plants.

FIVE ELEMENT FOOT BATH

Describe how all five elements can be represented in a footbath.

Reflective Moment
What is your favorite image representing nature?

The footbaths restore vital energy to the body as a whole.

FIVE ELEMENT FOOT BATH

1. Foot Bath Basin
2. One cotton bath towel. Use cotton towels, as they are absorbent.
3. Two cotton hand towels. These should be thin rather than plush as they will be used to wrap the feet later on; plush towels are harder to stretch and tuck around the foot.
4. Herbal bath infusion, oil, salt
5. Comfortable chair.
6. Blanket for shoulders.

METHOD

Take off your shoes and socks or hose and roll up your pant legs above the mid-calf area. Choose the remedies to include in the footbath. Plain water is healing, too, but the reason for considering a five-element footbath has to do, once again, with anatomy and physiology and the opportunity to absorb and release through the large pores in the soles of the feet. During a warm footbath, those pores open and are able to readily absorb the healing effects of herbal and other remedies through the feet.

Fill the basin two-thirds full. Make sure that the temperature of the water is hot enough (approximately 92 degrees F) to produce a relaxation response. In the summer, I often use cool footbaths when feet are hot, sore, and swollen from walking in the heat. If you work in air conditioning you may still have very cold feet even in summer, so the hot footbath can be used all year. Put the basin in front of your feet on a bath towel the long way.

Your feet are longer than they are wide and therefore fit more comfortably in the basin placed in the long direction. Fold two hand towels in half the long way and then in half again and position them on the bath towel next to the basin with the folded edge toward you. Have your towels ready to use quickly after the feet have been in the bath so as to retain the warmth of the feet. Put any remedies you have chosen into the basin and swirl the water with your hand using a figure eight motion. This pattern, known as "water coursing," reflects the same motion found in nature which can purify water. While your feet are in the water you can enter your safe place, meditate, pray, or center yourself during the footbath. When you take your feet out of the water be sure to cover your feet with the small towels immediately and dry them so that they do not get cold. Put on some warm socks and shoes.

Reflective Moment

Reflect on how your feet feel before
and after the five-element footbath.
Take some time to journal your experience.

CHAPTER 8
Fanning the Fire Element

Herbal interventions have the ability to catalyze major changes in body, mind, and spirit.

_____ and a _____
are the keys that open the door to plant partnerships and the release of energy for healing.

The price for partnering with nettle and all healing plants is knowledge and a caring heart.

What does it mean to have knowledge of a plant?

EVALUATING BEST SELF-CARE PRACTICE

Evaluate your Self-care plan. Are you able to determine whether or not your chosen gentle medicine interventions are helping? Are they bringing about your desired changes and results?

Name some plant science specialists and discuss how they might help you grow your knowledge of healing plants.

People respond differently to herbal remedies. Discuss the paradoxical effect of Valerian.

What are two herbs that work synergistically with Valerian to produce a calming effect.

_____ and_____lead to the development of knowledge and a caring heart and nurture the insights that can emerge from entering into the complexity of the living world of plant medicines.

GUIDELINE FOR BEST SELF-CARE PLANS

List 10 points for developing your best Self-care plan. Reflect on each one.

1.

2.

3.

4.

5.

6.

7.

8.

9.

10.

Plant partnership in Self-care is rooted in knowledge developed over many centuries of observation, trial, and evaluation.

FIVE RIGHTS OF PRECISION PLANT PARTNERSHIP SELF-CARE

List the Five Rights of Precision Plant Partnership Self-care. Discuss each and provide examples from your reading.

1.

2.

3.

4.

5.

The fire element reflects and is reflected in our _____ and _____.

Reflective Moment

How do communities and governments make decisions to protect the public from the potential harm from plants, and how great is the risk from plants?

RIGHT PLANT

Health decisions are made through the evaluative process of _____.

Research shows that there is an assumption that people make decisions in Self-care based on _____. But the assumption is not supported.

What supports the decision-making process is herbal opportunities that encourage _____ in Self-care.

_____ have a history of few to no adverse effects when applied according to tradition.

Explain what is important for people who partner with plants to be aware of in terms of safety considerations associated with specific herbs?

What is the purpose of legal regulation of herbs and what are some of the differences from country to country?

Discuss the significance of known interactions of herbal medicines and anesthetic drugs. Provide example from your reading.

RIGHT APPLICATION

When choosing an application, think of precision as
_____ and _____.

Herbs are catalysts for change.

Discuss how ephedra has been applied according to tradition and how this is different than the current application that is being cautioned against in the biomedical world.

Considering the right application for an herbal simple is part of your risk and benefit analysis.

Explain how a tea might pose less risk than does a standardized extract in a capsule.

_____ and other sensory experiences can activate one's common sense.

— *Gentle Medicine Self-Study #13—*
Home Garden Medicine

Onion (Allium cepa) is often easy to grow. Here is a simple but powerful remedy that can be made from your own garden and in your own home.

Onion Syrup

Slice 1 to 2 large yellow or white onions thinly. (Experience the onion's effects on your tear ducts!) Measure ¾ to 1 cup (180 to 360 ml) of honey (or any sugar). In a large container, alternately layer the onion slices and then the honey. Let it stand for three days in a dark corner of the kitchen and then strain the syrup into a colored glass bottle. Store in the refrigerator. The syrup can be taken in spoonfuls just like any cough syrup or can be added to a tea. Rest well after taking.

Seek the _____that carries the least risk but will achieve the benefit that you seek.

Continuing to apply an herb in a particular fashion when it is not effective is a waste of plant resources as well as a risk.

_____ is one reason that traditional herbal applications, such as teas and topicals, have a long history of safe use.

Discuss how we can evaluate the effectiveness of each herbal application in Self-care.

Common sense is demonstrated as an intuition or insight related to a particular experience.

Reflective Moment

How will you explain to people the safety not to mention the joy that can come from really knowing Self-care with healing plants?

Make a plan for applying your herbal simple that complements your daily routine and diet

RIGHT TIME

Determining the best time for an herbal application depends upon the herb and its constituents as well as your _____.

What does the example provided in your reading about coffee (*Coffea arabica*) decoction teach you about the importance of personalizing the timing of an herbal intervention?

All herbs and foods effect change in body, mind, and spirit.

What is the simple premise for Self-care with plants as partners?

What is Cytochrome P-450 and what is important about it?

Discuss some of the known benefits of herb-herb interactions known as "synergy."

Many people prefer to try gentle medicine and herbs before _____.

Herbs interact with everything.

RIGHT DOSE

What do you think about Paracelsus' statement that "the only difference between medicine and poison is the dose?"

What does toxicity mean?

Define median lethal dose (LD50). Give an example from your reading.

Another classification system to evaluate toxicity of plants includes GRAS _____, GRAF _____, and GRAP _____ Why is this system not really helpful in making regulatory decisions about plants?

What is the purpose of regulation when considering medicinal plants?

RIGHT PERSON

What is DSHEA?

What should a consumer consider about a company when buying herbs and herbal products?

PUTTING FEAR INTO THE FLAME

Explain how we add our consciousness to making our plant remedies.

Reflect on the following statement and discuss your thoughts and feelings here.

"Out of fear, we can spend so much effort seeking to assure that a plant will not harm us that we can actually miss the delight and the promise of healing that comes when entering the green world."

The fire of our consciousness transforms every herb into a gentle medicine

---

CHAPTER 9
Effecting the Ether Element

What is "Ether?"

Medicine is that healing energy we carry within us in balance and peace despite what is going on around us.

Those who have ears will hear.

ALCHEMY AND THE SECRET ESSENCE OF LEMON BREAD

Discuss alchemy and how it applies to Self-care.

What about herbs like lemon make them catalysts for change?

Reflective Moment

As you study your health patterns closely, notice any effects from interactions with the environment on your healing process, body, mind, emotion, spirit, or consciousness.

PLANT ALCHEMY

Discuss Spagyrics.

Give some examples from the reading about how the human body transmutes elements.

What is the goal of scientific exploration of anything in nature?

Describe the path of wholeness.

Life, like Lemon Bread, is full of secrets.

FORMULATION

Discuss the difference between a formulation and a simple. How might one recognize when it is appropriate to apply a formulation?

Like flower arranging, an _____ number of herbs is typically assigned to a formula.

Energy fields can be measured through _____.

Within every plant and every human is a seed of potential.

ADAPTOGEN ACTION AND THINKING PLANTS

Discuss the term "Adaptogens" and provide an example of an herbal adaptogen from your reading.

BACH FLOWER REMEDIES

What are the Bach Flower Remedies and how are they applied in Self-care?

Discuss how the Bach Flower remedies assist in adaptation.

"The Bach Flower Remedies move a person through an emotion." What emotions are you moving through? Journal your reflection.

REMEMBER THE HARMONY OF THE GOLDEN RATIO

The golden ratio describes _____.

_____

The shell of the nautilus has the same spiraling design as the inner ear of a human being.

_____

CONCLUSION
THE WAY OF THE THORNLESS ROSE

SELF-TALK

What is Self-talk? How do our patterns of Self-talk affect our health and plants?

— Gentle Medicine Self-Study #14—
Self-talk

As you work the process of creating plant partnerships, notice and journal your self-talk. Observe any thoughts that you have about the plants in your home and environment. Notice if you have any plants with thorns, prickles, and stingers. Can you discern a message in the pattern of these plants?

What peace offering might you give to the plants? Be patient and keep observing.

Journal what you learn.

Just as health is more than the mere absence of disease, peace for the people of Six Nations is more than the absence of conflict and war.

WISDOM OF ELDERS

Peace is promoted through _____ and _____.

How have trees come to symbolize life force and power in nature?

— *Gentle Medicine Self-Study #15—*
Power Object

This is an experiment in Peacemaking begins with understanding how you feel about power.

1. Choose an object that represents your personal power. Study it carefully and write down how you came to choose the object.
2. Make a list of the qualities of your personal power object.
3. Make a separate list of what power qualities you believe are your strengths.
4. Make another list of the qualities of power you need to fulfill as you pursue your Self-care plan.
5. Compare and contrast your lists.
6. Go to your safe place and ask the question, "What is the first step I can take to develop the qualities of power and peacemaking that I need for fulfilling my Self-care plan?"

What is symbolized by the bundle of five arrows?

Reflective Moment

Consider, what the role of Self-care with plants as partners wil be in the future.

> *Partnering with plants can inspire changes*
> *in your life, your rhythm, and your vibration.*

Describe the Five Nations Longhouse model for an ethic to guide the actions of any person who would cultivate peace within Self and community.

1.

2.

3.

4.

5.

6.

LEARNING FROM THE LEMON BALM LAWN

Discuss the difference between change and transition.

INVITATION TO PLANT NEW SEEDS AND TAKE THE NEXT STEP.

What is your next step after completing the Gentle Medicine Elements of Care® program?

To access more awesome courses, resources, information about joining the Self-care League, and becoming certified in the Elements of Care® program, please visit the Self-care Institute at:

www.GoldenAppleHealingArts.com

MARTHA MATHEWS LIBSTER.

Martha Mathews Libster, PhD, MSN, APRN-PMHCNS, APHN-BC, FAAN, is Founder and Executive Director of Golden Apple Healing Arts, an education and consultation company. Since 2006, she has led the Bamboo Bridge Global Tea House and the Nurse-Herbalist and Self-Care Institutes, innovative teaching and learning communities and forums for dialogue in health culture diplomacy. Dr. Libster is the author of ten books including: *The Nurse-Herbalist, Integrative Herb Guide for Nurses, Demonstrating Care: The Art of Integrative Nursing, Enlightened Charity,* and *Herbal Diplomats.* She is an inspirational speaker whose practice models are used by nurses on five continents. Dr. Libster is a professor and award-winning historian of nursing. She is an educational program designer, board-certified holistic Psychiatric Mental Health Clinical Nurse Specialist, and Herbal Diplomat® with 30 years' experience in the integration of traditional Chinese herbal medicine and nursing practice. She lives in Wisconsin, USA and can be reached at www.drmarthalibster.com and www.goldenapplehealingarts.com.